D1177574

THE LINDBERGH CRIME

Jurors

Foreman Walton

Schwarzkopf

Attorney General Wilentz

Justice Trenchard

Clerk Lloyd Fell

Defense Attorney Reilly

Deputy Sheriff Low

Hauptmann

Photograph by Acme

THE VERDICT . . . . . At 10:45 o'clock on the night of February 13, 1935, Foreman of the Jury Charles Walton spoke the words: "We find the defendant, Bruno Richard Hauptmann, guilty of murder in the first degree."

THE
LINDBERGH
CRIME

By

SIDNEY B. WHIPPLE

ILLUSTRATED

BLUE RIBBON BOOKS

New York

PRINTED AND BOUND BY THE CORNWALL PRESS, INC., FOR
BLUE RIBBON BOOKS, INC., 386 FOURTH AVE., NEW YORK CITY

Printed in the United States of America

TO MY MOTHER AND FATHER

THE LINDBERGH CRIME

THE LINDBERGH CRIME

CHAPTER ONE

COLONEL CHARLES AUGUSTUS LINDBERGH, SEEKING REFUGE from a world that insisted upon regarding him and his family as public property, chose as the site for his new home a region conveniently distant from New York by airplane, but not easily accessible by ordinary means of travel. His estate, hemmed in by the forbidding Sourland mountains of New Jersey, was suited to his temperament, provided the isolation he required, and offered that thing in life he most desired—personal freedom to live his own life as an ordinary American citizen.

He had planned his home from the air, marking out the proportions of his landing field and determining to place the house upon the crest of a knoll where it would dominate the five hundred acres of his undulating land. To the north and west of this spot stretched a tangled woodland reaching into the Sourland mountains. To the south were rolling meadows and occasional swampland, crossed by dirt roads connecting the villages of Hunterdon and Mercer Counties.

The house, as it rose during the winter of 1931, was of field stone, whitewashed with cement, and built in the fashion of a French manor, two and a half stories in height. From its small entrance hall a visitor would pass into an immense living room, distinguished by fireplaces at each end. Directly over this room, and attained by a staircase leading from the entrance hall, Colonel Lindbergh and his wife, Anne Morrow Lindbergh, had their apartments.

Two wings spread from the back of the house, one containing the garage and, above it, the servants' quarters. In the other, its windows catching the sun from the south and west, was the second-floor nursery and sleeping room of Charles Augustus Lindbergh, Jr., who was then seventeen months old and beginning to struggle with baby speech.

Around this home was a white picket fence, and the picturesqueness of the solid white buildings was enhanced by a towering windmill at the rear. Not far from the house was the already partially cleared landing field the Colonel had planned to use as the base for his easy air flights on business or pleasure, using as a guide the revolving light of a ten-mile beacon at the summit of the mountains.

To the average air pilot, the region was not pleasant. The territory, in fact, was so wild, so full of sudden traps, that army aviators used it for practice in mapping rough topography.

For a man of Colonel Lindbergh's known zest for air adventure—and his efficiency—this territory held no particular terrors, however. He had surveyed it from his airplane in all kinds of weather and from every aspect. He was happy with his choice.

This was the setting, early in 1932, in which the son of Charles A. Lindbergh was being brought out of babyhood and into childhood. When, on June 22, 1930, he had come into the world, he had been saluted and acclaimed with a public hysteria that passed far beyond the nation's boundaries. Telegrams of congratulation flooded the Morrow mansion in Englewood, where he was born. Embarrassing heaps of gifts were showered upon him from all quarters of the globe. The tidal wave of public interest was second only, perhaps, to that which swept the world when his father, three years before, had made his celebrated flight to Paris.

Yet even this chorus of thanksgiving had its sober implications. More than ever, the distasteful fact was apparent to the child's father that only by the most forceful of actions could he and his family escape the maudlin worship of the multitudes and achieve the desired solitude of an American family.

There was, in fact, a premonition of what was to come in some of the more serious writings of the day. It was Heywood Broun who said, with sure prescience:

> His background is that of wealth and fame, of courage and high reputation. But I am already moved with compassion. He cannot possibly realize yet the price he must pay for being a front-page baby. He will.

Something of that same feeling must have agitated the hearts of the Lindbergh family, but it was from the intrusion of worshipers rather than from predatory mankind that they sought to guard their child.

For seventeen days after his birth he was nameless. Then came a brief announcement that he was to take his father's name, and beyond that little news of him was vouchsafed the curious public. The few photographs that were taken of him were carefully retained by the closest members of the family. No bulletins were issued regarding his health. No news stories were released concerning his growth.

His first summer was spent, for the most part, at the Englewood home of his grandfather. During the following summer, while his parents were away on their spectacular air tour of the Orient, he was once more the "guest" of Senator and Mrs. Morrow at their home in North Haven, Maine. And in that summer Senator Morrow, weary and overworked, died, and Anne Morrow Lindbergh came home to her first great family sorrow.

Meanwhile, the great home in the Sourlands, rearing its walls while the Lindberghs were happily away, neared completion. Like all new houses, built under the changing temperatures of the Middle Atlantic climate, it had its little faults. There was, for instance, that shutter in the baby's nursery. Warped by the weather, it stubbornly resisted all attempts to close and lock it. All the other windows and shutters behaved admirably, efficiently. Only this one balked and could not be barred. Fate sometimes operates through petty and minute agencies.

In this home, Charles Augustus Lindbergh, Jr. led a normal baby's life. He had large blue eyes and a smile that, one day, would have flowered into the same attractive smile of his father. He had a Scotch terrier, which he lovingly ran ragged in childish devotion. He ate and slept and romped regularly, and suffered not at all from coddling, for Anne Morrow Lindbergh, a devoted mother, was nevertheless a sensible one.

Now and then, when the pressure of public demand for "news" became too great to withstand, or when ridiculous rumors reached maddening proportions, some of the real truth behind the baby's quiet life was permitted to go forth. To reports that the infant was already, at the tender age of four months, being prepared for aviation, Colonel Lindbergh, writing with a somewhat unusual burst of humor in the *Pictorial Review* of October, 1930, said:

> Our son has hardly reached the age to have his future determined for him, and, in any case, it is a question he can decide for himself when the time comes. Personally, I do not want him to be anything or do anything that he himself has no taste or aptitude for. I believe that everybody should have complete freedom in the choice of his life's work.

One seeking privacy or solitude could scarcely discover a more favorable spot than that chosen by the Lindberghs. The nearest village, three miles away, by dirt lane and paved road, is the small town of Hopewell. From Hopewell, it is eight miles to Princeton and fourteen to the state capital, Trenton. Scattered through this zone are a few clusters of houses forming themselves into hamlets and villages.

In spite of this rural seclusion, however, there were those who beat a trail to the Lindbergh estate—thrill hunters and curiosity seekers—parking their automobiles along that meandering roadway that rejoices in the name of Featherbed Lane, and stopping only at the private entrance to the estate. Of these unwelcome visitors to Hopewell there were thousands, and some one among them, watching this house from afar, found his mind tempted by a daring and diabolical scheme.

Within the Lindbergh home, on the first blustery evening

of March, 1932, there were as fascinating a group of persons as ever spoke their lines in a staged drama. The Lindbergh household was a smoothly running organization, dominated by that efficient but soft-spoken butler, Oliver Whately, who had come to the "Morrow children" from the Morrow establishment.

He was English—typically English—with a passion for reading and the gracious manners of a perfect gentleman's gentleman. He was forty-five years old, urbane but close-lipped, guarding his master's personal affairs with the firm dignity of an English mastiff. Daily it was his custom to make a pilgrimage to Hopewell, first to enjoy a spare moment in the village library, second to fill any requirements of his pantry or table. For three years he had been in service in America, in the homes of wealthy families in Long Island and Westchester, and at the end of his first year settling down to the comfort of the Morrow household.

With him, as housekeeper and cook, was his wife, Elsie, whose gentleness of character matched and was complementary to that of her husband. Below-stairs life with the Lindberghs was happy and harmonious.

Next in importance to this sedate English couple came Betty Gow, the twenty-eight-year-old nursemaid, an attractive brunette, to whom was entrusted the personal care of the infant. She had come well recommended to the child's parents, and her behavior during the eighteen months in which she had had the management of the baby's welfare had been everything wished for in a nurse. Little was known of her outside interests, although gossips might have found some food for reflection in her friendship with Henry

Johnson, a red-headed sailor who danced attendance upon her during her free hours. Yet every girl is entitled to her romance. "Red" Johnson was a personable young chap who had met Betty during the previous summer at North Haven, Maine. At that time he was a paid hand aboard Thomas W. Lamont's steam yacht.

These three, then, constituted the working branch of the Lindbergh ménage, and a more outwardly respectable and loyal trio would be hard to find in any American household of wealth and culture.

The Lindbergh home, however, had not in truth settled down to fixed domestic habits. Although the house itself was technically finished and livable, the completing touches that would transform bare walls into a permanent home were still in progress. Under these circumstances, it was natural that the youthful family should have divided its time between the Hopewell residence and the Morrow mansion in Englewood.

On the morning of March 1st, Anne Morrow Lindbergh looked out upon the dour landscape, observed the furious wind, and decided the weather was too unkind to risk taking her son to Englewood, as she had planned. Furthermore, Charles Junior appeared to be suffering from some congestion of the lungs, and his condition worried the young mother.

Shortly before noon, Mrs. Lindbergh called the Morrow home by telephone and talked to Betty Gow, telling her the baby's condition, and instructing her to "come to Hopewell right away." She had decided, she said, to remain in Hopewell "until the baby is better."

Betty came—but not at once. First it was necessary to let "Red" Johnson know of the change in plans. Betty might have had her usual evening with the young man, had she remained in Englewood. But "Red" was not to be found just then, and so the comely nursemaid left word that he was to call her at Hopewell later in the day.

At mid-afternoon, Betty arrived in Hopewell, and assumed charge of the sick child. Mrs. Lindbergh was relieved, though obviously the baby's condition was not dangerous.

Darkness descended and the gusts of wind whipped through the dismal, creaking branches of the forest behind the white house. It was not a pleasant night to be abroad, and the mother congratulated herself on her wise decision to stay comfortably in the brightly lighted, warm house at Hopewell.

As for the Colonel, he was in New York attending to his private business. He had, in fact, an engagement to speak before the Alumni Federation of New York University, a gathering of 2,000 diners who had been gratified at his unexpected acceptance of their invitation. Accordingly, the Colonel was not expected home for dinner, and the household settled down to its smooth evening routine.

At seven o'clock the baby's bedtime arrived. Both Mrs. Lindbergh and Betty Gow ministered to him in the nursery. His sturdy chest was rubbed well with oil. He was dressed warmly in his woolen "baby-bunting" wrap, tucked comfortably beneath the blankets of his crib, and left to slumber. On his thumbs—which, as with the commonest of children, have a mutual attraction for tired baby mouths—

were secured those metal cup devices used by the modern mother "so that his mouth won't be spoiled."

Betty Gow moved noiselessly around the room, straightening out the clothing and arranging the shutters. But there was one green shutter that resisted all attempts to latch it, and after several futile efforts in the sighing wind, Betty Gow gave up the attempt and went to her own room.

At about a quarter past eight o'clock, Colonel Lindbergh arrived home. By a strange quirk of fate, and in the pressure of his business, he had completely forgotten about his dinner engagement. As usual, he inquired after his son and was told the child was already asleep, but suffering from a slight cold. Ollie Whately, at eight-thirty, announced dinner.

With dinner over, the Colonel went to his study—directly beneath the nursery—for a little work before turning in. Anne went to her room on the second floor.

Some time later, Colonel Lindbergh was aroused from his concentration by a noise outside the window. It might have been that a bough had cracked. He thought it was the wind, and resumed his work.

At ten o'clock, as was her custom, Betty Gow decided to make a visit to the cribside of her charge. She mounted the stairs, turned on the shaded lamp and gazed blankly at the crib.

It was empty.

"Strange," she thought. "Either Mrs. Lindbergh or the Colonel must have picked him up."

So she casually walked to the bathroom, where Mrs. Lindbergh was preparing for bed, and asked:

"Did the Colonel take the baby?"

Equally casually, Anne Morrow Lindbergh replied:
"Perhaps you'd better go downstairs and see."

Wholly expectant of finding the child in his father's arms,
the nurse entered the library and then stopped suddenly—
for the Colonel was busy writing, and there was no child in
sight.

Puzzled, Betty Gow, with a feeling of strange disquietude
in her heart, said to the father, "The baby is not in his crib,
sir."

The Colonel and the nursemaid hurried upstairs, Lindbergh's long legs striding hurriedly in advance of the now
frightened maid. They met Mrs. Lindbergh at the head of
the stairs, and the three, in silence, surveyed the empty
nursery.

Still they refused to believe the truth. "He must have got-
ten out of his crib by himself—he is somewhere upstairs,"
they tried to reason. But the search, which they began to
realize in their hearts would be futile, revealed nothing. The
child had been stolen.

Colonel Lindbergh called Ollie Whately and told him to
phone Harry Wolf, Hopewell's chief of police. Then, in
desperation, he seized a rifle and, with no definite plan in
his stricken mind, rushed out of doors in a fruitless chase.
The wind, with rising fury, covered all other sounds. There
was no noise of fleeing criminals, no sound of speeding
automobiles—nothing but blank darkness, shrouding the
abduction in mystery and falling like a black curtain between Colonel Lindbergh and his child.

In keeping with his training, the least agitated member
of the Lindbergh household at this moment—to outward

appearances—was that efficient butler, Ollie Whately. He stepped silently to the telephone and called Harry Wolf.

"Colonel Lindbergh's son has been stolen. Will you please come at once?" he said. There was a gasp at the other end of the line. Wolf seized his hat and an automatic and within two minutes was speeding over the three miles that lay between Hopewell and the estate, with Constable Charles E. Williamson as a companion. Colonel Lindbergh had returned to the house, shocked by the realization of the pitiful futility of his chase, and steeled his nerves to call Major Charles Schoeffel of the New Jersey State Police.

The gathering of those tenuous clues that were soon to lead far and wide—into nothingness—began at once. The police officers and the family crowded into the nursery, peered into the empty crib, inspected the warped shutter, gazed long at a footprint on the window sill—and pounced upon an envelope conspicuously left there. With hands trembling from emotion, Major Schoeffel opened the envelope and extracted its contents, and it is noteworthy that even under the stress and strain of this dramatic moment, Colonel Lindbergh's brain operated rationally and bravely.

"Be careful of fingerprints," he said.

Major Schoeffel knit his brows over the penciled note. "Now, whom do you want to see this note, Colonel?" he asked meaningly. Harry Wolf, automatically ousted from command of the case in that simple phrase, stood by for a moment and then silently withdrew.

The note, scrawled in a script difficult to decipher and bearing evidences of illiteracy, read:

Dear Sir!
Have 50000$ ready 25000$ in 20$ bills 15000$ in 10$
bills and 10000 in 5$ bills After 2-4 days we will in-
form you were to deliver the money.
We warn you for making anything public or for
notify the Pol [remainder of word blurred] The
child is in gut [sic] care. Indication [?] for our
letters are singnature
                    Ans 3 holes [?]

Then followed the peculiar signature that was to identify
all subsequent communications from the kidnaper. It was a
symbol that would attract not only the interest of every
student of criminology but the "expert" analysis of cryptolo-
gists and psychologists—and that would provide the police
with one of their most maddening and baffling clues.

The symbol was composed of two intersecting circles,
which might have been drawn around a twenty-five cent
piece. Within the oval formed by the overlapping circles was
another smaller ring. The outer rings were drawn in blue
ink, the inner one in red.

This, then, was the ransom note. It was the first shocking,
stunning proof that little Charles Lindbergh, sleeping
soundly with his deeply dimpled chin snuggled beneath his
blue blanket, had been snatched from his crib for gain—
that the world's most noted baby, "America's child," was
the victim of the most fiendish plot devised in modern
criminal history.

The investigators, with Colonel Lindbergh striding in the
lead, went outside the now brilliantly lighted house, and
began a systematic search of the grounds. Fifty feet away
from the nursery window their flashlights, puncturing holes

in the darkness, fell upon a ladder. It was in three sections, each section seven feet long, built and joined with the skill of a craftsman. Yet here, if he had indeed used it, the kidnaper had made his first error. The ladder was not strong enough to bear his own weight combined with the weight of the sleeping child. It had been broken where two sections were joined together. Was it in the stealthy descent from the nursery? Probably.

Back to the house the police trudged, bearing with them the broken ladder. It fitted into two depressions left in the soggy earth beneath the baby's window. As they reared the ladder against the wall, two of its sections nearly reaching the window sill, the police found their third clue—a chisel lying on the ground nearby. Presumably intended to pry open the shutter, it had been abandoned by the fleeing child-snatcher.

And there was a footprint, a heavy, almost shapeless track, from a shoe perhaps wrapped in a stocking, just below the window.

For the moment, those comprised the sum total of the clues presented to the agonized parents and the luckless police.

Within the home, where Anne Morrow Lindbergh waited, dry-eyed and brave, other activities were being pressed forward. Within thirty minutes after Ollie Whately's calm telephone call to Chief Wolf, three states had received the alarm by police teletype. State troopers were speeding to Hopewell. Every New Jersey and New York road was guarded. Every policeman was routed from his regular duties and bidden to watch for a fleeing automobile which would contain—it was hoped—a sleepy boy clad in a woolen sleeping garment.

At ten o'clock that evening the city rooms of New York's morning newspapers were almost deserted. There would be no news tonight. Politics would dominate the front pages. Governor Franklin D. Roosevelt was considering a special session of his legislature to consider unemployment relief. Congress was angrily debating national prohibition. The Japanese were still fighting at Shanghai. And a persistent bandit robbed a Childs restaurant for the third time—once too many—and had been shot for his foolhardiness. Copydesk men were yawning.

Then the telephones began to jangle. The explosion came. "Colonel Lindbergh's baby has been kidnaped."

Switchboards in telephone exchanges began flashing madly. Airplanes and private automobiles were chartered. Reporters were summoned from their beds. Maps were consulted. Early front pages were swept into the hell-box to make room for the news—real and astounding news. An army of news men, paralleling an army of police, began rolling out of New York and converging on Hopewell, forty-seven miles away.

The night telephone operator at Hopewell, operators at Princeton, operators at Trenton became swamped by a crescendo of demands for lines—lines—lines.

At Englewood, Mrs. Dwight Morrow, the baby's grandmother, replied in agitation to frantic calls: "Yes, we have heard the baby was kidnaped. We don't know any more."

In Hopewell, a reporter, forerunner of a regiment of news

men, banged insistently on the door of Paul T. Gebhart's general store and hotel.

"Wake up, Pop!" he shouted. "You'll have three hundred here for breakfast."

CHAPTER TWO

ON THE MORNING OF MARCH 2ND, THE SMALL TOWN OF HOPE-well, with its little hotel, postoffice and modest telephone building, became the center of the world. The kidnaping of Charles Augustus Lindbergh, Jr. had aroused the nation to a pitch of hysteria and horror comparable only to the wave of anger that followed the assassination of Abraham Lincoln. The world dropped its business, that day, to discuss in horrified and angry accents the most revolting crime of the century.

Long lines formed in front of news stands to snatch at the newspapers as they came, with blaring, hot headlines, from the press. Millions of mothers sat constantly by their radios, straining to hear the wearisome repetition of the story, with prayers in their hearts that the next bulletin would bring glad news.

Hopewell, at dawn, seethed with activity. A hundred, two hundred, three hundred reporters, camera men, amateur and professional detectives, state police, city police, federal sleuths, augmented by throngs of purposeless curiosity seekers, swarmed into town. They came by airplane and automobile, by train and bus, and with Gebhart's store as a base, they spread, fanwise, out through the country. They marched along the dirt roads to the Lindbergh estate and tramped over the sticky hillsides. They listened to, and amplified, a thousand rumors. They swooped over the white house in planes, and dotted the hillsides overlooking the scene in black swarms.

Moving with them came the signal corps of this army, linemen in overalls, with vanloads of cable; radio engineers with truckloads of paraphernalia.

The Lindbergh home was in a state of siege.

Earlier in the long night those fortunate few who were first to arrive at the house found the way made easy. They were received, gravely, by Ollie Whately. They were escorted to the living room and made comfortable with sandwiches and coffee. They were obligingly told all there was to tell—the now familiar story of the abduction, without embellishment and without theories, for no one, at that hour, had been able to form any theories.

Colonel Lindbergh, his face haggard and drawn, his boyish smile vanished, himself greeted these first messengers of outraged public opinion. He shook hands with them, thanked them for their interest, and excused himself to watch over Anne. Yet it was he, as greatly as Anne, who needed at that moment every possible word of comfort, for he was very close to the breaking point.

The Colonel had called to his side, among the first, his counsellor, friend and business associate, Colonel Henry C. Breckinridge. With the lawyer, Major Schoeffel and Colonel H. Norman Schwarzkopf, commander of the New Jersey State Police, he had already attempted to outline a plan of procedure. His plan, understandable to any parent, was to buy his baby back—with all his worldly goods, if necessary—regardless of the police, regardless of the majesty of the law, regardless of eventual justice. He wanted his child. The return of the baby was paramount. The police might theorize and speculate and plan punishment for the criminals when they should be captured. But just now there was only one issue, and that was the happy return, safe and sound, of Baby Lindbergh to his parents' arms.

With the influx of ever-increasing hordes of newspaper men and tramping squads of police, however, it became evident that morning that something must be done to bring order out of the chaotic scrambling for news and clues, that some defense must be raised against the importunate throngs beating at the gates. The Lindbergh estate therefore became the field headquarters of a semi-military encampment.

Automobiles were moved from the roomy garage to prepare quarters for the state police who were given control of the campaign. Here, with a trooper to man each telephone, was installed a switchboard from which radiated twenty lines. Army cots were set up. The scene was that of a general staff base in France on the eve of a drive.

Neither for Colonel Lindbergh nor for his wife had there been a moment's rest that night. With her voice under control, though her eyes were reddened from lack of sleep and weeping, Anne Lindbergh took the detectives over the scene of the kidnaping.

"We've counted all the blankets and none is missing," she told them. "When he was taken, they didn't wrap him in anything. All he had on was his little sleeping suit, and he had a cold."

At dawn, bareheaded, and wearing a pair of old gray trousers and a leather flying jacket, the Colonel once more emerged from the house with a group of detectives, and resumed his search of the estate, covering the ground so hurriedly tramped the night before under the flickering flashlights.

At six o'clock in the morning he returned for a single hour alone with Anne and for a breakfast which he could not eat. Then, in the broad daylight, he resumed his search. Back at the big house, the flood of telephoned and telegraphed messages from the world began arriving. Messages from the great and near great; from the humble and lowly; from friends and would-be counsellors—and from cranks whose weak brains had reeled under emotion and whose insane babblings were later to provide maddening obstacles in the way of the man-hunt.

With magnificent fortitude the closer relatives of Charles and Anne Lindbergh had rallied, without hysteria or public outcry, to the comfort of the stricken parents. Mrs. Dwight Morrow and Anne's sister, Elizabeth, drove to Hopewell from Englewood early in the afternoon. Out in Detroit, Mrs. Evangeline Lindbergh, the baby's grandmother, "very worried" but confident of a happy outcome, insisted upon teaching her classes of high school youngsters.

The little telegraph office at Hopewell mushroomed into a central metropolitan terminal. A dozen cables twisted their way from Trenton, across fields and farms and by-paths, and spread their manifold filaments to the impatient keys of a full score of telegraph operators, each pair of wires immediately pouring in a torrent of consoling words.

Never before had it been demonstrated what the name "Lindbergh" actually meant to the world—not alone the world of America, but the far away world of the Orient, the Eastern Continent, and South America. The President of the United States and the President of Mexico, the Premiers of Great Britain and France, the great ones of Japan and China were as one with their people in horrified condemnation of the criminals.

European and South American newspapers printed "extras" throughout the day and their switchboards, too, were deluged with inquiries from people who, whether in Paris or in Buenos Aires, had found a common, emotional understanding of the real Brotherhood of Man.

In New York, Catholic, Jewish and Protestant clergymen joined in a service of prayer for the safety of the lost infant, and their prayers were broadcast to the world. In Oklahoma City, the General Missionary Council of the Methodist Episcopal Church South suspended its session for twenty minutes, while four hundred laymen and members of the clergy, including seven bishops, knelt in prayer for the Lindberghs.

Bishop William T. Manning, head of the Protestant Episcopal Diocese of New York, sent a diocesan letter to all ministers within his see, asking them to offer prayers for the immediate restoration of the child "and for those who are guilty of this act, that their hearts may be softened and that they may realize the full meaning of their heinous crime."

Also, that afternoon, Dr. John Grier Hibben, President of Princeton University, drove to the Lindbergh home and offered the services of the entire student body to help the police in tracking down the abductors.

Around the Lindbergh home there was chaos. The wheels

of justice had begun to roll, but with a ponderous creaking that foretold a rough journey. It would be days before even the first semblance of orderly procedure could be established. For the present, however, there was the undeniable necessity of searching every inch of the estate, and of extending the search far and wide, into the Sourland hills, for additional clues to be added to the meager threads already in their nervous hands. And there were interviews—hundreds and hundreds of interviews—to be staged. The questioning of neighbors, the routing out of witnesses, the hunt for residents who might have seen suspicious figures in the neighborhood was a stupendous task, even for Colonel Schwarzkopf's brave array of uniformed troopers. And there was the "ordinary" police work to be done, the guarding of the estate from the hordes of curiosity seekers and, horrible to state, souvenir hunters. Furthermore, even on this first day after the crime, there were scores, no, hundreds, of would-be detectives, already tramping down the brush and weaving new tracks in the muddy hills, aimlessly destroying many of the possibilities of striking a warm trail.

Something had to be done, as well, about the press. Here were these swarms of persistent news hounds, tumbling over each other and the police, demanding news, insistent upon answers to questions, eager to earn the glory of solving the greatest mystery of their careers—and eager, from the heart of them, to restore the child to his father and mother. They were a gigantic force—a force for good or evil, for while with one blast they might electrify the world and speed to the consciousness of every good American his duty as a citizen to join in the apprehension of the kidnapers, with another they might give ample warning to the criminals themselves that the chase was becoming warm and force them into hiding. It was a delicate problem.

Here the tact of Colonel Lindbergh asserted itself. As night fell, he called for a conference with the leading representatives of the press associations and the more prominent New York newspapers. He greeted them courteously, shook their hands grippingly, and sat down for an informal, and unpublished, chat. He was tired. There were lines in his worn face and deep circles beneath his frank eyes. Then he explained his problem.

He appreciated, he said, that it was the desire of every man, and every institution he represented, to do everything humanly possible to obtain the return of his son. He explained his position that the safety of the child was the paramount consideration, and that he was ready to pay the ransom, without question and without regard to the activities of the police. But, he said (and there was logic behind his reasoning), there would be little hope of establishing the slightest contact with the kidnapers so long as his home was besieged not only by reporters but by the hordes of outsiders who, to satisfy morbid cravings, had encamped in the neighborhood.

He had therefore arranged, he said, for the press to receive its news of the progress of the hunt from other sources.

The representatives of the press, moved by his plea and recognizing the justice of his position, pledged there would be no interference, accepted for their fellows the terms laid down by the Colonel, and withdrew. Their pledge was not violated.

Of the clues which then presented themselves to the detectives, that of the ladder first attracted—after, of course, a study of the ransom note itself—the microscopic attention of the police. The examination and development of this clue was given into the hands of Captain Henry Gauthier, of the Jersey City police. With the ladder sections strapped to the side of a police car, Captain Gauthier set forth on a journey that was to carry him hundreds of miles through New Jersey, and which was to take the wooden rungs before the eyes of more than five hundred people. Nearly every family within a radius of twenty miles inspected it. And all of them, in a disappointing chorus, disclaimed any knowledge of its manufacture. The ladder, however, was not without its usefulness in determining the nature and the characteristics of the man who committed the crime, provided always that the man who constructed it and the man who used it were one and the same.

A Trenton lumber expert told the police it had been put together by one who was proficient in the handling of carpenters' tools. The nails were cleanly driven. The saw cuts were smooth and true. Every rung was even. Its three sections fitted together perfectly, round pins fitting easily into grooves cut for it as each section joined its neighbor. New eight-penny nails had been used, and it was of new lumber except for the topmost rung and the uprights of the second section—the very spot where it had given way presumably under the weight of the kidnaper and his burden.

Temporarily disregarding the blurred footprints on the window sill and in the soft ground, as they trailed off into

nothingness, the police turned to the most important clue—
the ransom note itself.

First of all, there was a decided foreign tone to the note.
Its letters were curiously made, reminiscent of an Old World
language. The kidnaper had written 50000$—20$—10$—
not an American or an English custom. This alone, unless
the entire note was cleverly faked, would stamp the writer
as a Continental. And there were other evidences of foreign
origin. "We warn you for making anything public . . . the
child is in gut care. . . ."

On the single word "gut" the detectives based their first
decision. The word "gut" is Teutonic. Therefore, they said:
"The kidnaper of Charles A. Lindbergh, Jr. is a skilled
carpenter of German extraction."

This was progress. Except that there are thousands of
skilled German carpenters in this land. Were any of them in
the vicinity of the Lindbergh home? What construction had
there been, except on the Colonel's estate, within the neighborhood? The detectives turned their thoughts to the
Skillman Hospital for Epileptics, eight miles from the Lindbergh home and five miles from Hopewell. Lumber had
been left over in the construction of a number of cottages on
the hospital grounds. And some of the workmen at Skillman had been employed in the building of the Colonel's
new home. Emissaries drove post haste to the hospital—and
found every inmate accounted for during every moment of
the day and night of March 1st, and every workman was
absolved. But some of the discarded fragments of wood had
been given to the poorer inhabitants of the Sourlands, to
use for kindling. Could it be . . .?

Another fantastic theory presented itself. Among these hill people are some descendants of Hessian soldiers who fought under Lord Cornwallis, and who remained on American soil, to intermarry with the Indians and remain, until they died, exiles in a foreign land. Could it have been possible that some descendant, more Hessian than Indian, was the writer of the ransom note? The theory was discarded almost at once because of the nature of the crime and the careful planning with which it had been accomplished. These people were noted neither for their ambition nor for their clear thinking. For the most part, they desired nothing but to be left alone in their shacks.

The sensation seekers, however, went bounding into the forest or toiled painfully up the wet and sticky hillsides, and weird and wonderful were the tales they brought back to feed to the wires into New York newspaper offices. "Clues" developed by the thousand, some plausible, some ridiculous, all of them erroneous. Doddering old men and half-witted women were gravely interviewed. Many of them remembered the strangest of coincidences to bolster suspicions that this or that neighbor had a hand in the crime.

Joan Lowell, in her capacity as a lady of the press, came across such a one, interviewed her at length, and recounted in shuddery language the results of her investigation. In impressive blackface type it was recorded how "the Sourland Mountain midwife" who apparently lived in a shack at Zion, N. J., "blanched" when Joan asked her if she knew where the baby might be. And "sent a significant look to her half-grown son who sat behind me." The interview ended with the Sourland Mountain midwife shouting like a Billingsgate fishwife, and chasing the author of *Cradle of the Deep* out into the deep woods at the end of a rifle. The Sourlanders were an uncommunicative lot, but everything they said or did under the harrying of the police and "reporters" had its special significance that blossomed into "today's best clue" in the fertile soil of imaginative minds.

And a great deal of attention was paid (with a consequent loss of valuable time) to the vague suspicions of two elderly widows, Mrs. Matilda Morrison and Mrs. Antonia Cholowski, with whom Matilda lived. Mrs. Cholowski, it appeared, had overheard some conversation in which the words "Lindbergh," "kidnap" and "baby" were used. So, accompanied by state troopers who towered over her, she put on her little bonnet and trotted with them through the hills, hither and yon, pointing out places where the baby might be concealed. In the end, Mrs. Cholowsky who, for a time, appeared to be assuming the rôle taken by the "pig woman" in the famous Hall-Mills murder case, went back to her little yellow house between two scraggly hills and the police decided they would be more careful in the future.

The reporters and the police continued their systematic tramping through the woods, criss-crossing each other's trails, stumbling over each other's footprints, interviewing the oldest inhabitants and the youngest children and all in between. If the reporters found anything suspicious it was blazoned to the world. If the police found anything it went into the secret archives of the chief.

Unfortunately for the progress of the investigation, it was obvious that each one of the myriad "clues" voluntarily offered must be traced to its end. Solution of the crime might hinge upon the most insignificant of incidents. It was impossible to say of any story, however fantastic, "this is absurd—not worth pursuing." The entire fabrication of the crime was so unbelievable that it would tax the imagination to go beyond its bare facts. Even the astonishing conclusion of Joan Lowell who, *privatim et seriatim,* had interviewed many Sourlanders, not forgetting the loquacious Mrs. Cholowski, that the kidnaping had been planned and executed by mountaineer dim-wits, looked plausible at the time.

But there was one young man to whom the police gave attentive ear. He appeared to have something. Ben Lupica, a Princeton Preparatory student, intelligent, quiet and firm in his convictions, lived in a modest house a mile and a half from the Lindberghs. On the afternoon of March 1st, he had stopped his car by the roadside near the gateway of the Colonel's estate, to peruse a letter just taken from his R.F.D. box. As he was reading it, another automobile intruded upon his consciousness. It appeared to be a Dodge, and two sections of a ladder projected from its vacant, right-hand seat. As the car passed him, Lupica looked curiously at the driver. Strangers are rarely seen on this strip of road. The driver, he told the detectives, "had a thin face, and wore a black overcoat and a fedora hat."

The police took the young student over and over his story. It was fool-proof. And it was the more significant because at that moment no "outsiders" knew a ladder had been found. Lupica's information went into the general repository of police information, to be revived dramatically after two years had gone by.

Another man there was, one Millard Whited, a woodsman as knotted and gnarled as the lumber he cut for a living, who produced startling incidents for the consideration of the sleuths. On two occasions, as he was driving along the dirt road bordering the Lindbergh estate, he saw a man in an automobile which also contained a ladder, on the road. The two dates fixed in his mind were February 18th and February 25th or 27th. He said he would never forget the looks of the prowler.

Another promising clue was afforded by Herbert Garwood, salesman for a shrubbery concern, who had tried to sell Ollie Whately some landscaping equipment. He recalled that while he was talking with the butler, a man and a woman drove to the house in a green automobile and without so much as a by-your-leave began taking photographs of the building. They were promptly and indignantly hurried on their way by Whately, but later, after he had departed, without a sale, Garwood said he came upon the woman, hidden in the underbrush, and focusing her camera on the nursery windows. It was a promising clue, to be sure, but millions of promises were never fulfilled.

On the afternoon of March 2nd, Edward Copner, the rural mail carrier from Hopewell, drove to the Lindbergh home and threw down three large sacks crammed with mail—more than he had ever carried in the years through which he had plodded over the route. This was the beginning of a flood that, growing into stupendous proportions, so deluged the household that an entire corps of workers had to be assigned to inspect it. The rapidity with which false clues from this deluge developed was amazing, and the entire postal force of the United States government was set to work on the case.

At Washington a letter demanding $50,000 ransom and threatening death to the baby was intercepted and turned over to the police. The letter said the baby was safe. Police could not decipher much of it.

A letter was opened at the Granville, Ohio, postoffice. Signed with the figure "4", surrounded by X's, it read: "Tell Anne not to be nervous. Everything O.K. Give us time."

From Pottsville, Pennsylvania, a letter written in a feminine hand urged the searchers to concentrate their manhunt "eight miles west of Hopewell." Enemies of the Morrow family, it said, had devised the plot for revenge.

Another letter, mailed to the chief of police of Springfield, Illinois, said the writers had the baby and that they would return him for $50,000 in cash. "We need the money, not the baby," they said.

And John Johnson, a seventeen-year-old youth, was arrested at Bridgeport, Connecticut, and confessed he wrote a postcard to Colonel Lindbergh, advising him to "obey instructions or suffer consequences" because he "wanted to see what the newspapers would say."

Meanwhile, with these manifold clues, a majority of them contributed by crack-pots, nit-wits or maliciously insane, came the immediate necessity of checking the history, antecedents, associates and movements of every member of the Lindbergh and Morrow households. Colonel Lindbergh, from the outset, insisted it could not have been an inside job. He knew and trusted every servant in the two households. All of them loved and were loyal to little Charles.

Yet how did the kidnaper know the baby was home in the Sourland mansion on the night of March 1st, when, but for the mischance of a serious cold, he would have been in Englewood? How did the kidnaper know about the warped shutter? How did he know the hour of the child's retiring and the hour when he would be alone and unattended in the nursery?

Often, in crimes of this nature, the persons most blandly innocent on the surface conceal the most guilty of consciences. Often, too, it is the insiders who, with an unfortunate and mistaken friendship, unthinkingly reveal the most intimate details of family life above-stairs.

With whom, then, were that estimable couple, the Whatelys, most familiar outside of the Lindbergh home? Who was this red-headed young man, Henry Johnson, whose "date" with nursemaid Betty Gow had been broken by telephone that afternoon, and who had talked to her by telephone from Englewood at nine o'clock that evening?

CHAPTER THREE

HENRY JOHNSON WAS AN AMIABLE YOUNG MAN WHO HAD NO business being in the United States. He had arrived from Norway as a seaman and casually jumped his ship in order to see something of the country. What he saw, particularly of the young women with whom he made chance acquaintanceships, pleased his youthful fancy so greatly that he decided to remain in America, unmindful of the immigration laws. Nobody bothered him. Nobody demanded to see his papers. And if there happened to be, at divers times, no work for him to do, he could at least descend upon his brother John, in West Hartford, Connecticut, until times were better.

In the summer of 1931 he was employed aboard Thomas W. Lamont's yacht, then cruising in Maine waters. At North Haven he met the attractive Betty Gow, nursemaid to Charles A. Lindbergh, Jr., then little more than a year old. They liked each other at once. There was something frank and genuine about Henry's broad grin, and something very appealing about his red hair. And Betty was a delightful companion, a little reserved perhaps because of her important position in the household of a world hero, but always ready to enjoy such mild forms of entertainment as the coast towns of Maine provided.

When summer was over the friendship continued. Betty

took up her duties at the Morrow home in Englewood where the Lindberghs were staying. Henry, the yachting season being over and his job gone, spiced his hunt for work by occasional visits to New Jersey and became a favorite with the below-stairs world at the Morrow mansion. It was obvious that he should be called "Red." It was also obvious to the other servants that his attachment to Betty was becoming serious, although when they first met Betty was twenty-seven and he was two years younger.

Now the timing of the kidnaping had been perfect. On another night or at another hour the child would not have been in his crib. The first questions that presented themselves naturally to the police were these:

How did the kidnapers know the child would be in the Hopewell house at the hour they chose for the commission of the crime?

How did the kidnapers know Mrs. Lindbergh had suddenly changed her plans about taking the baby to Englewood?

There were three possible answers. The first was that it was sheer chance—a successful stab in the dark. The second was that informants from within the house had deliberately told the kidnap gang and were therefore a part of the conspiracy. The third was that servants had, unwittingly, revealed the information to some of their associates.

The detectives, questioning the servants with soft insistence—for there was no rough work in this inquisition—were particularly interested in Betty Gow's movements. With her they went patiently over every moment of the day and every moment of the previous week-end. At every point they checked and rechecked her story. Considering the young woman's distracted state of mind it was a clear and straightforward account.

"I tried to get Johnson on the telephone at Englewood before I left for Hopewell," she said, "but I couldn't reach him because he wasn't at his boarding house. So I left word for him to call me in the evening at Hopewell. We had intended seeing each other that night. He called me from Englewood between eight and nine o'clock that night and I told him how it happened I wasn't at the Morrow house. I told him the baby had a cold."

And where was "Red" Johnson just now? Betty didn't know, but he had a brother living in West Hartford, and perhaps——

The police of Hartford, swooping down on the small home of John Johnson in the western suburb, found "Red" Johnson calmly asleep, unconscious of the hue and cry. Yes, he knew of the kidnaping. In fact, he admitted, he had tried to telephone to his friend, Betty Gow, to find out more about it, but he couldn't get his call through. He was neither perturbed nor alarmed at this sudden descent of the police, although the thought occurred to him that they might make some embarrassing inquiries into his history, and that would mean he would have to go back to Norway.

They took him to the police station and subjected him to as thorough a grilling as any well-schooled group of police and detectives might stage. Throughout the ordeal he was calm—almost bland. He had a ready answer to every question and seemed to conceal nothing. He admitted he had seen Betty Gow Sunday night and Monday night, and that he would have been with her on the fateful Tuesday night if she had remained in Englewood.

The telephone lines between Hartford and Hopewell were busy. State's Attorney Hugh M. Alcorn, County Detective Edward J. Hickey, Captain George J. Sullivan and Chief of Police Joseph Grogan took turns plying the youth with questions and then turning to the wires to collect more questions from the state police heads at the Lindbergh home.

How had Johnson reached his brother's home in West Hartford? The answer was:

"Driving my green Chrysler coupe, license number NY-3U 9680."

The coupe had been found, where it should have been, at John Johnson's home, and busy detectives had inspected every square inch of it. Thrown carelessly in a corner they saw an empty milk bottle. A white film remaining in it showed it had been used for nothing else but milk. They asked Johnson about it.

"Oh, I'm fond of milk," he said. "I very often buy a quart and drink it while I'm driving."

The very simplicity of "Red's" explanation made it appear flimsy to the sweating detectives. State's Attorney Alcorn viewed the finding of the milk bottle, logically, as "highly important." What would a convivial sailor be doing with a bottle of milk? The police net began to tighten around "Red" Johnson, who knew too much about the events inside the Lindbergh home.

"I do not think," said State's Attorney Alcorn, "that Johnson has been entirely frank. We are going to hold him, on the strength of the story he tells, for further investigation."

Further incidents and coincidences began to involve the sailor in the mesh. While Johnson was being questioned in the County Building at Hartford, postoffice employees intercepted a special delivery letter addressed to Mrs. Lindbergh and a postcard addressed to the Colonel, both mailed in the Connecticut city and both written in pencil. The message on the postcard read:

Baby still safe. Get things quiet.

The hook on the "J" in the New Jersey address was turned to the right instead of the left, a peculiarity identical with that of two postcards already received by the Lindberghs, one mailed from Newark, New Jersey and the other from East Orange, New Jersey. All three were addressed to "Chas. Linberg, Princeton, N. J."

Then there was the belated story of James L. Dalton, toll collector at the Outerbridge Crossing, which links Perth Amboy, New Jersey to Tottenville, on Staten Island.

At 10:45 o'clock on the night of March 1st, Dalton stopped a green automobile at the toll bridge. In the car were two men, a woman and a baby. The child appeared to be clothed in a white zipper suit of brushed wool. The three adults appeared to be about thirty years old, and the baby an infant, perhaps a year and a half old.

Dalton couldn't seem to remember the automobile license number—one can't keep track of all the licenses that roll over the bridge in the course of a night—but he thought the first letters and digits were NY-3U. Then there was a figure he had, quite frankly, forgotten, but thereafter came the figures 680.

Both of the men in the automobile, Dalton said, were light complexioned, apparently well dressed, and spoke good English. They made several inquiries regarding directions, and then drove on.

Captain of Detectives Henry Gauthier of Jersey City rushed to Hartford and joined in questioning the red-headed youth. Photographs of his coupe were sent by air to Hopewell and Jersey City, for comparison with descriptions of "suspicious" cars seen hither and yon by New Jersey residents on the day of the kidnaping.

"Red" Johnson, exhausted and shaken by the ceaseless interrogation, lost his bland composure and for a time it appeared he was about to "break." But he stubbornly insisted he had given the detectives the truth about his movements, particularly as they revolved around the controversial hours of the kidnaping.

"All through the evening of March 1st, I was with Johansen Junge and his wife, Marguerite," he insisted. Marguerite was a seamstress employed by the Morrows. There the matter rested until the Junges could be seen and interviewed. And when Detective Captain Gauthier talked with them they corroborated, in part at least, "Red" Johnson's story. Except that they weren't sure but that "Red" had left them, for a few hours, on the night of the kidnaping.

"Positive identifications" of Johnson's coupe, seen scurrying over New Jersey roads before and after the kidnaping, poured into police headquarters. A majority of them were manifestly incorrect because one object cannot be in two places at the same time. But the number of persons who recalled having seen "a man, a woman and a baby" during the night of March 1st was truly astounding.

James Bistany, proprietor of a roadside lunchroom at Norwalk, Connecticut, came forward to report that the usual "man, woman and baby," in a green car, stopped at his counter only a few hours after the kidnaping. He looked at "Red" Johnson, in a police lineup, examined his features intently, and shook his head. Johnson certainly was not one of his midnight customers.

Johnson was finally taken to New Jersey, unshaken in his account of his movements, but held as an important witness. By this time even the police were convinced that his alibi was iron-clad, and constant observation of his mental reactions impressed them with the belief that whatever else he might have been, "Red" Johnson was not the criminal type.

"He wouldn't hurt a fly," they agreed.

There still lingered the suspicion, however, that he might have had friends who were not so innocent and that, perhaps boasting of his friendship for Betty Gow and his knowledge about the daily activities of the world's most noted baby, he might inadvertently have dropped valuable information to the gangster world.

Furthermore, they still had the undeniable proof that he was in the United States illegally. It was their duty, therefore, when they were done with their inquisition, to hold him for the immigration authorities. They did it joyfully. It was fitting and proper that something should be done to the young man who had been so annoying!

It was not until March 20th that Johnson was officially exonerated of all complicity in the crime. In the interval the police had run down and checked every known friend and every possible acquaintance of the sailor. Their operations took time. And produced a result of nothing, net. Johnson was turned over to the immigration officials and by them sent back to his native land. He went in rather good humor for a man who had undergone such an ordeal, and avowed his determination some day to return—legally, this time— and become an American citizen.

Activities of the Jersey State Police, under command of Colonel H. Norman Schwarzkopf, were by no means halted during the fruitless investigation of the Johnson phase. While the municipal police were engaging themselves with that once-promising lead, the troopers and detectives, headed by Captain John J. Lamb, were tracing scores, hundreds, even thousands of possible clues. The very mechanical operations involved in handling telegrams, telephone calls and floods of mail—many of these communications obviously coming from cranks—taxed the resources of the department. The thorough search of the Sourlands, hampered and blocked by the hordes of private investigators, morbidly inclined citizens, and newspaper men and women, required large squads. The simple police duty of protecting the Lindbergh home from intruders occupied the attention of still further platoons of men. Hopewell swarmed with humanity, and it was even possible that within this motley gathering the actual kidnaper himself might be lurking.

The police of the nation responded quickly and eagerly for duty. From his capitol at Trenton, Governor A. Harry

Moore sent an appeal "to all the forces of law and order in the nation" to concentrate on the hunt for the kidnapers. To President Herbert Hoover and to the governors of states as far west as Illinois the governor sent the following telegram:

> Entire country shocked at kidnaping of Lindbergh baby. Imperative that coordinated effort be made to apprehend abductors and restore child. Have called conference at my office at State House in Trenton for tomorrow, at 11 a.m. of police officials of leading American cities. Regard it as plain duty of everyone to cooperate. I earnestly urge you to send a representative best qualified to assist.

The response was immediate. It resulted in the largest assemblage of famous American detectives in the history of the country. By train and by airplane they poured into New Jersey, the "aces" of metropolitan police forces, from the famous "Pat" Roche of Chicago to the equally famous J. Edgar Hoover, chief of the Bureau of Investigation of the Federal Department of Justice.

The detectives, each with his own set of theories, met behind closed doors in a large assembly hall of the State Capitol. For more than an hour Colonel Schwarzkopf, presiding over this unusual meeting, outlined the known facts surrounding the baby's disappearance and turned over to the crime detectors what few positive clues had been developed in the few hours since Betty Gow had made her appalling discovery in the Lindbergh nursery.

A hubbub of suggestions and counter-suggestions resulted. As with many other professions, so in the nation's police

departments there existed, and continue to exist, great or
petty jealousies. The lines of demarcation between federal
investigators, state police and metropolitan departments
were finely drawn and forbade encroachment. The metropolitan detective had little but scorn for his country cousin.
Private detectives were viewed by the regularly constituted
force exactly as press agents are viewed by journeymen news
writers.

A few of the sleuths visited Hopewell, inspected the ladder, looked at the ransom note, stared at the footprints in
the ground and offered one or two vague theories. The
others, promising their hearty coöperation, departed for
their own cities and went about their business in their own
way, using their own methods, working out their own plans.

Colonel Schwarzkopf himself returned to Hopewell to
begin the painstaking task of sorting, checking, elaborating,
running down the tangled threads of evidence.

Schwarzkopf, a graduate of West Point and a thorough
soldier, with the build of an athlete and a mind trained for
quick thinking in an emergency, made no pretensions to
being a detective. His job was military. It was the super-
vision of a body of armed men, the maintenance of dis-
cipline, the training of a police army. He had with him,
however, and in complete charge of the highly specialized
detective branch, Captain John J. Lamb. Lamb's name was
already well and favorably known to the police world. It
was he who, more closely than any other official of New
Jersey, had approximated a solution of the baffling Hall-
Mills murder case—melodrama of a small town Lover's
Lane involving an amorous pastor and a susceptible lady of
his choir.

Working under the direction of these able officers were more than five-score troopers, engaged eighteen hours a day —or until exhaustion forced them to drop to cots for a little sleep—in guarding the Lindbergh estate, searching the kidnap zone, investigating every household within a ten-mile radius, and interviewing the more than three hundred residents of the section who were brought to the house for questioning in those first few days.

They were working, furthermore, against great odds. Public opinion was sharply divided on the major question of whether the police should step out of the case and permit Colonel Lindbergh freedom to deal with the kidnapers, or whether it was their paramount duty to use every bit of energy and brains they possessed to capture the gang.

One side said: "The return of the baby is the prime duty of all officials." That was the majority opinion.

The other side said: "The duty of a police force is to catch malefactors, and they are sworn to that duty." They were in the minority.

Yet it was imperative to protect the Lindberghs from the hosts of cranks and well-wishers who were bound to interfere, either maliciously or unintentionally, with the progress of justice. And it was manifestly impossible for Colonel Schwarzkopf to call off his forces, however devoutly such a move might have been desired by Colonel Lindbergh. So Colonel Schwarzkopf grimly clung on, permitting the Lindbergh family as much freedom of operation outside the ken of the police as he could, in all conscience, allow.

At noon, on March 4th, after three days of almost sleepless vigil, Colonel Lindbergh decided to make an appeal, over his own and Anne Morrow Lindbergh's signatures, to the world at large. Their statement, pathetic in the light of subsequent events, was issued on a typewritten slip, in unemotional language. It said:

> Mrs. Lindbergh and I desire to make a personal contact with the kidnapers of our child.
>
> Our only interest is in his immediate and safe return and we feel certain that the kidnapers will realize that this interest is strong enough to justify them in having complete confidence and trust in any promises that we may make in connection with his return.
>
> We urge those who have the child to select any representative that they desire to meet a representative of ours who will be suitable to them at any time and at any place that they may designate.
>
> If this is accepted, we promise that we will keep whatever arrangements that may be made by their representative and ours strictly confidential and we further pledge ourselves that we will not try to injure in any way those connected with the return of the child.
>
> CHARLES A. LINDBERGH
> ANNE LINDBERGH

This overture to the kidnapers was accompanied, however, by an official statement from Attorney General William A. Stevens of New Jersey, who announced that whatever the Lindberghs might or might not promise, the officers of his state had no power to offer or grant any immunity to criminals.

To the cry of the Lindberghs, "we will not prosecute," the state answered, "but we will."

Colonel Henry C. Breckinridge, Lindbergh's chief advisor, explained the reason behind his appeal.

"We are counting," he said, "upon the personal statement to create a feeling of confidence in the minds of the persons who now have the baby, so they will feel free to establish a contact with us. Colonel Lindbergh is not afraid. Certainly the kidnapers cannot believe he would trifle with them in a matter of such extreme importance to him. He will meet them anywhere, under any conditions they may wish to lay down, even to going into the underworld itself, to meet the men who have his baby and arrange for his return."

On the day this appeal was issued, an additional cause for worry fell upon the Lindbergh household. Mrs. Lindbergh, who had slept only a fitful six hours since the night of March 1st, developed a cold. In itself the illness was not dangerous. But coupled with her fatigue and the fact, which became known simultaneously, that within a few months she would become the mother of a second child, it became a new source of alarm. The reasons behind the parents' appeal to the kidnapers, spread on the front page of every newspaper in the United States and read into the microphones of every broadcasting station, were the more understandable.

There was a substantial belief, in the minds of most lay investigators and some of the higher officials, that the entire crime was the work of an underworld crime syndicate; that professionals rather than amateurs had plotted and executed the abduction. Such a crime demanded nerves of steel and a bold imagination, clock-work efficiency and a recklessness of public opinion that fitted in well with what was known of some of the nation's best-known gangs.

The name of Morris Rosner, who had connections leading

from the government down to the New York underworld, had been suggested to Colonel Breckinridge as that of a man who could give vast assistance, if the baby were actually being held by gangsters. Rosner was called to Hopewell and entrusted with many of the official secrets, much to the displeasure of the police heads who viewed his operations with suspicion.

Rosner believed firmly that the crime was the work of professionals, and hinted, in fact, that its solution might lie within the membership either of the notorious Purple gang, of Detroit, or the Scarface Al Capone mob, of Chicago. His idea, he told Colonel Lindbergh, was to gain the confidence of the underworld by appointing two of their lowly citizens as official emissaries.

Thus, on March 5th, twenty-four hours after issuing their appeal to the kidnapers offering virtual immunity from prosecution, Colonel and Mrs. Lindbergh sent out a second announcement, a pitiful demonstration of their anxiety and of the strange lengths to which they had been influenced to go by their advisors. The following notice appeared in the newspapers:

> If the kidnapers of our child are unwilling to deal direct we fully authorize "Salvy" Spitale and Irving Bitz to act as our go-between. We will also follow any other method suggested by the kidnapers that we can be sure will bring the return of our child.
>   CHARLES A. LINDBERGH
>   ANNE LINDBERGH

Neither Salvatore Spitale nor Irving Bitz was regarded as a "big shot" in New York's world of rackets and rum.

Theirs was a modest partnership, based on the ownership of two or three speakeasies in Manhattan, one of which, in Forty-first Street at the rear of the *New York Daily News* building, was a comfortable hangout for newspapermen. But their official appointment as agents for the Lindberghs immediately raised them in rank and importance—and incidentally assured them effectively of immunity for their own illegal business so long as they should be engaged in the meritorious work of running to earth the nation's most daring criminals.

So, in the haunts of these two men, there was for a time a flurry of hurried comings and goings, of conferences with mysterious visitors, a whispering behind closed doors.

Unquestionably, the estimable Messrs. Spitale and Bitz would have delighted to have turned up the Lindbergh child's kidnapers. So would millions of other less sinister citizens. But if those two had turned the trick, what a triumph for the "honest" speakeasy!

The unfortunate fact remained, however, that Spitale and Bitz had no more idea who kidnaped Charles Lindbergh, Jr. than they did of who kidnaped Charley Ross. If the incident served any purpose at all, which is doubtful, it was merely to give the authorities some cause to believe that they were wrong in assigning the crime to professed criminals of the gangster type, and to turn their attention to the possibility that a daring amateur, wily, perhaps working as a lone wolf, conceived the plot and carried it out.

For many a long day Rosner and Spitale and Bitz fuddled around with the problem while they basked in public acclaim.

CHAPTER FOUR

THE CRANKS, THE WEAK-MINDED, THE CRIMINALLY UNBALANCED
made a cackling holiday, for a time, over the events which
had stimulated their crazy emotions and further shattered
their reason, and they added immeasurably to the pains and
heartaches of the Lindbergh family and the labors of the
police. Unfortunately, it had been reasoned, the deed itself
might have been accomplished by just such a cunning
maniac, and it was necessary to deal with every clue, from
whatever source it came, sane or lunatic.

More than once, Mrs. Lindbergh was aroused from her
bed to talk with persons in Maine or California, in Michigan
or Mexico, who were "positive" they had found the child.
Parents of children from one to three years old, innocently
touring the country, were suspected, trailed, held up and
arrested from coast to coast.

The Lindberghs had carefully withheld from the public
certain distinguishing marks by which their baby might
have been identified. The world knew, from the child's
photographs, that he had a deeply dimpled chin and a smile
like his father's. In a general way it could picture his blond,
curly hair and blue eyes. But it did not have the secret, the
key to his identification.

Therefore, after each excited informant had given his
"proof" over the telephone that he had seen or found the

infant and failed, in his description, to say the convincing words the Lindberghs were waiting for, it became more and more apparent to the watchers that the whole country was pursuing a maze of false clues.

Colonel Lindbergh was still insistent upon receiving and listening to every person who had a tale to unfold. So it happened that an impressive man "with a secret he would tell to no one else but Anne Morrow Lindbergh" was able to penetrate to the home and the very room where she was lying ill. He stood in the doorway while the worn and distracted parents waited for his message. Then, to their amazement and horror, he began a Shakespearian declaration. He was unquestionably insane, and the police gently removed him from the scene.

Spiritualists and pseudo spiritualists also made the occasion a field day for their operations. One of them professed to have seen, in a trance, Ollie Whately the butler handing the child to someone who stood outside on a ladder. Her seance concluded, triumphantly, "the baby is at 123 Ivy street, Bloomfield, New Jersey." Detectives, rushing to that city, found no such address.

Two others, professing to be in communion with the spirits, offered their services. Unable to "break through the light," they told Colonel Breckinridge, who was listening, that he would do better to go back to his office in New York and "await a message there." The couple, who incidentally came from the Bronx, had quite by accident given the lawyer some good advice, as subsequent developments proved.

This was on March 4th, three days after the kidnaping. And it was on this day that the Lindberghs received their

first genuine message from the kidnapers after the brief note
that had been deposited in the baby's room at the time of the
actual kidnaping. This message, mailed from Brooklyn,
read:

> Dear Sir. We have warned you note to make
> anything public also notify the police now you have
> to take consequences—means we will have to hold
> the baby until everything is quite. We can note
> make any appointment just now. We know very
> well what it means to us. It is (is it) realy necessary
> to make a world affair out of this, or to get your
> baby back as soon as possible to settle those affair
> in a quick way will be better for both—don't by
> afraid about the baby—keeping care of us day and
> night. We also will feed him according to the diet.
> We are interested to send him back in gut health.
> And ransom was made aus for 50000 $ but now we
> have to take another person to it and probably have
> to keep the baby for a longer time as we expected.
> So the amount will be 70000 20000 in 50$ bills
> 25000 $ in 20$ bill 15000 $ in 10$ bills and 10000 in
> 5$ bills Don't mark any bills or take them from
> one serial nomer. We will form you latter were to
> deliver the mony. But we will note do so until the
> Police is out of the cace and the pappers are quite.
> The kidnaping we prepared in years so we are pre-
> pared for everyding.

At the bottom of the letter were the strange, interlocking
circles in blue and red, duplicate of the symbol on the nursery kidnap note. There was no question but that it was
genuine.

On the following day the kidnapers again communicated

with the family, through Colonel Breckinridge's New York office. The soothsayers had been right. Colonel Breckinridge was needed back in New York!

The third ransom note was, in a sense, a repetition of the second. It appeared that the kidnapers were worried lest their messages be intercepted by the police before they reached Colonel Lindbergh's hands. In the same peculiar script characterizing the first two communications, it said:

Dear Sir: Did you receive ouer letter from March 4. we sent the mail in one off the letter—near Boro Hall, Brooklyn. We know Police interfer with your privatmail. How can we come to any arrangements this way. in the future we will send ouer letters to Mr. Breckenbridge at 25 Broadway. We believe polise captured two letter and let not forwarded to you. We will not accept any go-between from your sent. We will arrangh theas latter. There is no worry about the boy. He is very well and will be feed according to the diet. Best dank for intorma- tion about it. We are interested to send your boy back in gut health.

It is neccisery to make a world-affair out of it, or to get your boy back as soon as possible. Why did you ignore ouer letter which we left in the room the baby would be back long ago. You would not get any result from Polise becauce our dinaping was pland for a year allredy. But we were afraid the boy would not be strong enough.

Ouer ransam was made out for 50000 but now we have to put another to it as propperly have to hold the baby longer as we expected so it will be 70000$ 20000 in 50$ bills 25000 in 25$ bills 15000$ in 10$ bills and 10000 in 5$ bills. We warn you

again not to mark any bills or take them from one
ser.No. We will inform you latter how to deliver
the mony but not before the polise is out of this cace
and the pappers are quite.

Again there was the tell-tale symbol at the foot of the note,
and the watchers were convinced they had established contact with the true kidnapers. Among other phrases in the
letter was one—"why did you ignore ouer letter which we
left in the room"—which provided a double check on its
genuineness. No one in the world, save the kidnapers and
the responsible principals in the case, knew a ransom note
had been left in the nursery.

Analysis of the notes, their twisted, Teutonic expressions,
their German construction and occasional spelling, confirmed the original belief of the detectives that they were
dealing with a man of foreign extraction. But for all their
awkwardness, the notes were direct and to the point. The
kidnaper wanted to bargain. He would not bargain until
the police were removed from the case. He reassured them
that the child was in "gut" health—preying on the parents'
sensibilities to force a quick deal.

It was also evident that the kidnaper was watching the
newspapers and perhaps listening to the almost hourly radio
broadcasts. His reference to the baby's diet proved that, for
it had been published in all the newspapers of March 3rd at
the request of a mother who was greatly worried over the
health of her baby.

"Mrs. Anne Morrow Lindbergh," the announcement read,
"asks that the baby's complete diet be adhered to, as follows:
One-half cup orange juice on awakening. One quart of milk

a day. Three tablespoons of cooked cereal morning and evening. Two tablespoons of cooked vegetables once a day—preferably peas, carrots, spinach or potatoes. The yolk of one egg. One baked potato or rice. Two tablespoons stewed fruit. One-half cup prune juice after the afternoon nap. Fourteen drops viosteral (a cod liver oil preparation) during the day."

At a moment when the kidnaper was thus stealthily approaching the Lindberghs to bring his plot to the desired conclusion, events were occurring in the Bronx which were eventually to provide the case with one of its most fantastic and sensational phases. A certain John F. Condon, holder of an honorary doctor's degree, educator, lecturer and patriot, entered the case.

In the welter of news surrounding the kidnaping, the *Bronx Home News,* a community journal circulating almost exclusively in the northern sections of Greater New York, printed an interview with the Doctor.

In the course of his statement, Dr. Condon had said:

> I offer all I can scrape together so a loving mother may again have her child and Col. Lindbergh may know that the American people are grateful for the honor bestowed upon them by his pluck and daring.
>
> Let the kidnapers know that no testimony of mine, or information coming from me, will be used against them. I offer $1,000 which I've saved from my salary (all of my life's savings) in addition to the suggested $50,000. I am ready, at my own expense, to go anywhere, also to give the kidnapers

the extra money and never utter their names to
any one.

If this is not agreeable, then I ask the kidnapers
to get any Catholic priest, with the knowledge that
every priest must hold inviolate any statement
which may be made by the kidnaper.

This was not the first such offer that had been made by
public-spirited citizens. John Grier Hibben, President of
Princeton University, Warden Lewis Lawes of Sing Sing
prison, Dudley Field Malone, noted New York lawyer, and
many others had offered to act as intermediaries, always
upon a pledge that no harm would befall the kidnapers.
Dr. Condon was in good and respectable company.

Dr. Condon was a prophet who was not without honor in
his own county. At seventy-four, a cheerful, kindly man, he
boasted that in forty-eight years he had never missed teaching a scheduled class. He was an outdoor man, imbued with
the gospel of exercise, clean living and health-building
sports.

More than six feet tall, and of a powerful build, he had
distinguished himself in athletics in his younger days, and
even now found a zest in refereeing football games or acting
as a baseball umpire. He had given Fordham University,
where he was now teaching pedagogics, its first football,
taught many of his students the art of swimming, and
preached to them the necessity for body building.

He was devoted to youth—and youth responded by giving
him their friendship, loyalty and devotion. Thousands of
the younger generation knew him by sight for he had lec-

tured to them or played games with them, and thousands more knew him by reputation.

Dr. Condon was a sentimental man, emotionally patriotic, steeped in a belief that American institutions, American history and American heroes—among them Colonel Charles A. Lindbergh—were God's gifts to world civilization.

In later days there were those who professed to see something strange in Dr. Condon's intervention in the Lindbergh case. They asked questions. Why should the kidnapers pay any attention to a communication from the Bronx? How would it happen that their eyes would light on the columns of a community newspaper? What inspired Dr. Condon to give his interview and with it the offer of his life savings for the return of the Lindbergh baby?

In the course of events, those first two questions were to be answered. At the time of the first hue and cry for the kidnapers, Dr. Condon himself answered the third and his answer was genuine and simple.

"The only thing I wanted," he said, "was to see that baby's arms around his mother's neck once more."

When Dr. Condon's interview appeared on the front page of the *Bronx Home News* it created no stir in other public prints. Few editors paid much attention, in those days, to neighborhood newspapers. They had interviews of their own, some from the highest executives of the nation, with which to fill their columns, and the incident passed unnoticed. Unnoticed, that is, save by a few readers in the Bronx, among them one man with grim lips and a pointed chin. This man read it and acted at once. He sat down and wrote the Doctor a letter.

In Hopewell, where a hundred newspaper men were begging for "just one interview with Colonel Lindbergh," to be met with the response that the Colonel must be excused, it was quite evident that the family and the police were drawing apart in the matter of procedure, and that the child's father was holding himself more and more aloof from the authorities. Early on March 7th, Captain Lamb admitted to the press that the police had not been taken into the Colonel's confidence regarding any possible dealings through his gangland emissaries, Spitale and Bitz.

Police activities, in fact, appeared slowed down, although in the garage where they had established field headquarters, Colonel Schwarzkopf, Major Schoeffel and Captain Lamb continued to map their strategy. Out in the fields, the troopers kindled bonfires against the snow and cold winds, and maintained their constant guard duty.

A woman, Annette Wilcox, who said she was a waitress in a Philadelphia restaurant, arrived to tell the police a story that—for a few hours—interested them deeply.

On the Friday after the kidnaping, she asserted, two men entered the restaurant where she was employed, and talked in her hearing about the case. From their conversation she "learned" that the kidnapers had flown over the Lindbergh estate, meaning to return the child, but that when they saw the heavy concentration of police they flew away.

She did not know, of course, that the numbers of every plane that flew within spy-glass distance of the estate were already checked, and her story fell flat, of its own weight, when it was investigated.

The insistence of the press upon having "official statements," tangible, credible reports on the progress of the case instead of the myriad false clues they were themselves digging up, had led to new arrangements for handling news reports. The newspaper men, it was agreed, would twice a day present what questions they cared to ask, in written form. The police would thereafter, as soon as convenient, make whatever replies they deemed fitting and proper—or no reply at all if none was indicated.

The entrance of Spitale and Bitz into the case had captured the imaginations of the news men and served the unintentional purpose of dragging a red herring across the trail. While they should have been watching the Bronx, they were, figuratively, watching the back doors of Manhattan speakeasies. They had reasoned that Spitale and Bitz would not have been appointed as mediators unless there had been some indication that they "knew something." They could not conceive of the move as a mere chance shot, and their conviction was strengthened by reports from Chicago that Al Capone was beginning to stir up his henchmen, to muscle in on the proceedings.

Capone, from his cell in the Cook County jail, where he was being held before his trip to Atlanta for the long stretch, had professed his horror at the kidnaping.

"It is the most outrageous thing I ever heard of," the man who was himself graced with the title, Public Enemy No. 1, had said. "I know how Mrs. Capone and I would feel if our son were kidnaped, and I sympathize with the Lindberghs. I'll give $10,000 for information that will lead to the recovery of the child unharmed and the capture of the kidnapers."

The $10,000 was small change for the racketeer. He could

have afforded, and actually would have been glad to give half a million to restore America's most famous baby to his father's arms. Capone was under a long sentence. He knew that if, through any one of his agencies, the baby were safely brought back to Hopewell, millions of citizens would have forgiven his past and implored a presidential pardon for him.

The day's questions of Colonel Schwarzkopf as outlined by the reporters had, therefore, very little to do with what actually was transpiring, but were directed largely at the vacant-minded activities of the petty rum-runners and racketeers, the gangsters and gunmen whom a large section of the public and not a few police heads insisted upon regarding as the mainspring of detective activity.

Among the questions they asked that day were these:

Q. Have Spitale and Bitz, or either of them, ever been in the Lindbergh home?

A. Not to my knowledge.

Q. Have they communicated with the Lindbergh home or with Lindbergh or with any one connected with the case?

A. Not to my knowledge.

Q. Are there any indications that the introduction of Spitale and Bitz will ensure the safe return of the baby?

A. We have no knowledge of their being introduced into the case.

Q. Has any communication purporting to come from the kidnapers reached the family saying "Baby alive and well?"

A. Not to my knowledge.

Q. Have you determined or can you learn who suggested the names of Spitale and Bitz to the Lindberghs or how these two underworld characters were suggested?

A. We do not know whether or not the names were suggested to Colonel Lindbergh and therefore could not say by whom they were suggested, if they were suggested.

Upon such scraps of non-information the press fed and, in some instances, waxed fat. The chief source of what real knowledge they gained about the case was through what the newspaper trade calls "pipe lines." Favored reporters, striking up friendships with minor officials, troopers or witnesses, and keeping the friendships alive through the divers means familiar to every earnest newspaperman, obtained many a tip that approximated, if it did not quite, hit the truth.

Considering the material they had, they did fairly well, these reporters, against overwhelming odds and the utmost secrecy that cloaked every movement in Hopewell. And considering the material the state police had, they did very well too. They were forced to lie, at times, about leads that looked promising. They were forced to hedge and take refuge in silence at other times, and they did it with straight faces and easy consciences, in the interest of justice.

Nevertheless, during the first few weeks following the kidnaping there was constant antagonism and friction between the authorities and the press. To every personal request from Colonel Lindbergh the newspapers had acceded. They had withdrawn their reporters from the close pre-

cincts of the estate. They had "killed" true stories bearing on
the case, in the interest of returning the baby alive and un-
harmed. Yet the tale of their relationship with the police
was, according to *Editor and Publisher,* organ of the trade,
one of "official suppressions, official misrepresentations of
fact and official denials of officially sponsored statements."
It described the office of the New Jersey State Police as "a
breeding spot for misleading statements" which was a bar-
rier to the communication of legitimate news to newspaper
offices in New York.

The police tapped all press telephones. A reporter, tele-
phoning from his room in the Hopewell House, was able
to look from his window into the switchboard room of the
telephone exchange. When he called his number he had the
pleasure of watching a state trooper pick up a set of head
phones and plug himself in on the line.

"I'll have to go to Elizabeth or New Brunswick to talk to
you," he told his editor. "From where I sit I can see a state
trooper listening to us." The trooper dropped his ear phones.

Three agencies—the Lindbergh family and their advisors,
the police, and the press—were thus working at cross-pur-
poses throughout the early progress of the chase, and the
police, being in the middle and bearing the brunt of the
criticism, were very cross about it all.

As the "discovery" of children, all over the United States,
who bore some faint resemblance to the kidnaped child
came to their attention, they became further annoyed. As,
for example, when a ragged, dirty little urchin, accompanied
by four adults "traveling about," was found at a cross-roads
town in Tennessee. Because he had curly, blond hair the

Tennessee constables at once jumped to the conclusion that he must be Charles A. Lindbergh, Jr. Telephone calls to Colonel and Mrs. Lindbergh proved beyond a doubt that the Tennessee officials were wrong, but for twenty-four hours the luckless tourists were held in jail while telephotos of their baby were sent to Hopewell.

"We've been stopped by the police and investigated twice before," the companions of the infant declared. Upon their release they printed a sign which read: "See the Baby that Looks like the Lindbergh Baby—15 Cents," and for a few days did a circus business on the strength of the resemblance.

Such incidents, repeated over and over again, were as annoying as they were distracting, and their repetition caused the weary police to view with understandable skepticism many of the developments which were later shown to have had a direct bearing on the case. To them the entire world seemed to have gone mad, and the amiable activities of Dr. John F. Condon, Patriarch of the Bronx, appeared to be part and parcel of the madness.

On the night of March 9th, Dr. Condon, tremendously agitated, entered Max Rosenhain's restaurant on the Grand Concourse, where he was accustomed to take a nightly cup of coffee, and beckoned his friend, the proprietor, to his side. It was almost midnight. With fluttering hands, he drew from his wallet a letter and thrusting it into Max's hands commanded: "Read this!"

The letter, in the same misshapen characters of the original ransom note, said:

> Dear Sir: If you are willing to act as go-between in Lindbergh cace please follow strictly instruction. Handel incloced letter personally to Mr. Lindbergh. It will explain everything. Don't tell any one about it as soons we find out the police is notifyed everything are cancell and it will be a further delay. Affter you get the money from Mr. Lindbergh put 3 words in New York American
>
> > Money is ready
>
> After notise well give you further instriction. don't be affrait we are not out for your 1,000$ keep it.
>
> Only act stricly. Be at house every night between 6-12 by that time you will hear from us.

Rosenhain told Dr. Condon that, in his opinion, the thing to do was to get in touch with Hopewell at once. But when the Doctor, whose telephone call was put through after the usual delays, was asked to tell his story to Colonel Lindbergh's advisor, his heart failed him and his tongue clave to the roof of his mouth. Seeing the doctor was unable to make himself understood, Rosenhain seized the telephone and explained carefully how the Doctor had received the note through the mail that day, and how another sealed note, addressed to Colonel Lindbergh, accompanied it.

The Colonel, after a moment's hesitation, directed that the sealed letter be opened.

Rosenhain tore open the letter and read:

> Dear Sir: Mr.Condon may act as go-between you may give him the 70,000$ make one packet the size will be about (here following the drawing of a box, 7 x 6 x 14 inches in dimensions).
>
> We have notifyd you already in what kinds of

bills We warn you not to set a trapp in many way
If you or someone els will notify the Police there
will be a further delay. after we have the mony in
hand we will tell you where to find your boy.

You may have a areplane redy it is about 150 mil.
awy. But before tell you the add. a delay of 8
howers will be between.

There was silence at the other end of the telephone for a
moment, and then Colonel Lindbergh asked if there was
any distinguishing mark on the note. Rosenhain described
the strange device at the bottom—the intersecting circles in
red and blue, and the three marginal holes.

"Hire a fast car at my expense and come to Hopewell at
once," Colonel Lindbergh said. "I'll have a police car meet
you at Princeton, to escort you over."

CHAPTER FIVE

OUTSIDE THE RESTAURANT, WHEN DR. CONDON AND MAX ROS-
enhain rushed breathlessly out of doors to seek a conveyance
to Hopewell, was Milton Gaglio, a clothier who was a friend
of both men. He had a fast car and was eager to give his
services. So they drove, at top speed, to a drug store in the
New Jersey college town, where, in accordance with the
prearrangements, a police car was waiting. On the outskirts
of Hopewell they picked up Colonel Breckinridge, who
entered the car and questioned the men until they pulled up
in front of the Lindbergh home.

The Colonel met the party at the door, greeted them ex-
citedly, and led them into the living room, where sandwiches and coffee were waiting. While the Doctor warmed
his tired body by the fireside, he told his story. The conference lasted until dawn, and the Doctor was so close to exhaustion at its end that he was directed to bed, while his
companions returned to the Bronx.

There was no doubt in Colonel Lindbergh's mind that
they were at last on the right track. This was no hoax. The
symbol at the bottom of the note to Condon and that at the
bottom of the message left in the child's room were identical
—made with the same mathematical precision and attention
to detail.

At nightfall, much rested, Dr. Condon returned to his

home. Shortly after his arrival his telephone rang, and a hoarse voice told him he would receive another message sometime during the evening of March 12th.

On that fateful evening, a tense group of watchers—the Doctor, his friends Rosenhain and Gaglio, Colonel Breckinridge, and Al Reich, a former prize-fighter who acted as bodyguard and chauffeur—waited nervously in Dr. Condon's living room. At 8:30 o'clock there was a ring at the doorbell. There stood a taxicab driver, with a crumpled note in his hand. He walked away, somewhat startled at his reception by five men, and by the fact that one of them, Gaglio, had slipped out of doors, run to the sidewalk, and jotted down the number of his cab. The taxi driver was Joseph Perrone, who more than two years later was to figure heavily in the case.

Back once more in the house, the five men inspected the note. Again it bore the distinguishing marks that stamped it as genuine, and it said:

> Mr.Condon: We trust you but we will note come in your Haus it is to danger even you can note know if Police or secret servise is watching you
> Follow this instruction, take a car and drive to the last supway station from Jerome Ave.line 100 feet from the station on the left seide is a empty frank-further stand with a big open porch around. you will find o notise in senter of the porch underneath a stone. this notise will tell you where to find uss.
> Act accordingly
> After ¾ of a houer be on the place bring the mony with you.

Dr. Condon already was putting on his coat. With Al Reich as his chauffeur, he followed the directions in the note, and drove to the "frank-further stand" near the subway. Beneath a rock on its broad porch, he found, as he had expected, his second instructions.

> Cross the street and follow the fence from the cemetery. direction to 233 street.
> I will meet you.

Reich remained in the automobile some distance away, while Dr. Condon nervously paced the dimly lighted sidewalk. Minutes, seeming like years, dragged by and the Doctor began to fear the whole affair was a monstrous hoax. Then, from the blackness of the cemetery, he saw something white waving over the fence. He walked toward the signal. It was a white handkerchief and behind it was the dim outline of a man.

The emissary's next movement was surprising. Like an athlete in a German Turnverein exhibition, he climbed up the other side of the high cemetery gates and seemed to drop from the skies, landing easily, cat-like, on his feet. Dr. Condon approached him, palms outstretched, to show he was unarmed.

No sooner had the two men come together, however, than a uniformed cemetery guard, on regular patrol, approached. Hearing the crunch of the third man's step on the gravel walk, the mysterious conspirator took to his heels, with Dr. Condon after him.

The doctor, a sprinter despite his age, caught up with the fleeing man and took him by the arm.

"See here," he said, "there is no reason to be afraid of me. I am alone."

The kidnapers' negotiator allowed himself to be persuaded to walk a short distance and sit down on a park bench, fifty yards from where Al Reich was waiting.

The first concern of the extortioner appeared to be whether the ransom money was ready.

"Did you bring it with you?" he asked.

The Doctor explained, in simple language, why that would have been impossible. First, he said, it would be necessary to establish to the satisfaction of the Lindberghs the fact that the gang to whom they paid any ransom actually was in possession of their child.

The purported kidnapers' representative then asked for proof, in turn, that Dr. Condon was authorized to deal for Colonel Lindbergh. The Doctor turned over Colonel Lindbergh's simple note agreeing to appoint the Doctor as an intermediary, and Condon bolstered this evidence with the story of how he had visited the nursery at Hopewell, talked with the parents, and gained their consent to his action. Nor could he refrain, from this point, at delivering a little homily on the heinousness of the crime. "What would your mother think?" he asked the man, sorrowfully.

As additional proof that he came from the Lindberghs, Dr. Condon afterwards told how he showed the agent two large safety pins and asked him whether he knew what they were. The man beside him identified them as the pins that had held down the blankets over the sleeping baby. He even went further and described intimate details of the nursery. *There was no doubt in the Doctor's mind at that moment that the man to whom he was talking actually was in the nursery at the time Baby Lindbergh was stolen!*

The mysterious agent, sitting with his chin buried in the collar and lapels of his short coat, apparently trusted the Doctor, but was fearful of police interruption. Under the gentle prodding of the go-between, however, he seemed to gain confidence, and even responded to some of Condon's highly personal questions.

His name was John, he said, and he came from Boston. He explained his foreign accent as Scandinavian, and said he had no relatives in this country. To Dr. Condon's eye, he appeared to be about thirty-five years old, and perhaps five feet, ten inches in height.

To a suspicious mind, however, "John's" readiness to answer questions about himself might have led to certain conclusions, among them that the man's name was not John, that he was not of Scandinavian birth, and that he was not from Boston. A furtive man undoubtedly would attempt to mislead such a questioner.

The conference lasted for an hour and fifteen minutes. Dr. Condon was told there were five in the kidnap gang— three men and two women—and that this particular agent was the "Number Two" man in the case. The Chief, the Number One man, would not see the Doctor because the Doctor knew him, "John" said. Then he went on to explain why the ransom had been raised to $70,000.

"There are more of us in it," he said. "Our arrangement is that the Number One and Number Two men will get $20,000 apiece, and the other three will get $10,000 apiece as their share."

They reached no agreement about money at this time. Dr. Condon turned the conversation to other issues. He wanted particularly to know whether it would be possible to see the baby—to make sure he was alive and well, to reassure the parents of his safety, and to provide absolute proof that payment of the ransom would restore the child.

It would be impossible, he was told. The baby was hidden on a boat fully six hours away. But it might be possible to arrange for the delivery of some token, easily identifiable by the Lindberghs, to prove to them the child was in the negotiators' hands.

The Doctor told "John" he would do what he could about the $70,000, although at the time, he explained, he was authorized only to go as high as the first sum mentioned, $50,000. He promised to take up with Colonel Lindbergh the matter of arranging for delivery of a suitable "token" from the baby's belongings, to be turned over to the parents before the final negotiations were carried out.

The kidnapers' spokesman said he wanted to prove to his fellow conspirators that he had actually established contact with the Doctor, and suggested that Condon publish another advertisement in the paper, saying simply, "Baby alive and well."

The question arose as to how soon "John" could deliver the required token. "John" once more told how the baby was 150 miles from New York, and said he would have to have time. He did promise, however, to get in touch with the Doctor before six o'clock the following evening, and said he thought the token might be delivered some time Monday.

Dr. Condon, who had conceived the little fantasy of calling himself "Jafsie" (only a slight deviation from pronunciation of his initials, J. F. C.) was exceedingly contented with the arrangements, and returned to the automobile where Al Reich was waiting for him.

All through Sunday, March 13th, Jafsie remained home, expecting word from the kidnapers. None came, nor was there any communication from them through Monday's twenty-four hours. Dr. Condon was worried. On Monday he inserted a five-word message in the newspapers:

Come and see us. Jafsie.

On Tuesday night, however, a package arrived at Jafsie's home. Colonel Breckinridge was in the house, awaiting the "token." Sitting on a couch in Jafsie's living room, he unwrapped the coverings.

In the box was a small garment. It was the sleeping suit in which the child had been tucked into bed on the evening of March 1st.

Identification of this garment was repeated at Hopewell, where Anne Morrow Lindbergh examined and wept over it. The indisputable proof lay in the fact that nurse Betty Gow had sewn to its sleeves the little metal guards designed to prevent him from sucking his thumbs. The threads were still hanging. And the sleeping suit showed indications of recent cleaning.

It will be remembered that the conference at the cemetery took place on the night of March 12th. This was March 15th, and three days had been required to produce the pitiful evidence that the extortioners had actually conceived and carried out the kidnaping.

What caused this delay of three days, at a time when the kidnapers were nervous and wanting money badly, and why was it so significant? Because it marked the time, perhaps, needed to obtain the token from the infant—or from his body, wherever it might have been.

With the suit, the kidnapers sent another note, an impatient note, scolding, threatening. It said:

> Dear Sir. Ouer man fail to collect mony. there are no more confidential conferences after we meeting March 12 these arrangements to hazardous for us. Circumstances will not allow transfare like you wish. it is impossible for us. wy shuld we move the baby and face danger. to take another person to the place is entirely out of the question it seem you are afraid we are the right party and if the baby is all right. well you have ouer signature always the same as the first one, especially three holes.
>
> Now we will send you the sleepingsuit from the baby. bcsides it means 3$ expense becauce we have to pay another one.
>
> Please tell Mrs. Linberg note to worry the baby is well we only have to give more food as the diet says
>
> You are willing to pay the 70,000 note 50,000 without seeing the baby first or note. We want another way because we don't like to give up. If you are willing to accept this deal put these in paper
>
> I accept Money is ready

Dr. Condon, obeying instructions, advertised. But in addition to the words "I accept. Money is ready," he wrote, for emphasis, "package received was okay."

Evidently the kidnapers failed to see the advertisement,

for they were silent until March 21st, when Jafsie received another letter, postmarked from Manhattan, which was the essence of an ultimatum to the negotiators. The kidnapers wrote:

> Dear Sir: You and Mr. Lindbergh know ouer program If you don't accept den we will wait untill you agree with ouer deal. We know you will have to come to us anyway. But why should Mrs. and Mr. Lindbergh suffer longer as necessary We will note communicate with you or Mr. Lindbergh until you write so in the paper.
>
> We will tell you again; this kidnaping cace whas prepared for a year already so the Police won't have any looks to find us or the child. you only puch everyding further out did you send that little package to Mr. Lindbergh? It contains the sleepingsuit from the baby. the baby is well.

Certain that the negotiators had failed to see his advertisement, Jafsie advertised three times more, on successive days beginning the 23rd of March:

> THANKS. That little package you sent was immediately delivered and accepted as real article. See my position. Over fifty years in business and can I pay without seeing goods? Common sense makes me trust you. Please understand my position.
> JAFSIE

There was no reply to this advertisement, and Dr. Condon became worried. After a consultation with the principals in the case, he tried again. This time his advertisement read:

> Money is ready. Furnish simple code for us to use in paper.   JAFSIE

Two days later, Dr. Condon received a new note, mailed on March 29th. It said:

> Dear Sir: It is note necessary to furnish any code
> . . You and mr. Lindbergh know ouer program
> very well. We will keep the child in ouer save plase
> until we have the money in hand, but if the deal is
> note closed until the 8 of April we will ask for
> 30000 more. also note 70000 . . . 100000
> How can Mr. Lindbergh follow so many false
> clues he knows we are the right party ouer singna-
> ture is still the same as in the ransom note. But if
> Mr. Lindbergh likes to fool around for another
> month, we can help it.
> once he has to come to us anyway but if he keeps
> on waiting we will double ouer amount. There is
> absolute no doubt aboud the child. It is well

Dr. Condon advertised once more:

> I accept. Money is ready. Jafsie.

Three days before, believing the critical moment was at hand, Colonel Lindbergh had had the banking house of J. P. Morgan and Company assemble in the required denominations, the sum of $50,000. Jafsie was so sure that the kidnapers would finally accept the $50,000, and not press their demands for the extra $20,000, that he had the package made up in the form first requested, although the bundle was naturally far larger than the dimensions proposed. In it there were 5,150 bills in $5, $10 and $20 denominations.

Twenty thousand dollars in $50 bills, held in reserve in case the kidnapers demanded the full amount, were kept available.

On April 1st, Jafsie received his reply, and with it an enclosure for Colonel Lindbergh. The note to Jafsie read:

> Dear sir. It is in Mr. Lindbergh interest not to notify police. Don't speak to anyone on the way. If there is a radion alarm for police car we warn you, we have same equipment. have the money in one bundel we will give you ¾ hower to reach the place.

To the Colonel, the extortioners wrote:

> Dear Sir, have the money ready by Saturday evening. we will infor you where and how to deliver it have the money in one bundel we want you to put it in a sertain place. there is no fear that somebody els will take it, we watch everything closely. Pleace let us know if you are agree and read for action by Saturday evening, if yes put in the paper
> Yes, everything O.K.
> It is a very simble delivery but we find out very son if there is any trapp. After 8 houers you gete the adr. from the boy, on the place you find two ladies. the are innocence.
> If it is to late we put it in the New York American for Saturday morning. Put it in the New York Journal.

Dr. Condon hurried to insert the signal, "Yes. Everything O.K.," and on the evening of Saturday, April 2nd, the extortioners used the method that had been so successful previously—a taxicab driver messenger—to deliver the following directions:

> Dear Sir: Take a car and follow Tremont ave. to the east until you reach the number 3225 East Tremont ave.

> It is a nursery
> Bergen
> Greenhauses florist
> There is a table standing outside right on the
> door. You find a letter undernead the table covert
> with a stone read and follow instruction

Keeping their pledge that no police would accompany them at this dramatic meeting, Colonel Lindbergh and Dr. Condon obeyed the directions and drove to the "greenhaus" where Jafsie found, beneath a stone, the second instruction. In addition to the $50,000 in one package, the Colonel had $20,000 more for precaution. Jafsie thought he might talk the emissary out of the extra money, but the Colonel wanted to take no chances.

At the florist's, Jafsie was bidden to

> Cross the street and walk to the next corner and
> follow Whittemore ave to the soud
> Take the money with you come alone and walk
> I will meet you

Dr. Condon crossed the street and walked along in the darkness.

Whittemore Avenue, intersecting Tremont Avenue, is a dirt road bounding the northwest side of St. Raymond's cemetery. Its low white fence had not been completed at the time of this midnight rendezvous. The Doctor walked a few steps and then hesitated. In accordance with a pre-arranged agreement with Colonel Lindbergh, he said, loud enough for his voice to carry back to the automobile, "I guess there's nobody here—I'll have to go back."

As though in reply, a voice came from the other side of the fence:

"Doctor! Over here, Doctor!"

Colonel Lindbergh, listening, marked the guttural accents. He would never forget that voice.

Walking a few paces, the kidnapers' agent on one side of the fence and Jafsie on the other, the two men discussed the impending payment. Then they came to a point where the incompleted fence abruptly stopped, and were face to face.

"All right, give me the money," the man, by this time known to Jafsie as "John," insisted.

"Not until I get a receipt for it," said Jafsie stubbornly.

"But I haven't got a receipt. I'll tell you where the baby is as soon as you give me the money."

Dr. Condon continued to insist that he would break off the negotiations unless he were given a "paid in full" receipt for the money. The agent finally consented, saying it would take ten minutes, and meanwhile the Doctor could go back to the car and get the package.

More conversation about the amount. The Doctor explained that $50,000 was a lot of money. Colonel Lindbergh couldn't raise any more, in cash, at that time. Better take the $50,000 and let the other $20,000 go. The money was only a few feet away. And with the promise of a small fortune so near, "just across the street, in fact" the cupidity of the negotiator conquered. He agreed to accept the smaller sum. But he expressed fear lest the other members of the gang think he had double-crossed them.

Within ten minutes, Jafsie had returned to the spot where he had left "John," carrying with him the specially constructed package. The agent was there, with an envelope in his hand. He grasped the package of bills and in return passed Jafsie the note.

"You must promise not to open this for three hours," he warned the Doctor.

"Well, at least I've saved you $20,000," Dr. Condon said to Colonel Lindbergh cheerfully, as he took his seat beside him.

They drove back to one of the houses owned by Dr. Condon, only a short distance from the scene of the transaction, and faithfully waited the allotted time before opening the message.

The note itself appeared to answer their frantic question, "Where is the baby?"

> The boy [it said] is on boad [boat] Nelly It is a small boad 28 feet long. two persons are on the Boad. the are innosent. You will find the boad between Horsenecks Beach and Gay Head near Elisabeth Island.

The Doctor and the Colonel were jubilant. Here, at last, was the happy climax to their long negotiations. The Colonel made preparations to fly at once to the "save plase" where the gang, including the "two innosent ladies" had supposedly concealed the child.

The mockery of that pathetic two-day search was the epitome of human cruelty. Colonel Lindbergh set forth confident that the chase was at an end. The money he had paid was nothing. He was willing, as he had been from the first, never to take an avenging step toward the kidnapers, never to trace one of the ransom notes, never to lend himself to the police task of bringing the abductors of his child to justice.

Five hours before the passage of the money in St. Raymond's cemetery, the principal detectives were aware of the coming meeting. They had urged and implored the Colonel not to pay the ransom—or at least to be permitted to seize the kidnapers' agent after the payment. To all their protestations, Colonel Lindbergh was adamant. Even Inspector Harry Walsh, in whom he had every confidence, had failed to move him. The Colonel was insistent that he would play square with the kidnapers.

So Colonel Lindbergh flew happily along the Connecticut and Rhode Island shores, toward Buzzards Bay and Gay Head. Sailing over Elizabeth Island, he throttled down and scanned the sea for the "boad Nelly." A few boats were riding easily at anchor near the shore. None of them answered the kidnapers' description.

The Colonel wheeled his seaplane over Vineyard Haven, flying low, flying high. Occasionally he swooped almost to the surface of the sea when he spotted from above the outlines of a vessel that might have answered "John's" description of the *Nelly*. Gradually the suspicion came to him that there had been an interruption of the kidnapers' plans. It could not be, he thought, that they were deliberately lying to him.

At nightfall, when it became apparent that for that day at least he was doomed to disappointment, he turned homeward, to the southwest, and sadly brought his plane to rest at the New York airport he had secretly left early that morning.

On Monday, April 4th, he resumed the search at dawn. Coast guard cruisers spotted him flying above them. State troopers at Vineyard Haven watched him through binoculars as he criss-crossed the sky, hunting for the *Nelly*. Once, during the search, he landed and made some inquiries about the boat. What he heard was alarming. No person could be found who had seen any vessel answering the description of the one he sought.

Slowly the only possible conclusion was driven home to his mind.

There was no such boat. The directions were deliberately, fiendishly false. He had paid $50,000—for nothing.

(AUTHOR'S NOTE: Published versions of the ransom notes received by Colonel Lindbergh and Dr. John F. Condon contain several variations, and even the official court transcript is at variance with several interpretations of them. Many different spellings are due to the fact that the writer of the extortion notes made his letters imperfectly, and occasionally blotted, erased, or blurred his words, so that the authorities had to guess at many of them. It will be noticed, as well, that the spelling of many words in the later extortion notes differed from that in the earlier communications. The authorities always regarded this as an indication that the extortioner was using a German-English dictionary, and that he was watching the newspapers carefully, "educating" himself particularly in the spelling of proper names. Examination of the notes and the photostatic copies of them has convinced this writer that the above account of them is, under the circumstances, as accurate as possible.)

CHAPTER SIX

SO GREAT HAD BEEN COLONEL LINDBERGH'S FAITH THAT HE would return from his quest of the ship *Nelly* with his son, that he had taken along on the trip to Martha's Vineyard a small blanket to keep the boy warm on the return trip. There were lights blazing in the hitherto darkened nursery when, shortly before midnight on April 4th, the tired and disappointed father returned at last and admitted failure. So great, too, had been his trust in the honesty—if that is the word—of the kidnapers, that he had paid little attention to the persistent efforts of three Norfolk men to get his ear. He believed he was on the right path. It had been proved to him, by evidence set before his own eyes, that he was dealing with the actual kidnapers. Others who professed to have knowledge of the baby's whereabouts he regarded as conscious or unconscious fakers.

But when repeated visits to the scene to which he had been directed by Jafsie's man failed to reveal the slightest trace of any boat answering the description of the kidnapers' boat, he began to look in other directions. Still clinging to the incontrovertible knowledge that he had at least been in contact with the real abductors, he nevertheless listened to the story of John Hughes Curtis, boat builder and man-about-town of Norfolk.

Curtis had come to him well recommended, although

Norfolk citizens might have told him that the boat building trade hadn't been particularly lively in recent years, and Curtis's financial condition was not, at the moment, such as would inspire confidence. But associated with Curtis were the Very Reverend H. Dobson-Peacock, dean of Christ Episcopal Church of Norfolk, and Rear-Admiral Guy Burrage (retired) who had commanded the ship on which Colonel Lindbergh had returned to America after his history-making flight to Paris.

The rectitude of the latter two could not be questioned, although it was evident almost from the start that the clergyman was garrulous and gullible, and the retired naval officer was entering the case reluctantly.

John Hughes Curtis, hale and hearty, bluff and well-met, had been something of a social leader in the southern town. It was he who had led the cotillions at one of Norfolk's swankiest of dancing clubs. The fact that he had been forced into bankruptcy by the hard times had not affected his social standing. Many others were in the same boat with him. Nor did the suspicion that, at one time or another, he might have helped out his decreasing business by doing an occasional job for a rum runner weigh heavily against him. In this instance, in fact, the implied connection with seafaring men of the bootleg industry lent verisimilitude to the fantastic tales he told.

His entrance into the case began as early as March 10th, nine days after the kidnaping, when he visited Dean Peacock and made that gentleman's eyes pop out with the story of what had happened to him "last night, down at the Norfolk Country Club."

He had been called, he said, to talk over the building of a
new dock for the yacht clubs of Norfolk, and after the
meeting "a man whom I call Sam" jumped on the running
board of his car and swore him to secrecy. Sam then revealed
to him that he had been sent to Curtis by two other men,
who wanted him to get the boat builder to act as a go-
between in the Lindbergh kidnaping case.

"I told him," said Curtis to the clergyman, "that Colonel
Lindbergh must have a million people bothering him right
now, and that it would be impossible to get to him, but I
told him to get in touch with me again—that I'd think it
over and let him know. So in the morning, after I'd thought
about it all night, I decided to come to you."

The Very Reverend Dean was interested and enthusiastic.
Of course they could reach Colonel Lindbergh's ear. Wasn't
he, Dobson-Peacock, rector of the Episcopal Church in
Mexico City when his great friend, the late Senator Dwight
W. Morrow, was Ambassador down there? Together, the
men went to the telephone company and made arrangements for a "very secret" call to Hopewell. They asked to
speak to either Colonel Lindbergh or Mrs. Morrow.

Neither the Colonel nor Mrs. Morrow was at home, they
were informed, but they might speak confidentially to a Mr.
Rosner, "Colonel Lindbergh's secretary." Accordingly, it was
to that individual, who had so strangely become a sort of
personal detective, private secretary and general pooh-bah of
the Lindbergh household, that they breathlessly told their
story.

"Mr. Rosner gave us very little satisfaction," Curtis complained.

On Friday, March 11th, the husky boat builder appeared once more at the rectory and advised haste. He had been in contact with "Sam" again, he said, and the kidnapers were getting restless. Curtis thought it would be a good idea to bring Admiral Burrage in on the deal, in view of the Admiral's previous association with the Colonel.

"We went over to the Admiral's house," said the Dean, "and Mr. Curtis repeated to him, word for word, the story he told me. Admiral Burrage put a call through to Hopewell and talked with somebody who said he was Colonel Lindbergh, but he wasn't quite satisfied it was actually the Colonel. So he sat down and wrote a note suggesting that we go to Hopewell the following Tuesday—the 22nd—and that unless it would be inconvenient, we would arrive about four o'clock in the afternoon. We went to Hopewell, and saw Colonel Lindbergh, to whom Mr. Curtis once more repeated the story, exactly as he had told it to me and to the Admiral. Colonel Lindbergh, although apparently not convinced [he could not have been, since he had such convincing proof to the contrary in the Jafsie negotiations, then under way] requested us to follow up the clue."

Delighted with even this slight concession, Curtis and his two credulous assistants returned to Norfolk. Unable to keep such a glorious secret, someone—it is easy to surmise which one—"talked," and on the following day a Norfolk newspaper announced to the wide world that the baby was being held on a boat in Chesapeake Bay and that three distinguished citizens were negotiating for his return.

Norfolk's normal somnolence was alarmingly shattered within twenty-four hours. Attracted by the fresh scent a score of news hounds, diverted from the main chase, went baying into Virginia and drew up at the rectory door of the Very Reverend H. Dobson-Peacock. Some of the more cynical were inclined to sniff at the good cleric. As a negotiator in the most delicate transaction known to American criminality, he appeared to be too responsive, too eager, too ready to volunteer information. His ingenuous replies to their questions were not wholly in keeping with the importance of the occasion. But he was a splendid news source.

So, while Admiral Burrage, somewhat annoyed at the visitation, shut the door between himself and the interviewers with the finality of a command from the quarter-deck, the Dean obligingly posed for photographers, gave out interviews, prayed a public blessing on his endeavors, and bathed in the warmth of the ensuing publicity. Then he sent "the boys" back to their hotels with an admonition to "rest until tomorrow, because I may have some news for you then."

John Hughes Curtis, very tired after a mysterious weekend trip, returned to his home, rested for an hour, and then received the reporters.

"I can tell you very little," he said, "for too much publicity would ruin our work. In order to do certain work which began before all this publicity, I had to leave town. As to where, how, or to whom I talked, I am not in a position to say at this time. I left early Saturday afternoon and returned this afternoon."

The shipbuilder made it very clear, however, that he was embarrassed by Dean Dobson-Peacock's loquacity and thoroughly annoyed that reports of his activity had leaked out.

"Until it is proved to me that I am the victim of a hoax, or until, on the other hand, our negotiations prove successful," he said with virtuous indignation, "I'm going to see to it that all this unwise publicity is stopped."

Colonel Lindbergh turned back to his negotiations through Jafsie with the feeling that some person was deluding the Norfolk men, but it was not in his mind to shut the door against any other solution of the case, however bizarre, unreal or fantastic it might have sounded. He believed that if Curtis were in touch with the kidnapers, sooner or later he would receive proof, either through the symbol of the interlocking circles, or through some material evidence. He asked, first, for a photograph of the baby. After that, he suggested, he would like some written document, for comparison with the genuine ransom notes in his possession. Curtis promised to do his best.

For fourteen days, thereafter, a series of mysterious trips, now by Curtis alone and again by Curtis and the Dean, who was bubbling over with enthusiasm, ensued. After each trip the news "leaked out" that the Norfolk negotiators were "on the right track," that "progress was made," and that "the baby is alive and well."

Then came the sensational disclosure that Colonel Lindbergh already had paid $50,000 to the supposed kidnapers of his child, through Jafsie, and that he had received nothing in return. The news intensified Curtis's importance, and the Colonel himself began to listen more readily to his tales.

Until the negotiations were well under way, Curtis had never suggested what sum of money might be required by the kidnapers. Now, he began to indicate the necessity of depositing some money—say $25,000—in Norfolk "as an earnest" which would prove the Colonel's readiness to do business through him. Colonel Lindbergh insisted that he must have proof that he was dealing with the proper persons before he would make such a deposit, and the matter was not pressed.

On the 18th of April, there came an important conference at Hopewell. Curtis arrived in the company of E. B. Bruce, a manufacturer, of Elmira, New York, who had been his friend for twenty years, and volunteered the surprising information that he had actually seen, touched, and checked some of the ransom bills paid out by Jafsie and divided between the members of the gang.

Curtis's story was vivid. His dramatic account of the preliminary negotiations was peopled with a strange assortment of characters, described with infinite detail and provided by the author with families, homes, ships, secret radios, and even an old Ford automobile which, moving from point to point on the Virginia capes, provided an itinerant receiving station for messages from the "kidnap ship."

The piratical vessel in question, Curtis said, could be identified easily. It was a two-masted Gloucester fisherman, with Fairbanks Morse motors and a temporary cabin built aft. Its hull was painted so dark a green that it appeared black. At full speed, it was capable of doing fourteen knots.

A motley cast of characters, according to the boat builder, lived aboard the vessel. First there was Sam Truesdale or Torresdale. Sam had many aliases, among them: Sam Vernikoff, Sam Tarsdale, Sam Murray, Murray Thursdale, A. B. Murray, and Murray Green.

Then there was "John," of Scandinavian descent, like Jafsie's "John," whose last name Curtis said he did not know. And Olaf Larsen, whom his companions called "Dynamite," or "Din" for short. And two other tough characters called Eric and Nils. These five, said Curtis, constituted the actual gang.

Two other startling characters appeared in the dramatis personae. One of them was Dynamite's wife, Hilda. She was "about five foot six, Scandinavian, speaks with an accent, sort of muggy hair, good looking, fairly nice form and dresses fairly well, is about thirty-eight years old, weight about 135-140, has three boys, from twelve down to seven."

"And it was Hilda," Curtis added, "who always seemed to be forcing her husband on."

With Hilda the leading lady, "Inez" was the ingenue. Inez was married, but Curtis didn't know her married name. In fact, come to think of it, Inez wasn't her real name at all—it was just a name Curtis called her. He never heard Hilda address her by any name. At any rate, Inez was an expert radio operator, and it was she who received and sent the messages to the gang at sea, to and from the portable radio station.

Inez, as Curtis had nicknamed her, was "about twenty-five years old, round bosomed [Curtis thought of everything], fairly good form, dressed fairly neat, and had a husband who was captain of a boat supposed to be working at Hampton."

In the happy little household where the two females entertained Curtis while their husbands were at sea, there was a home-made crib—the very crib in which the kidnaped baby had been transported from Hopewell to the boat. As to the kidnaping exploit, the police had been wrong from the start, Curtis declared. His version, as told to him by the round-bosomed Scandinavian women, differed in its main essentials from the theories built up by the detectives in their reconstruction of the crime.

In the first place, Curtis said, the initiation of the plot began within the Lindbergh ménage when a servant met John in a roadhouse near Newark and discussed with him the possibilities of such an abduction. John and Eric, he continued, arrived at the Hopewell estate in a green Hudson sedan, which was parked, its lights extinguished, several hundred yards from the house. The two men had entered the nursery by way of the ladder, chloroformed the child, and then descended *through the house and out by the door leading into the driveway*. In the parked car was the cradle to receive the baby, and Hilda, the big blonde "nurse." Sam Truesdale's Buick was stationed several hundred feet down the road, and in it were the other members of the gang, acting as lookouts against the possibility of interruption.

Although there were many discrepancies in Curtis's stories, chief among them the fact that he had once said that the "inside" participant in the crime was a man-servant and again that it was a girl, Colonel Lindbergh decided he would at least go so far as to accompany the boat builder on one of his trips to the kidnapers' rendezvous.

Curtis had interested Colonel Consolvo, a wealthy Baltimore hotel proprietor, in his mission and obtained from him the use of his yacht *Marcon,* fully equipped, victualed for a cruise, and ready to go to sea at any moment. From April

2nd until April 22nd, the *Marcon* and its crew stood by for orders. Colonel Consolvo was paying the bills.

Before the expedition started on their first sea tour, however, Curtis elaborated the picture he had given the authorities, and told of a new meeting he had held, on board the ship *Theresa Salvatore,* fourteen miles off Cape May, with the gang. At this meeting, he said, he shook his fingers at the kidnapers and told them, "You ought to be hanged for this."

"I told them," said Curtis, "that Colonel Lindbergh would provide the money if proper means of identification were obtained, and that he would forget the names of their vessels. They said they had with them at that time $3,000 of the ransom money, four bundles of $500, and Larsen had $1,000. I took off five or six of the bills from Larsen's roll and checked them against the list [of serial numbers provided by Colonel Lindbergh]. They said they had spent approximately $1,000 of the entire amount up to then, including $500 to a party of rum runners for John to buy some liquor. They said the child was safe and they would pick him up off Falmouth, Mass., and then transfer him from a small boat to a big boat.

"John sent his love to Condon," Curtis continued, "and said the Doctor was okay in every respect. Although I was in their power and they knew it, I wasn't scared of the whole crowd. I shook my finger at each and every one of them, and told them I could beat hell out of them with my bare hands. They saw I had them in check and I just shook my finger at all of them. At this stage, John said he would like nothing better than to kidnap Lindbergh himself. They asked me what I thought would happen to them if they got caught. I told them I didn't know, but that they deserved a noose around their necks. When I asked them for some of the ransom money to take back to Colonel Lindbergh as proof they had received it, they wouldn't give it to me. 'We have confidence in you, why hasn't Colonel Lindbergh?' they asked."

After this spectacular meeting, Curtis said, he persuaded Dynamite Larsen to go with him to Trenton, for the express purpose of calling Colonel Lindbergh on the telephone and making an appointment at Hopewell. After they had tried unsuccessfully to reach the Colonel, however, Dynamite became alarmed and refused to go through with his bargain.

"He was extremely angry," Curtis related. "All the way back to Cape May he insisted we were being followed, and he made me take a roundabout way to the cape."

Captain John J. Lamb of the New Jersey State Police, to whom Curtis told the whole story, didn't believe a word of it. Colonel Schwarzkopf was no more credulous. Colonel Lindbergh himself, partially suspicious but anxious to leave nothing undone that would bring back the child, at last consented to spend a day hunting the phantom Gloucester fisherman from the speedy yacht *Marcon*.

At 5:50 o'clock on the afternoon of April 22nd, Curtis boarded the *Marcon* and told the skipper, Captain Frank H. Lackman, that a man who desired to be known as "Alex Swanson"—but who was actually Colonel Lindbergh—was coming aboard soon with a party, and that he should prepare to go to sea within two hours. A little later an automobile drove up to the dock, and from it stepped "Mr. Swan-

COL. CHARLES A. LINDBERGH AND ANNE MORROW LINDBERGH ". . . . . they wanted only to rear their son as an ordinary boy."

The LINDBERGH MANOR AT HOPEWELL " . . . . far from the city, to provide seclusion for a private American family . . . . . a shutter at the nursery window resisted all efforts to close it."

CHARLES A. LINDBERGH, JR. " . . . . . his first birthday party."

THE RANSOM NOTE . . . . . was written in a script and with expressions that betrayed the foreign origin of the writer—a German.

FIFTY THOUSAND DOLLARS . . . . . Dr. John F. Condon gave it into the hands of a mysterious figure in St. Raymond's cemetery, and received in return—nothing.

JAFSIE . . . . . Dr. John F. Condon, educator, lecturer, Grand Old Man of the Bronx.

GASTON B. MEANS . . . . . He smirked and smiled when he took fifteen years for swindling.

JOHN HUGHES CURTIS . . . . . Norfolk boat builder, building a fabric of fantastic lies.

THE VERY REVEREND DEAN H. DOBSON-PEACOCK . . . . . a guileless cleric with a trusting heart.

A HURRIED GRAVE . . . . . here, perhaps, the fugitive kidnaper stopped, feared pursuit, and hastily disposed of his burden, and here was found the body of Charles A. Lindbergh, Jr.

OLIVER WHATELY . . . . ."the perfect servant . . . a gentleman's gentleman . . . the Lindbergh butler."

BETTY GOW . . . . . "a comely Scottish nursemaid . . , she had cared for Baby Lindbergh since his birth."

HENRY ("RED") JOHNSON . . . . . "a personable young man, who had to explain away a bottle of milk."

VIOLET SHARPE . . . . . "maid in the Morrow establishment . . . she died a suicide, in hysterical fear."

THE RANSOM ZONE . . . . . wherever a ransom note was found, they
stuck a pin. The criss-crossing lines fixed the operations of the ransom
passer within the Bronx and Upper Manhattan.

COL. H. NORMAN SCHWARTZ-
KOPF . . . . . not a detective,
but a military man, he
commanded the New Jer-
sey State Police.

FRANCIS FAY . . . . . a silent figure, responsible chief of the
New York Division of In-
vestigation, in the Department of Justice.

THIRTY MONTHS OF WORK . . . . . brought congratulations from J. Edgar
Hoover, head of the Division of Investigation, to his brilliant corps of
man-hunters.

JOHN LYONS AND WALTER LYLE . . . . . Hauptmann paid $10 at their station for gasoline. Lyle wrote down the number of his car. Trapped.

The Garage . . . . . demolished, inch by inch, it yielded nearly $15,000 in musty ransom bills.

THE SECRET HOARD . . . . cleverly hidden in the wall, a two-by-four panel had been neatly bored with holes that provided concealment for $840 in ransom money and a small revolver of German manufacture.

BRUNO RICHARD HAUPTMANN . . . . . "he was a man with flat cheeks and a pointed chin."

JUSTICE THOMAS W. TRENCHARD . . . . . Humane . . . . . "if the weather is inclement, I would prefer the jury remained indoors tomorrow, but if you do go out, wrap yourselves up warmly and wear your rubbers. If one of the jurors lacks rubbers, I will be glad to provide them."

EDWARD J. REILLY . . . . . "The Bull of Brooklyn." . . . . . "This case is a police frame-up, from beginning to end. There is not a shred of evidence to place Bruno Hauptmann in New Jersey on the night of the crime."

DAVID T. WILENTZ . . . . . Attorney General of the State of New Jersey . . . . . "I have never before, in all my career, prosecuted a criminal case."

ARTHUR KOEHLER . . . . . "Why, through this man's testimony, the State will wrap this kidnap ladder around the neck of Bruno Richard Hauptmann." (From Attorney General David T. Wilentz's declaration in court.)

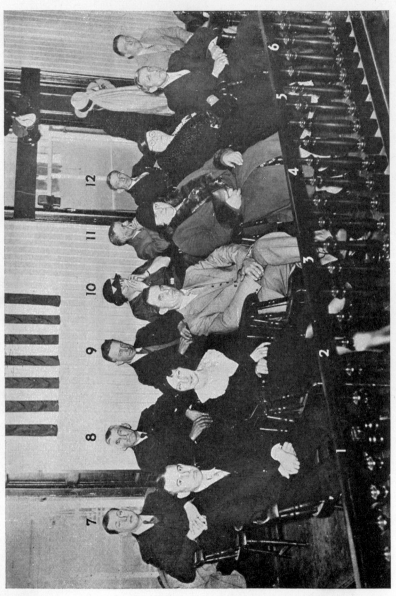

THE HAUPTMANN JURY . . . . . No. 1, Elmer Smith; No. 2, Mrs. Ethel Stockton; No. 3, Charles F. Snyder; No. 4, Verna Snyder; No. 5, Mrs. Rosie Pill; No. 6, Foreman Charles Walton, Sr.; No. 7, Robert Cravath; No. 8, Philip Hockenbury; No. 9, George Voorhees; No. 10, Mrs. Mary Brelsford; No. 11, Liscom C. Case; No. 12, Howard Biggs.

son," Manufacturer Bruce of Elmira, Lieutenant George L. Richard, a navy pilot, and the commandant of the Norfolk naval air station. A Browning machine-gun and a number of smaller firearms were deposited on the *Marcon's* deck.

One airplane from the station was to make occasional contacts with the *Marcon,* and in the event the child was rescued, Captain Lackmann arranged to display a white sheet on top of the awning as a signal to the escorting plane.

At 7:40 o'clock in the evening the *Marcon* cast off and headed down the Roads. About two hours later, Curtis entered the pilot house and told the skipper that he was to hunt for the *"Mary B. Moss,* a Gloucester fisherman, with a black hull." Colonel Lindbergh, or "Alex Swanson," turned in for some sleep, asking to be called at four in the morning. Curtis told the Captain to go twenty knots due east of the lightship, where he was sure to find the *Mary B. Moss* cruising.

The *Marcon* reached the supposed rendezvous at 2:50 o'clock in the morning, and loafed around in circles, awaiting the appearance of the Gloucesterman. No ship was sighted until 6:30 o'clock, when the men in the pilot house saw through their binoculars a fishing smack, east by south of the *Marcon's* position. The little party armed themselves and the machine-gun was set in position on the deck. The *Marcon* approached the stranger at top speed and began circling the craft. But as they approached the boat, Curtis, in disgust, announced that it had no resemblance to the ship he was chasing.

Through the long forenoon, the yacht zigzagged, north and south, in the vicinity of the position Curtis had marked on the chart, but when afternoon came it was apparent they would make no contact that day. So the *Marcon's* sharp prow was pointed homeward, landing the party at the government dock at dusk.

Colonel Lindbergh leaped from the *Marcon* to the pier and helped moor the vessel. He was bitterly disappointed, but he gave no sign that the day's events had shaken what little confidence he may have felt in Curtis's melodramatic story. He agreed to await developments and the Norfolk negotiator promised to establish a new contact with the gang that night.

The various members of the expedition scattered to separate establishments for the night, and Curtis set forth on another nocturnal adventure, seeking, he said, to find out whether John and his gang of bullies had double-crossed him. He returned before midnight and aroused the others with good news. He had been to Yorktown and there received a message from the *Mary B. Moss.* "Has yacht double exhaust?" the message inquired. "Heard your exhaust. Had company. Be patient. Will break through."

"I talked on the phone with Hilda," he explained, "and she told me Dynamite had been at the location we agreed upon, but that he hadn't been able to carry through the agreement."

Thus reassured, the party assembled once more in the *Marcon's* cabins, and at two o'clock on the morning of April 24th once more passed through the Virginia Capes, making for the same position where they had found nothing but disappointment the preceding day.

The next twenty-four hours were a repetition of the preceding trip. An all day cruise over the same course brought little more than further glib excuses—or expressions of anger—from Curtis.

Then began a succession of sea trips, all with negative results, and all attended by the same encouraging reports from Curtis's Hilda, together with such excuses as "the weather was bad" or "we had trouble with our engines" or "John couldn't persuade the other members of the gang it was safe today."

Believing that perhaps it was dangerous, or futile, to use the yacht *Marcon* any further, Colonel Lindbergh transferred the party to the yacht *Cachelot*. On May 8th, Curtis informed the Colonel that he had made one last desperate attempt to make a personal contact with John, Sam, Eric and the other freebooters, and that he had gone alone to Freeport, Long Island, where he met Hilda at her bungalow. He found Hilda very nervous, Curtis said, because of the messages she was getting from Dynamite about rough seas and the necessity of getting the child safely out of the hands of the gang.

The kidnapers, it seemed, had split into two factions, one headed by John, the other by Dynamite. John, by far the most vicious of the gang, threatened to sell the child to the highest bidder, and it was only the pacifying argument of Sam Truesdale (who by this time had become "Sam the Gasman," a Scandinavian Jew with greasy hair) that the crew were persuaded to hang together.

Meanwhile, between trips to sea and to Hopewell and New York, the Norfolk negotiator had found time to visit Atlantic City, where he enlisted the secretarial services of

Miss Ruth Gay, a stenographer once employed by him. Miss Gay made telephone calls for him, took notes of various conferences, and began to prepare, under his dictation, a set of memoirs that was to startle the world when, as, and if they were ever published. He suggested to William E. Haskell, Jr., assistant to the President of the *New York Herald Tribune,* that an "advance" of $25,000 might be proper upon the signing of a contract granting the exclusive rights to such a production. Mr. Haskell thought such an amount might be proper, but there would be no contract and no advance until the child was returned.

Curtis stimulated Mr. Haskell's desires for the exclusive rights, incidentally, by telling him how, on one trip, "we actually established contact with the kidnapers' boat, and it was all we could do to restrain Colonel Lindbergh from diving overboard and swimming over to the other ship."

Back in the Bronx, at this moment, Dr. Condon was striving desperately to restore the broken threads of his contact with the man he knew as "John." For weeks he advertised, in pleading repetitions of his earlier successful messages, "Come and see us. Jafsie." "Money is ready. Jafsie." "What is wrong? Have you crossed me? Jafsie." "Please. Better Directions. Jafsie." There was no response from the kidnapers.

Colonel Lindbergh, his mind beset by doubts, his logic moved by the insistence of police that he was following a false trail, decided he would make one final voyage on the yacht *Cachelot* and then abandon the clue.

CHAPTER SEVEN

IN THE LATE AFTERNOON OF MAY 12TH, WILLIAM ALLEN AND Orville Wilson, truck drivers, were rattling over the Mount Rose-Hopewell road with a load of lumber which they had hoped to deliver before nightfall. As they reached the top of the hill, Mr. Allen became alarmed by certain internal warnings and decided he would do well to halt the truck and, as he delicately phrased it, "stretch his legs." To obtain privacy, he entered a thicket of tangled underbrush not far from the fringe of the highway and there lowered his haunches until only the crown of his battered hat was visible from the road.

Mr. Allen remained in this posture for approximately three seconds. Then, his face an ashen gray, he rushed to the truck where Mr. Wilson was reclining at ease over the wheel, and galvanized him into action with the words, "My God, there's a dead child in them woods!"

The two men debated whether to go to Hopewell and put the matter into the hands of the police, or to re-enter the thicket and investigate further. The more he thought about it, the more it seemed to Mr. Allen that he might have been mistaken. Curiosity won the debate, and they broke through the underbrush, casting fearful sidelong glances, until they reached the spot where Allen had made his discovery.

Fifty feet from the highway there was a little knoll, and

on the other side of it a slight hollow. In the hollow, partially concealed by a covering of dirt and leaves, was the form of an infant. One small foot protruded from the dirt.

Allen and Wilson remained just long enough to assure themselves it was no illusion—they brushed away enough dirt to discover clothes clinging to the skeleton frame—and then rushed to their truck and down the hill to Hopewell. At the small town police station, they found Assistant Police Chief Charlie Williamson, to whom they related their discovery. Williamson, Chief Wolf, and a group of state police and detectives accompanied the couple back to the "grave," over Allen's protestations that he had a load of lumber to deliver, and after viewing and photographing the surroundings, carefully removed the body. They noticed particularly that only a few feet away, strung along the ground, were emergency telephone wires which had been put in place only a few days before. It seemed strange to them that linemen, passing so close to the burial scene, should not have stumbled across the grave. Yet every indication pointed to the probability that throughout the seventy-three days since the kidnaping of Charles A. Lindbergh, Jr., this body had been exposed to the elements.

They sent a messenger to the Lindbergh home, to seek the aid of Betty Gow. The nursemaid, they recalled, had been able to describe, in the minutest detail, every article of clothing in which she had wrapped the baby on the night of March 1st. Betty Gow produced from the baby's wardrobe a little shirt she had made herself. It had scallops, done in blue thread, at the edges. A spool of thread from which the stitches had been made reposed in Betty's sewing box.

The messenger returned to the hilltop and handed the garment to the detectives. They knelt and compared it with the material that clung to the frame. The stitches were the same and the blue thread—which rain and snow had been unable to dim—had come from the spool in Betty Gow's basket.

This, for the detectives, was sufficient for temporary identification. The body was that of Charles A. Lindbergh, Jr., murdered and thrust into a hurriedly scraped grave, probably within a few hours after his abductors had climbed the ladder and removed him silently from his cradle.

Coroner Walter H. Swayze was summoned, and the body was removed to an undertaking establishment in Trenton, where Dr. Swayze and Dr. Charles H. Mitchell examined it before making an official report.

As gently as possible, the news was broken to Anne Morrow Lindbergh and her mother, who fortunately was there to comfort her. There were no tears. The courage and self-control that brought Mrs. Lindbergh through the tortures of ten weeks came to her aid at that moment. Her first thought was for Charles—Charles who was somewhere off the Virginia Capes, cruising on a now hopeless quest. Coast guard patrols and the Navy's fastest cruisers set out to intercept him. Radio messages were sent out, directed to the small yacht *Cachelot*. But it was hours before he was to be reached.

Throughout that dismal afternoon it had been raining, and the soggy Sourland hills never looked more dreary. Few of the reporters, clinging to the warmth of Pop Gebhart's general store, or hazarding new guesses as to the

identity of the kidnapers, suspected there was anything
unusual in the little burst of activity on the part of the state
police. They had been told, by lookouts, that two or three
of the officers had been observed going up the Mount Rose
road, but that was not unusual.

A telephone call came to press headquarters at Trenton
and Hopewell.

"There will be an important announcement at Colonel
Lindbergh's garage," a voice announced. "You are requested
to be there as soon as possible."

They leaped from their chairs and jumped into automobiles. This was the first time since they had been barred
from the Lindbergh estate that an invitation of this sort had
come to them. It presaged one of two events—either that the
baby had been restored, or that the child had been found,
dead. They speculated on the news as they sped over the
short distance from Hopewell to the big white house.

At the garage they were welcomed in silence. Colonel
Schwarzkopf, grim and uncommunicative, announced he
would have a statement "when all of your representatives
have arrived." By "all," he said, he meant also those of the
press who were still in Trenton, but who were on their way.
For an hour, the early arrivals from Hopewell fidgeted and
guessed, in whispers, at what the impending announcement
would reveal. With the last man from Trenton in place,
Colonel Schwarzkopf, a stiff, military figure, cleared his
throat and read:

> We have to announce that apparently the body of
> the Lindbergh baby was found at 3:15 p.m. today
> by William Allen, Negro, of Trenton, who was

riding on the Mount Rose road toward Hopewell.

He was riding with Orville Wilson on a truck load of timber. They stopped the truck so he could answer a call of nature.

He went into the woods for this purpose on the Mount Rose Hill, in Mount Rose, N. J. Going under a bush, he lowered his head, and as he raised his head he saw a skeleton on the ground. He says, in his statement, that what he saw had a person's foot on it. He called back to Mr. Wilson. Mr. Wilson ran into the woods, saw what it was and decided to go to Hopewell and get the police. He notified Chief Wolf, who notified these headquarters. Inspector Walsh, of Jersey City; Sergeant Moffatt, of the Newark police; Lieutenant Keaton, of the New Jersey State Police, and a number of other detectives immediately went to the scene. They reported finding the body of a child estimated to be between a year and a half and two years old, in a bad state of decomposition, but having blond hair and wearing what appeared to be an undershirt and a flannel band around the body.

Not satisfied with this identification, men were sent back into Hopewell to the Lindbergh estate, to get samples of the undershirt the baby wore and of the flannel shirt the baby had on the night of the kidnaping.

This flannel shirt had an embroidered scallop edge on it. These articles were taken back to the scene and compared with the clothing found on the body, and were matched closely enough to afford an identification of the body as that of the Lindbergh baby.

The statement of William Allen and Orville Wilson says that the body was pretty well con-

cealed by leaves, dirt and brush. The skull had a
hole in it about the size of a quarter, just above the
forehead. The body was lying in a depression, as
though an attempt had been made to bury it, face
down.

Mercer County Physician, Dr. Charles H. Mitchell, and the County Coroner, Walter Swayze, were
immediately called in.

The silence while Colonel Schwarzkopf was reading his
statement was broken when he reached the word "body."
There was a rush for the doors as some of the reporters
tried to break through and reach telephones.

"No! No!" Colonel Schwarzkopf shouted. "Not a man
is to leave this room until I have finished reading my statement." Then, when he had concluded, he said, "That's all,
boys. I shall answer no questions for the present."

Within five minutes the world knew the ghastly truth.
The hunt for kidnapers had been transformed instantly to
a hunt for murderers.

Far off the coast, in its fruitless patrol of the seas, the
yacht *Cachelot* made its last turn southward. Colonel Lindbergh had decided that any further observation for the day
would be of no avail. It had been dark for two hours. There
were no lights anywhere on the horizon.

E. B. Bruce, the Elmira manufacturer who had accompanied the Colonel through the phantom world of kidnap
ships and mysterious Scandinavian pirate rings, approached
him and said, in a low voice:

"Colonel, I have just received a message from shore for
you." He hesitated. "The baby has been found." The Colo-

nel tried to frame a question and Bruce saw he must tell him the truth. "He is dead."

Colonel Lindbergh stared into the darkness for a moment. Then he walked over to John Hughes Curtis.

"Curtis," he said, "I want you to come to Hopewell with me."

Back in Hopewell, where the renewed activity had restored something of the charged atmosphere of the early days, Colonel Schwarzkopf was elaborating on his first statement. Amplifying the preliminary identification, he said:

> Betty Gow has positively identified the garments found on the body discovered today as being the garments in which the Lindbergh baby was clothed on the night of the kidnaping. The sleeping suit was not on the baby, but the two shirts on the body have been positively identified by Betty Gow. Mrs. Morrow and Mrs. Lindbergh were at the Hopewell home when it became known today that the baby found today was the Lindbergh baby.
>
> The body was found on the left side of the road going from Mount Rose to Hopewell. More than twenty additional troopers were immediately ordered to duty upon the discovery of the facts which have come to light today. Additional men are also being detailed.

In Trenton, Dr. Mitchell completed his examination of the body, analyzing particularly the injuries to the head. His formal report said that death had been due to "a fractured skull caused by external violence." To the reporters he admitted that the "external violence" might have been a bullet, a stroke with a club, a crash against a tree, or an automobile accident. At any rate, the child had been dead for at least two months.

With the finding of the body the authorities were now able definitely to demonstrate two facts. First, the kidnaped baby was dead while Jafsie's negotiations were in progress, and Colonel Lindbergh had paid his $50,000 to persons who knew they could not restore the child to his arms. Second, the supposed kidnapers who had been negotiating with John Hughes Curtis—if, indeed, they existed at all—also had empty hands while they were bargaining.

But the finding of the child proved something of far greater import. It demonstrated, conclusively, that Jafsie's negotiators were the actual kidnapers. They had sent back to the Lindberghs the little woolen suit that had clothed the baby on the night of March 1st. There was no such garment on the body. It had therefore been removed by the kidnapers—and *it had taken them three days,* the detectives recalled, *to obtain the token, clean it, and return it to the family.*

The police added another scene, therefore, to their previous reconstruction of the crime.

The wooded tract where the body was found was on the summit of a hill which is crossed by the Hopewell-Princeton road. From this vantage point the white walls of the Lindbergh home could plainly be seen, and at night an observer, particularly one armed with binoculars, could see the lights in the house as they might have been turned on or off. Accordingly, it was reasoned, the kidnapers had walked from the house to Featherbed Lane, where their automobile was parked. That would be a matter of ten minutes. Another fifteen or twenty minutes would have been consumed in reaching the top of the hill. There, looking backward, it is supposed, the kidnapers saw the Lindbergh home ablaze with lights. They knew the police had been notified—that the family had discovered the empty crib.

If an alarm already had gone out, any chance of fleeing with the child was hopeless. Every road would be guarded. Every automobile containing a baby would be stopped. They were trapped. Thereupon they decided to dispose of the incriminating evidence. Here there were two possible police deductions. Either the child, injured in a fall when the ladder gave way beneath the kidnaper's bulk, had died —or else he was callously killed. In either event, the kidnapers scratched away a little earth in the hollow near the roadside, using whatever implements they had at hand, and there left the baby's body, a prey to the elements.

The first move made by the police, now freed from all restraint in handling the case, was to call for Dr. John F. Condon and John Hughes Curtis. Condon, shocked by the tragedy, was now ready to reveal the entire inside history of his dealings with "John" to whom he had paid over Lindbergh's $50,000. Curtis was on his way back to Hopewell with Colonel Lindbergh.

The Colonel arrived with his "friend" shortly after midnight, a tragic figure with reddened eyes and haggard face. He strode into the house and remained in communion with his family for a time. Then he scanned the reports of the police and the findings of the medical authorities. Nothing remained for him to do except a few painful formalities. The case had left his hands.

On Friday the 13th of May, he drove, bareheaded as usual, to the small mortuary of Walter Swayze in Trenton, pushed through a throng of morbid spectators, and entered the gray frame house. He remained inside for only ten minutes.

"Colonel Lindbergh," asked the Prosecutor of Mercer County, Erwin E. Marshall, "are you satisfied that this is the body of your baby?"

"I am perfectly satisfied that it is my child," the Colonel replied. Then he walked to the table where the covered body was lying, and requested the removal of the sheet. He stood, a flush of color mounting to his cheeks, for a few seconds, and then walked from the room in silence.

Skeptics, some of them close to Hopewell, professed to doubt whether the body actually was that of the kidnaped infant. But the identification had been absolute. The Lindbergh child had a peculiar, or unusual, conformation of his toes, two of which overlapped the great toe. He had been treated for this by a New York specialist. The tiny bones of the body discovered the previous day presented indisputable proof that this was Charles A. Lindbergh, Jr.

Finally, making the identification complete, chemists analyzed wisps of hair found with the body and compared them with the strands the baby's grandmother, Mrs. Morrow, had treasured at her home. They were the same.

The sun was setting that afternoon as two automobiles rolled over the New Jersey hills to Linden, not far from the home of the Morrows. They stopped at the Rose Hill Crematory, and black-clad attendants took the child's body within. From the second automobile, Colonel Charles A. Lindbergh alighted and followed the little group inside. There was no religious service. The small, battered body was given to the consuming flames in the presence of only one man—Colonel Charles A. Lindbergh, walking through the shadow of the Valley of Death with his little son.

The hue and cry for the perpetrators of America's most frightful tragedy swelled to gigantic proportions. For more than seventy days, the public had been satisfied that everything humanly possible was being done to restore the baby. Now there arose a demand for vengeance. The Federal Government, throwing the entire resources of its Department of Justice back of the hunt, was urged to pass laws making kidnaping a capital crime—placing it in the same category as murder. Heavy rewards were offered for the capture of the criminals. Expressions of horror and proffers of help came from national and state executives and from foreign rulers.

In their anxiety to determine, first, how the Lindbergh baby met his death, the police turned once more to the broken ladder by which the kidnapers gained entrance to the nursery. As closely as possible they duplicated the original ladder, and then tested its construction by sending men of various weights up its rungs. The ladder they made broke under the weight of 184 pounds. Subtracting the weight of the child, which was 30 pounds, they deduced that the kidnaper must have weighed 150 pounds or more.

They found that when such a ladder collapses, the man who is climbing or descending is not thrown from the lad-

der, but into it. If he is carrying a bundle, that burden may
be hurled against the wall or, in falling, strike against a
lower sill.

They remembered that Colonel Lindbergh, sitting in his
library on the evening of March 1st, had heard a noise
resembling the crack of a tree branch outside the window.
And the most probable conclusion they could reach was
that in the collapse of the ladder, the baby was injured, to
die before the fleeing criminals reached the top of the hill
where they buried the body.

It was quite natural, in the state of public horror and
tension and the rising anger of the police and the people,
that particular attention should have been directed to Dr.
Condon, the benign Bronx mediator whose efforts had so
dismally come to grief. It was also quite natural that many,
formulating their own theories, should have pointed a finger of suspicion at his activities. At any rate, one of the first
legal processes to be observed was the calling together of
the Bronx County Grand Jury, and the hailing before it of
Jafsie, that he might tell his story and assist in the indictment of any John Does or Richard Roes whom he might
implicate in the extortion plot.

For four hours, on the day after the cremation of the
child, the elderly educator answered questions in the office
of District Attorney Charles B. McLoughlin. He repeated,
over and over again, his story of the cemetery negotiations,
and described, as accurately as it was possible, the mysterious "John" with whom he dealt. And he prepared, willingly, to go before the Grand Jury four days later, with his
friends, Gaglio, Max Rosenhain, and Al Reich, and lay

before the jurors the complete tale of the monstrous swindle.

The federal forces, meanwhile, swung into action on the John Hughes Curtis angle. A. L. Foster, a Brooklyn manufacturer who had obligingly lent the second yacht, *Cachelot*, used by Colonel Lindbergh and Curtis, was interviewed by Department of Justice agents who advised him to make no statements. Curtis himself, ignored in the first rush of activity that followed discovery of the body, was permitted to wander—but not too far out of sight—within the Lindbergh grounds.

Even at that moment, it appeared, the police were not positive that Curtis had not been in communication either with the kidnapers, who might have been attempting a double-extortion, or with "chiselers" who were trying to capitalize on the abduction.

The Navy Department and Coast Guard therefore continued, for a day, their search of the Virginia waters for the piratical craft described by the Norfolk boat builder. Six United States destroyers, three amphibian airplanes, and fifty coast guard vessels criss-crossed the ocean north and south of Cape May. From the Cape station itself thirteen cutters were dispatched, their crews armed with machineguns and sub-machine guns.

In Norfolk, the good Dean H. Dobson-Peacock was aghast. But he not only clung to his belief that he and his fellow negotiators had been dealing with the actual kidnapers, but he gave forth another interview in which he revealed further lurid details of his own participation in what he fondly believed was "excellent detective work."

He had gone to New York on April 22nd, he told police, in response to a telephone message from that city bidding him hurry there "if he wanted to insure the success of the negotiations." He was told to register at the Park Lane Hotel under the assumed name of "Hill." He met Curtis in New York, and was puzzled to learn that it was not his fellow townsman who had telephoned. Later that evening, according to the Dean's story, he was invited to a room in the Park Lane where five "gangsters" of sour mien were awaiting him.

"They crowded around me menacingly," said the clergyman, "and told me I wouldn't get out of there until I had promised to turn the baby over to them."

Like his friend Curtis, who was "not afraid when the five piratical gangsters surrounded him on board their ship," Dean Dobson-Peacock was unalarmed by the display. He protested, he said, that the entire negotiations were in the hands of John Hughes Curtis, and that he had nothing whatever to do with the ransoming of the child.

"That makes no difference," he said he was told. "You'll have to double-cross Curtis and Admiral Burrage. If you don't, you'll regret it."

Dean Dobson-Peacock refrained from relating this "incident" to the police until after the discovery of the child's body. Later he identified a picture of Gaston B. Means, a new and sensational entrant into the case, as one of the five men who had threatened him. Officials at the Park Lane Hotel said they knew nothing about the incident.

Official Washington now sent out a recall signal for its concentration of naval searching strength on the seaboard.

The *Mary B. Moss,* it was decided, was as mythical as the Flying Dutchman. But official Washington, through the Attorney General of the United States, sent a significant message to Governor A. Harry Moore at Trenton. It said:

> As a result of the recent disclosures in the Lindbergh case, and by direction of the President, I desire to renew the offer of the Federal authorities to hold themselves at the disposal of the authorities of New Jersey to render every possible service and assistance and the use of our facilities to aid you in apprehending the guilty persons.
>
> We recognize, of course, that the offense is not one against the Federal Government and that the Federal authorities have no police jurisdiction over the case, but there may be many ways in which the various detective agencies of the Federal Government may be of assistance to police of your state.
>
> Several of the executive departments of the Federal Government have investigative forces whose aid you may desire, and in order to avoid confusion, it has been suggested that J. Edgar Hoover, of the Bureau of Investigation of the Department of Justice, co-ordinate such services as the Federal agencies are called upon to render.
>
> If you will advise me what police official in New Jersey is to have general charge and control of the investigation, Mr. Hoover will get in immediate touch with him.

Thus, for the first time and still without official standing, the federal detective agencies were given an opportunity to pit their experience and skill against the wiles of what was regarded as a desperate and clever band of murderer-kidnapers. From that time on, their work never ceased.

From the moment he returned to Hopewell from Cape May, Colonel Lindbergh scarcely spoke to John Hughes Curtis. Curtis ate at his table, slept on a divan in the living room, was permitted to wander through the house as he chose. In the silent treatment accorded him he was never asked, "Don't you think you were mistaken?" Nor was he bullied by accusations or threats. It was patent, however, that he was worried, uneasy, fidgety; that he was uncertain as to his next move—whether to suggest that he could be of no further assistance and withdraw from the estate, or to remain at the house as a "guest."

He presented a forlorn picture, this usually high-spirited and jovial President of the Norfolk German Club, and there were many who felt extremely sorry for him.

For four days the principal inhabitants of the rambling white house treated him with polite indifference. Presently he began to show certain indications, unmistakable to psychologists and crime-detectors, that he was almost ready to "say something."

CHAPTER EIGHT

THERE WAS PEACE FOR JOHN HUGHES CURTIS, STILL A GUEST IN the Lindbergh home, through the quiet Sunday, May 15th. The day before he had been extremely busy and important, running over to Cape May City to "assist" in checking over his previous information, accompanied by a none-too-congenial police sergeant who objected to wetting his own legs in knee-deep grass while the Norfolk man was identifying abandoned cottages as the scenes of his various rendezvous with Hilda and others of her ilk.

In the first place, the sergeant didn't believe there was a scintilla of truth in what Curtis was telling him, and he didn't believe they would ever find the locale so nimbly described by his companion. Nor did they.

So, on Sunday, there had come a welcome rest for the "negotiator," and on Monday a little more work was found for him to do. He was invited to go to Newark to look into the rogue's gallery there and see if he could identify any of the photographs as those of Sam the Gasman, Dynamite, Eric or Nils. He pointed a finger at one of them.

"I think," he said, "that might be the man. He looks very much like one of them." The photographic subject upon whom he had touched had for many months been an inmate of the State Hospital at Morris Plains.

In company with detectives Curtis then made a futile tour of the entire City of Newark, "trying to point out the

house where he once held a conference with the gang."
Late that evening he returned to Hopewell, and sank to a
chair, manifestly disconsolate.

Shortly after midnight, Inspector Walsh made a friendly
approach. "Let's have a game of checkers," he suggested.
Curtis agreed, but his mind wasn't on the game, and after
a few minutes the Inspector said, "Well, I guess you're too
tired for games. Let's go for a short walk and then you can
turn in."

As they strolled outside, the Inspector talked, softly,
insinuatingly. In all of his phrases there was just the suggestion that Curtis ought, in the interests of everybody,
including Colonel Lindbergh and himself, to tell the truth.

For nearly an hour, Curtis pondered the matter. Then
he told Walsh there was at least one thing he wanted to
correct. He had never, he admitted, seen or handled any
of the ransom bills. But, so help him, the rest of his story
was true. He had made the statements about the money in
order to impress the authorities with the need for haste, he
said.

The two men returned to the house, and for two hours
more the inspector plied him with questions. Suddenly, at
four o'clock in the morning, Curtis asked for a typewriter
and chair, and began to write feverishly. Within thirty-five
minutes, Inspector Walsh and Lieutenant A. J. Keaton,
with whom he was working, had the following "confession"
in their hands:

> Made of my own hand and my own free will.
> Referring to the two statements made previously
> by me in regard to Lindbergh case.

At the present time I am sane, but I honestly believe that for the last seven or eight months, I have not been myself, due to financial troubles.

I was apparently brought back to my senses by my telephone conversation with my wife this afternoon, when she told me of the troubles she was having and how the children missed me; also by my conversation with Inspector Harry Walsh.

I desire to state that my remarks about the newspapers are true and can be verified. This is in reference to my story about Mr. Haskell and Mr. Wilcox of the *Herald-Tribune*.

Mr. Lee of the "News" and Mr. Twin and Fox offered me money for my knowledge of the Lindbergh case or pictures of the baby.

The matter was brought to my attention during a conversation and due to what I now believe was a distorted mind, by brooding over it, I became insane on the subject for the time being, which caused me to create the story in its entirety, which was untrue in every respect.

I never knew such people that I named to Colonel Lindbergh, they were creatures of a distorted mind, with the exception of Marie Truesday, who had no connection with the crime.

I exceedingly regret that I caused Colonel Lindbergh and others any inconvenience, and wish it were in my power to correct the wrong.

In justice to my wife and two children, I trust it is in the power of Colonel Lindbergh to forgive the inconvenience, worry and injustice I did him in his time of grief.

This statement has been brought about by the realization of the wrong I have done.

Submitted:
John Hughes Curtis.

Curtis's reference to the newspaper men involved in the confession was explained by the executives of the various public journals which had endeavored to tie Curtis up with exclusive contracts after the baby should be found.

Grafton S. Wilcox, of the *New York Herald Tribune,* announced that his newspaper made no contract with Curtis, and that it had stipulated that it would make no arrangement with him until after the baby had been returned safely to Colonel Lindbergh.

Richard Lee, of the *New York Daily News,* entered an immediate disclaimer that any tender had been made to Curtis, except that "on his recovery of the child" the newspaper stood ready to pay a certain amount for exclusive picture of the child and the story of his recovery.

The United Press had flatly refused the offer of "a prominent Norfolk citizen" (not Curtis) who had wanted to sell "the story of the return of the Lindbergh Baby for $7,500." The information at hand, the news service said, did not point to the negotiations as being authentic.

Having relieved his mind and unburdened his soul, Curtis let forth a loud blast against his associate, the Very Reverend Dean H. Dobson-Peacock, in a supplementary statement which accused the gentleman of being a publicity hunter.

Curtis told the police he would willingly have dropped the whole matter on March 15th, knowing the story to be untrue, but that the man of the cloth was urging him on.

"Many of the stories," said Curtis, "that appeared in the newspapers were manufactured by Peacock and were untrue, and he had knowledge of their untruthfulness at the time he released them for publication. I know from my own experience with the Dean that the only interest he had throughout this matter was one of satisfying his desires for publicity, and the more he got, the better he liked it."

The Dean, who professed to be highly shocked by such harsh words from a parishioner, tearfully disclaimed any desire for publicity, and proved his desire to shun the light by retiring within his shell-like rectory and issuing only a few brief bulletins in which he said he had been hoaxed, like everybody else.

But the Dean was also subjected to considerable fire from the police themselves, who asked him embarrassingly whether he wouldn't like to come to Hopewell and repeat some of his stories, particularly the tale about his trip to New York and the gangsters he met.

Colonel Schwarzkopf, in fact, gave the reporters, in a formal report, something to write about.

"Two telegrams have been sent to Mr. Peacock," he said, "both of which he has ignored, although we have the assurances of the telegraph companies they have been personally delivered. Investigation has developed that the alleged anonymous telephone call which summoned Mr. Peacock to the Park Lane Hotel in New York, where he was registered under the name of Hill, was apparently put in by Curtis. Upon his arrival in New York, Peacock went directly to Curtis's apartment in the Prince George Hotel and interviewed Curtis.

"In a telephone conversation with Peacock this morning, he said he would not come to Hopewell today, and indicated he did not know whether he could get to Hopewell at

all. He would give no definite answer as to when he would
come to Hopewell and shows no desire to coöperate with
the authorities at this point, although he was told that he
was involved by the statements of Curtis and his presence
was wanted for the purpose of facing Curtis."

To this the Dean retorted that he did not see why he
should have to go to the bother and expense of traveling to
Hopewell, since he had acted "in perfect sincerity," and
since he had other important work to do.

"And in reply to Mr. Curtis's statement that I might have
prevented this enormous deception," he said, "I feel called
upon to say that I cannot understand what Mr. Curtis
meant unless it was that he had told me in the beginning
that he would not undertake the negotiations alone."

Thereupon the boat builder, with some spirit, revealed
more incidents of the start of the hoax, and in particular
accused the Dean of trying to prevent the inclusion of
Admiral Burrage in the negotiating party.

"You know what sort of an old fogey he is," the Dean
was quoted as saying.

"Because of the manner in which the Dean pressed me
for news and because of the news he was manufacturing
for his own publicity and his desire for it," Curtis continued, warming up to his subject, "I became annoyed and
went to Admiral Burrage about it, and it was agreed that
in the future the Admiral would handle the publicity and
nothing but the real facts as delivered by me would be
released for publication.

"In connection with the stories he released to the press
stating that he had been held up by gangsters on the eighth

floor of a hotel in the City of New York on a visit to that
city to meet me, I made mention to Admiral Burrage upon
my return to Norfolk that in my opinion this was another
bid for publicity on the part of the Dean."

Colonel Charles H. Consolvo, who had generously put
his yacht at Curtis's disposal, paying all the expenses
incurred on the various trips, was deeply shocked—sickened
—by the truth. "It is the most colossal deception I have
ever heard," he said. "It is one of which I would never have
dreamed."

And Skipper Lackman, of the *Marcon,* who had spent so
many sleepless hours in the pilot house of his neat little
craft, would cheerfully have wrung Curtis's neck.

The authorities, while the battle of statements was raging,
thumbed through the statute books to find what law, if any,
John Hughes Curtis had violated. In his penitent mood,
Curtis was a pitiful figure. They had no desire to be too
harsh upon him, although their hate glands swelled almost
visibly when they thought of the trick he had played and
the hours of labor he had caused.

The statute books of the State of New Jersey, it developed, had very little to say about the cases of gentlemen
who, for gain or glory, befuddled the police while they were
at work on important cases, unless the gentlemen themselves
were part and parcel of the subjects for whom the police,
at that particular moment, happened to be hunting.

"Obstructing justice," however, was a broad term, which
might include almost anything, from tripping up a running
policeman to snatching a criminal from his hands. They
believed the phrase might fit Mr. Curtis's activities, so they

put him under arrest and booked him on the general charge of obstructing justice, to which they added another phrase, "giving false information."

A court of arraignment was set up at once in Colonel Lindbergh's library, and the Colonel, a gaunt spectator, never said a word during the short session. George Webster, justice of the peace, listened to the charge against Curtis, made by Prosecutor Anthony M. Hauck, Jr., which related that the said Curtis "for the purpose of hindering the apprehension of the person or persons guilty of the said crimes, did knowingly or willfully give false and untrue reports of the person or persons guilty of the commission of the crimes aforesaid."

The phrasing of Prosecutor Hauck's affidavit was, though a legal requirement, unfortunate. In order to convict Curtis of anything at all, it appeared, it would have to prove that he told his stories "for the purpose" of hampering Colonel Schwarzkopf and his men from catching the kidnapers, and this in turn would make it essential that Curtis himself knew who the kidnapers were.

However, leaving the knotty legal points to be untied at a later date, the gendarmes clapped Curtis's felt hat on his head, and took him away to the Hunterdon County Jail, in default of a $10,000 bond. Sheriff William B. Wean met Prosecutor Hauck and his charge at the jail door, and took the prisoner in tow. "You'll have to give me a receipt," said the Prosecutor.

The Sheriff pondered a moment and then wrote:

"Received one John Hughes Curtis." He took a look at Curtis, and added the words—"in good condition."

The angriest man of the group that had been working to restore the baby to the Lindberghs, however, was Dr. John F. Condon. Jafsie gave vent to his feelings in an explosive interview after he emerged from a grand jury session.

"I knew it," he said. "I knew it all along. I was sure this man was a faker. And he was not only a faker and guilty of a cruel hoax, but he did more than that. He ruined my chances ever of restoring my contacts with the real kidnapers."

Jafsie made much of the fact that Curtis had permitted word to "leak" to the underworld, through the newspapers, that he was "authorized" to pay as high as $100,000 for the return of the child.

"He spoiled my work when he came out with that announcement," he declared bitterly. "The sleeping garment of the stolen baby was the only authentic means of identification and it was sent to me by the kidnapers. It was the only definite lead and I was working on it. Then the Norfolk man came on the scene and the actual kidnapers, with whom I was dealing, threw in my face his announcement that he could pay $100,000—and I could pay only half that amount. No wonder they wouldn't deal with me!"

There came another brief moment of excitement that day, when a Long Island rum runner named Frank Parzych "confessed" that he was the real kidnaper. For an hour or two he resisted every effort to break down his story. Then it collapsed, as rapidly as it had been blown up. The police discovered he was a narcotic addict.

The Very Reverend Dean H. Dobson-Peacock went back to his study. Admiral Burrage sank deeper into retirement —although from the start his part in the drama had not only been wholly innocent but much against his will and better judgment—and John Hughes Curtis remained lodged in the Hunterdon County jail at Flemington, until such time as the authorities deemed it wise to go to trial with his case.

One week later, acting under a suspension of the rules, the New Jersey Senate voted unanimously to authorize the Governor to offer a reward of $25,000 for the apprehension of the criminals.

At this point, the law enforcement agencies of the nation were circularized, for the first time, with specimens of the handwriting on two of the notes received by Jafsie. Experts had compared them with the original ransom note left in the baby's room, and found they had absolutely corresponding characteristics. And logically, the man who received the money from Dr. Condon and gave him in return the false directions for "finding the baby on board Nelly" had been in the nursery on the evening of March 1st. He had been able to describe it to the Doctor.

Jafsie himself, worn out by the developments of the month, left for New England, to rest at the summer home of his friend, Walter Goodwin, at Becket, Massachusetts. He had with him, and the fact was duly recorded in the public prints, a note from Colonel Lindbergh expressing esteem and appreciation for all his efforts, and confidence that he had sincerely done his best to accomplish a highly desired end.

William Allen, the Negro laborer whose discovery startled the world, was offered $300 a week to display himself to gaping multitudes from the stage. The salary was tempting, particularly to a man who had only irregular work and a family to support. But the authorities stepped in and admonished him rudely. This was no time, they said, to be capitalizing on his service. Accordingly, William's toying with the idea of becoming a vaudeville artist came to an abrupt end.

The Norfolk tale-spinner was brought to trial on Monday, June 27th, at the Flemington Court House. In anticipation of the drama all Flemington turned out and with the populace came a host of sensation seekers from other towns and cities, all of whom seemed to know, many of them being able to read the newspapers, that Colonel Lindbergh was to be the State's star witness.

The legal authorities had pursued their hunt through the laws of the State for some other statutory offense upon which they might hold Curtis, but found none. Accordingly, for want of something better, he went to trial on the charge of obstructing justice—a misdemeanor carrying a maximum penalty of three years' imprisonment and a fine of $1,000.

Colonel Lindbergh, straight and tall and stalwart, told his story to the jury of seven men and five women and never once looked at the face of the prisoner. For two days he related the circumstances of his meeting Curtis, his first disinclination to believe the Norfolk man could by any chance have been in contact with the kidnapers of his son, and finally his readiness to listen after the disappointment of the Condon negotiations.

Lloyd Fisher, counsel for the defense, who cross-examined the Colonel during his second day on the stand, did as well by the accused man as could have been done. His handling of Colonel Lindbergh was smoothly sympathetic, and at least elicited responses not wholly unfavorable to Curtis.

The Colonel said that only once had the question of giving Curtis any money arisen, and that was when it had been suggested that $25,000 be deposited in a Norfolk bank, in trust, "to show good faith." He also said that to his personal knowledge, Curtis had not benefited to the extent of a penny during the entire transaction. And he also admitted that upon one occasion, when Curtis telephoned him that he "had one of the men in tow, and would like to bring him to Hopewell at once," he had been too busy to make the engagement.

"Do you believe Curtis was ever in contact with the actual kidnapers?" Fisher asked the Colonel.

"I do not believe he had any contact," Colonel Lindbergh replied. "I don't believe he knew who took the child or who had the child in their possession."

A succession of police officials followed Colonel Lindbergh to the stand and added their weight of evidence against him. And all of them swore to a belief that Curtis had imagined the entire story and that his supposed contact with the criminals was fanciful, false and absurd on the face of it.

A legal dilemma was thus passed on to the jury. Under the law, as carefully expounded to them by Judge Adam O. Robbins, the jury could not find Curtis guilty of obstructing justice unless the State had proved Curtis had actual knowledge of and contact with the criminals. Practically every important witness had declared, to the best of his belief, that no such knowledge or contact existed.

If, then, the jury found John Hughes Curtis guilty, it thereby proclaimed its own belief that Curtis's original story was the truth. And if it were the truth, where then did the "obstruction of justice come in?" And Curtis himself had branded his story as a tissue of lies, the product of a disordered brain.

It was a difficult problem, but the jurors solved it by finding Curtis guilty as charged, and adding a rider recommending the court's mercy upon him. Judge Robbins fined Curtis $1,000 and sentenced him to serve one year in jail. Justice smiled and was satisfied with the verdict.

But Curtis was never to serve his year in jail. There was an appeal from the Hunterdon County verdict, and before the appeal could be heard by the higher court, a little group of persons once more appeared before Judge Robbins. Among them were Prosecutor Hauck, Attorney Fisher, Curtis, and Assistant Attorney General Joseph I. Lanigan.

Curtis, who had been at liberty on a $10,000 bond while his appeal was pending, had driven all night from Norfolk to be in court. It was evident that previous conferences had been held between the attorneys.

When Judge Robbins took his seat on the bench, Defense Counsel Fisher prayed the honorable court that his client might be resentenced.

Lanigan and Hauck announced to the court that they

would not oppose the motion, and Judge Robbins announced:

"It is now within the province of this court to suspend operation of the jail sentence, which I now do."

Curtis stepped to the bench, paid his fine with a $1,000 bill, shook hands with the judge, the prosecutors and his own lawyer, and departed.

None of the principals in this adventure had any statements to make after the procedure save Curtis, who remarked when he reached his home town that this action was "a vindication" and that he had paid the fine rather than bother any longer with "the uncertainties of Jersey justice."

The entire case and the handling of it, however, left many questions, some practical and some in the realm of psychology, to be answered.

Granting that Curtis's entire story was a fantastic fabrication from beginning to end, what was its purpose? Money? The answer to that was that Curtis knew he could not receive a penny, whether for ransom or for his own services as a *litterateur,* until after the baby had been returned. The hope of gain, indeed, might otherwise have been a plausible motive, for Curtis's personal finances were in a parlous state.

Was it to gain time from his creditors, who were pressing him? Perhaps, because no creditor would dun a man who was engaged on an errand of mercy such as this.

Was it, perhaps, the clever conceit of the man that once it became known he was engaged as a negotiator, the real kidnapers might come to him and thus secure for him the glory and the pecuniary rewards that were bound to come if the issue were successful? The suggestion is plausible.

Or, finally, was it the result of a moment's sudden twist of the mind in which John Hughes Curtis saw himself glorified, for a little while, in the eyes of the public? This would seem to be one of the most logical explanations for the entire hoax. It exemplified the ancient copybook maxim —"oh, what a tangled web we weave, when first we practice to deceive!"

Finding himself inextricably tangled in the first web, and with him a respectable admiral and an innocent of the cloth, he was forced to go deeper into the "plot." Having invented "Sam the Gasman," he was forced to invent "Dynamite." Having created "Dynamite," and "Eric" and "Nils," he had to erect houses to house them and ships to carry them, and to provide them with an assortment of round-bosomed wives—the sort a seafaring man would approve.

Ever wanting, in accordance with his better nature, to pull out of the mess, the force of circumstances pulled him in the deeper. He had to invent lies to explain lies, and other lies to bolster up the first prevarications.

And throughout the sorry business, he undoubtedly had within himself the fantastic hope that a Divine Providence would throw his way a solution of the case, enabling him to leap clear of the trap he had constructed.

If the baby had been alive the outcome of his deception might have been vastly different. Instead, the child's body was found. His patchwork fabrication collapsed.

CHAPTER NINE

FROM THE BEGINNING OF THEIR INVESTIGATIONS, ONE OF THE major problems presented to the police was contained in the question: "How did the kidnapers know the Lindbergh child would be at Hopewell on the night of March 1st?"

It was recalled that Anne Morrow Lindbergh had intended, until almost noon of that day, to go to Englewood and to remain at her mother's home until the following weekend, and that her contrary decision was recalled only because of her baby's illness.

It was possible, of course, that the timing of the abduction was merely by chance, and that the kidnapers watched the house until they saw lights in the nursery, noted that they were dimmed, and seized the opportunity. But if this were so, still another question would arise, and that was: "How did the kidnapers know in what room Charles A. Lindbergh, Jr., was sleeping?"

The criminals had made no errors. They had reared the ladder directly at the nursery window, and at the only window in the large house that could not be fastened. Was this, too, mere chance?

Criminals seeking information of the Lindbergh family's habits would have had only two original sources—members of the family, or some of the servants of the two households at Hopewell and Englewood.

There were twenty-nine servants at the Morrow mansion, and three at the Lindbergh estate. The staff of the latter included the estimable Ollie Whately, his wife Elsie, and nursemaid Betty Gow. Extensive questioning had determined, beyond a doubt, that none of that trio had anything to do with the kidnaping or had given, wittingly or unwittingly, any information to outsiders which might have been passed on to the plotters.

Major Schoeffel of the New Jersey State Police had spent weeks in Great Britain and, with the aid of Scotland Yard, had inquired with patient thoroughness into the antecedents and past associates of every servant known to have been born on the other side of the ocean. In each case—Whately, Gow and certain members of the Morrow establishment— he found nothing but clean records.

Hundreds of hours had been spent going over with these thirty-two manservants and handmaidens the story of their activities during the entire year preceding the kidnaping. They provided the police with long lists of names of friends "on the outside," with whom they might have whiled away some of their off-duty hours.

There was a fine rapprochement between the two household staffs. Members of the Morrow establishment often visited the Hopewell estate and, with Ollie Whately, went swimming in the river near Zion, two miles from the Lindbergh home. It might be assumed that the Morrow servants knew as much about the interior of that house and the habits of its inmates as did the Lindbergh servants.

Heading the Morrow staff was the impeccable Septimus Banks, butler for Senator Morrow over a long period of years and held by him in vast esteem. He was a quiet individual, not given to much roistering, and the limit of his social indulgence appears to have been an occasional visit to a speakeasy in 125th Street, New York, and once in a while to some of the local taverns. He was neither loquacious nor given to associating with low characters. He felt the dignity of his position, like the suave Ollie Whately, as a gentleman's chief servitor, a major domo, a prime seneschal.

There was below-stairs romance in the Morrow household, and all, save perhaps the Morrows themselves, knew what was going on. Septimus Banks had fallen head over heels in love with a jolly serving maid, the brown-haired, snappy-eyed Violet Sharpe, who came to America from the little village of Tult's Clump, Bradfield, England. She was twenty-seven, and had worked in the Morrow household for two years.

When Violet went to work, under the orders of the irreproachable Septimus Banks, she gave the New York Y.W.C.A. as her address and as a reference the name of a Toronto woman who described her as "sober, industrious, willing and loyal."

Violet had a sister, Edna Sharpe, who was also in service. Edna was maid for Miss Constance Chilton, a friend and associate of Miss Elizabeth Morrow in the management of a school for young children.

Now, although Violet was popularly supposed to have been betrothed to the staid butler, the fact did not prevent her from an occasional bit of flirtation on the outside. Violet was rather one to have a good time—without, of course, the knowledge or sanction of her fiancé who, she realized, would be frightfully miffed if he heard of such carryings on. At twenty-seven, with her figure showing signs of plumping out a bit, it would never do to be jilted.

On the Sunday before the kidnaping, Violet and her sister, Edna, had taken a long walk. As they were returning to town, a cheerful young man waved to them from his green coupe and the girls, thinking him a friend, waved in return. The young man stopped his car, and although they then recognized their mistake, he persuaded them to let him drive them home. Before they reached the house, he had made a "date"—according to Violet—to take her to the movies on the following Tuesday night. That would be March 1st.

Violet insisted to the police, throughout their early rigorous questioning, that she didn't know the last name of this new friend. His first name, she declared, was "Ernie," and that was all she knew about him.

At one o'clock on the afternoon of March 1st, Ernie called her on the telephone, to confirm the arrangements for the evening. She knew, at that time, that Betty Gow was going to Hopewell and that the Lindberghs would not arrive as guests of the Morrow family.

Violet said that Ernie brought another couple with him that night, and that the four of them went to a movie house, remaining throughout the evening.

Of all the servants questioned by the detectives, Violet Sharpe alone adopted a defeatist attitude. She was flip and saucy with her replies. Occasionally she refused to answer questions, on the grounds that "that is my own business."

It was quite evident she was afraid that Septimus Banks might find out something to his displeasure. Her attitude was puzzling. She appeared to have no realization of the gravity of the case, and once in a while threw a wink toward the housekeeper when she had made a particularly "smart" or confusing reply.

It was easy to be seen that she was trying to throw the detectives off the scent. But was it because of her knowledge of the inside story of the kidnaping, or because she knew she had been guilty of making revelations to the plotters, or because she wanted to conceal certain incidents of her private life from Septimus Banks?

While she was undergoing her inquisition, the officers ransacked her room. They found little—a few letters from home, the names and addresses of friends, a batch of cards advertising the Post Road Taxicab Company, of White Plains, N. Y., and some books, among them *The World's 100 Best Detective Stories* and *Murder on Broadway,* a current thriller. And finally, there was a little written note, reading, "Banks promises to try and be straight for twelve months." It would have appeared from this that the estimable Banks had been slipping.

The police had dropped, temporarily, the questioning of Violet Sharpe in the interest of what appeared to be more important investigations, and the serving maid was not again annoyed until after the body of the baby had been found. And four days after that event, Edna Sharpe sailed for England. The police had no knowledge of her intention to leave the country, and the flight appeared to be hurried, for Edna obtained the visa to her passport only three days before sailing.

In June, the police moved their headquarters to Alpine and proceeded to resume their interviews with the Morrow servants. Once before they had been checked by Violet's illness. On the advice of the Morrow family physician, she had undergone an operation for adenoids and diseased tonsils, and she was in the hospital on the day the child's lifeless form was taken from its makeshift grave in the Sourlands.

Upon their return to the attack on Violet's story, with its discrepancies and contradictions, the officers found themselves faced with a changed young woman. Where she had been flippant, she had become sullen; defiance had given way to nervousness and hysteria; more than ever she appeared to be concealing some dreadful knowledge.

The police asked her the title of the motion picture she had seen with Ernie. She named it, but was unable to tell a word of the plot or the name of an actor in it. Then she broke down and confessed that she hadn't been to the movies at all; that, instead, she and Ernie and their two companions had spent the evening drinking beer at the Peanut Grill, near Orangeburg. Still she couldn't remember Ernie's last name. All she remembered, she said, was that he "wasn't so hot as a dancer."

The half a dozen or more cards advertising the Post Road taxi firm had, however, given the police a new lead. Investigating the concern they found that it had expired of malnutrition some six months before, but that it had been

operated by a man named Ernest Brinkert. And Brinkert
had a police record.

They showed Violet Sharpe a rogue's gallery picture of
Brinkert and asked her whether he had been her escort at
the Peanut Grill. She burst into hysterical weeping and said,
"Yes, that's the man." Then, giggling again, she winked
over her shoulder at another servant.

At that point it was decided to give the girl a rest. Her
heart, the Morrow family physician said, would not stand
the strain. But the police told her they would return, and
that she would have to go to the Alpine headquarters for
another session.

On June 10th, Inspector Harry J. Walsh and a group of
detectives called once more at the Morrow home and
announced they would proceed with the questioning of
Violet Sharpe. They did not know that the night before, in
an hysterical outburst before the other servants, she had
exclaimed, "They'll never take me from this house again—
I'll not go to Alpine."

Inspector Walsh told Arthur Springer, formerly secretary
to Senator Morrow, to tell Violet to prepare herself for
questioning. It had been arranged that a physician would
be in attendance, in order to protect the young woman's
health. Springer found the maid and told her she was
wanted.

Violet went to her room. Five minutes later another
domestic, Emily Keritarium, walked through the butler's
pantry and found her lying on the floor. She had taken
cyanide of potassium, and rushed downstairs, to die.

The police hurried to her room. A drinking glass with a

few crystals still clinging to it told the story of her suicide. The poison had been used in a preparation for cleaning silver.

Violet Sharpe's suicide intensified the search for Ernest Brinkert. In official circles it was regarded as an almost positive proof of guilt.

"The suicide," said Colonel Schwarzkopf, "strongly tends to confirm the suspicions of the investigating authorities concerning her guilty knowledge of the crime." And he sent out the following alarm:

> Arrest on sight Ernest Brinkert, wanted in connection with the Lindbergh kidnaping and murder. Description as of April 19, 1926, 24 years old, five feet four and one quarter inches, 144 pounds, stockily built, medium chestnut hair, light complexion, green eyes, occupation chauffeur, roofer and painter. Two moles left side of nose; a one-inch vertical scar from left eye to mouth; scar back of right hand. Small scar near right eye. Drives Nash coach, green, 1926, license 3V-1983, N.Y.
> Record is as follows:
> April 21, 1922, Westchester county, petty larceny. No disposition.
> April 7, 1926, Westchester County, assault, Westchester county penitentiary.
> April 19, 1926, Westchester County, as Ernest "Brown," assault. No disposition.

Ten hours later, Brinkert was in custody and the police believed they were nearing a solution of the case.

Brinkert's first words to the police in response to their questions convinced them he was a colossal liar. He said he not only didn't know any Violet Sharpe, but that he had never even heard of her! And he was quite willing to waive extradition and travel back to New Jersey from New Rochelle, New York, where he had been picked up.

Jafsie was called into the play. First, he examined a picture of Brinkert and declared he noticed a strong resemblance in it to the "John" to whom he had paid the $50,000 ransom in the cemetery. But when he was brought face to face with him, the Bronx intermediary announced it could not have been the same man. "John," he was sure, was at least five feet, nine inches tall. This man was much shorter.

Brinkert's marital adventures also came in for some questioning. In 1927 he had married a Miss Helen Pugmore, who left him and went home to her mother after a brief honeymoon. After that, without bothering with the formality of a divorce, according to his wife, he had taken unto himself another spouse, with whom he was living. The first Mrs. Brinkert had much to say about her husband, and none of it was good.

Other circumstantial evidence that appeared to link the one-time taxicab owner with the case came to light. Claude W. Moody, a real estate man at Larchmont, for whom Brinkert had worked, told police the young man had left work on February 28th, taking his wife away with him. After he had gone, it was found that a ladder was missing.

"I don't know anything about the ladder. I don't know anything about the case, and I never heard of Violet Sharpe," Brinkert repeated, "and if you'll give me time, I'll prove everything I say."

The police took him to New Jersey, and while they were

checking on his alibis, sent cablegrams to England asking Scotland Yard to place Edna Sharpe under arrest, if necessary, and by all means to get her story. They found, from Violet's bank book, that she had saved $1,600, and announced that "several deposits were made recently." Her wages were $85 a month.

As though to forestall an expected wave of criticism for "hounding a poor girl to her death," Colonel Schwarzkopf issued an explanatory statement of the police activity leading to the maid's suicide.

"Violet Sharpe," he said, "has been under constant suspicion in this investigation since she was first interviewed at Englewood, N. J., in the early days of the kidnaping, because she gave conflicting statements as to her whereabouts on the night of the kidnaping, and because she refused to reveal the identity of the man with whom she went out that night. She also refused to reveal the places visited on their trip that night. It has since been found that she had been in communication with this man at one o'clock on the afternoon of March 1st. She knew that the Lindbergh family expected to remain in Hopewell."

As long as Brinkert was held at police headquarters while the detectives were investigating his alibis, the press and public withheld judgment on the inquisition that preceded Violet Sharpe's death. Like the police, the whole world regarded that act as a probable admission of guilt, and waited breathlessly for an official announcement that the case was solved.

No such announcement came, however, and presently it was announced that taxicabman Brinkert had been released from custody, after presenting a thorough alibi and definite proof that he had never met Violet Sharpe or had any connection whatsoever with the case.

Thereupon another of those amazing coincidences among the thousands that had plagued the police from start to finish arose to add a further mystery. Another "Ernie," one Ernest Miller, of Closter, New Jersey, walked into the police station and announced that he was the young man with whom Violet had her "date" on the night of the kidnaping, and that he had taken her—as she finally admitted before her death—to the Peanut Grill. The police found ample corroboration for the story.

The question the detectives asked themselves at this point was: "Why did Violet Sharpe lie, in her identification of Ernest Brinkert as her escort on the night of the kidnaping?"

Such a general question naturally created further questions. Was her lying conscious or unconscious? Was she trying to protect someone else? Did she lie "for spite"? Because she hated and distrusted the police? Did she actually fancy she saw a resemblance in the rogue's gallery picture of Brinkert, to the honest face of Ernest Miller?

To this day, so far as anyone knows, neither time nor logic has provided an absolutely true answer to those questions. The most probable theory is this:

Violet Sharpe treasured her association with Septimus Banks, the butler. She expected and hoped to marry him. From the beginning she may have had the fear that revelations of her little wanderings in the company of another man, or men, might not only have broken her romance but even cost her a position in the Morrow household where she was comfortable and well liked.

That she was temperamental and high strung, of a nervous disposition and inclined to be headstrong, there was no doubt from her actions during the early questioning of all the servants at Englewood. She had been ill, and had undergone hospital treatment at the time the body of the child was found.

Under those conditions, there was only one theory—and it has never been more than a theory—that she committed suicide in a hysteria of terror that was wholly unconnected with the Lindbergh abduction; that she was another innocent victim in the chain of tragedies that followed the initial crime.

At any rate, once the public discovered that Violet had actually been out upon a mere frolic with Ernest Miller and his friends, Elmer Johnson and Catherine Minners—who also came forward and proved their innocence—the customary public clamor arose against the police, the "third degree," supposed brutality, and the "grilling" of an unfortunate young woman who was "forced to take refuge in self-destruction."

The British were particularly indignant. Labor members of Parliament said with some heat that they would ask the Government to make representations to the American Government on the question of infringement upon the rights of a British citizen. The *Daily Herald* of London accused the New Jersey officers of "venting their chagrin at their failure in the Lindbergh case on a poor English servant girl." Under the heading "Disgrace to American Justice," the *Tele-*

graph declared the police had "tortured" her, thereby darkening the record of the Lindbergh case and "making it more horrible."

Scotland Yard officials questioned Edna Sharpe, Violet's sister, at Beenham, and announced that both Edna and Violet appeared to have been "respectable girls." They discovered, however, one other fact hitherto overlooked by the investigators. Violet had been married before she came to America. Her husband's name was George Payne. Neither her sister nor her mother had ever met Payne, and her mother had never even been told Violet was married.

Many of the American tabloid newspapers, particularly those whose efforts at sensationalism had outrun the limits of truth and brought down upon them the enmity of the police, joined in the howl against Colonel Schwarzkopf and his men, and in yelping headlines demanded: "Punish Cops Who Drove Morrow Maid to Death!"

The occasion was also seized upon avidly by politicians opposed to the Democratic administration in New Jersey. Senator Emerson L. Richards, Republican leader, declared, "The Lindbergh case has been slaughtered to make a Democratic holiday," and listed "five major blunders" he said had been committed by the state police. In the order of their importance, he said, they were:

The detention of Henry (Red) Johnson, Betty Gow's lovelorn suitor.

The fruitless payment of Colonel Lindbergh's $50,000 ransom through Jafsie.

The hoax perpetrated by John Hughes Curtis.

Failure of the police to find the child's body, within five miles of the Lindberghs' home.

And, finally, the fatal questioning of Violet Sharpe.

In reply to the Senator, who was manifestly trying to turn this Democratic "holiday" into a Republican festival, the authorities pointed out mildly that if they had neglected to question Henry Johnson and all other associates of the Lindbergh servants, they would have been guilty of gross negligence; that they had nothing to do with the payment of the ransom money and that they not only advised against it, but asked the Colonel to permit them to arrest the negotiator; that from the beginning they had discounted entirely John Hughes Curtis's yarns, and had asked the Colonel to ignore them; and that hundreds of state police, volunteer searchers, and even the general public, had tramped over the Sourland hills for weeks without finding a trace of the child.

As for the questioning of Violet Sharpe and its consequences, the records and their own statements showed that no "third degree" methods had been permitted or used at any time. The questioning took place either in the presence of the Lindbergh family or their representatives.

"The questions and answers were taken down during the examination of Miss Sharpe and there wasn't any attempt at intimidation," said Inspector Walsh. "She was always questioned either at the Lindbergh home or the Morrow home in Englewood, never in the station house. She was always treated gently and kindly—never roughly. Colonel Lindbergh would not have permitted any rough treatment. We really pleaded with her to help us."

To this, Colonel Schwarzkopf added that a thorough questioning was warranted by the fact that the police knew Violet was not telling the truth, and that it had been discovered that she actually knew "Ernie's" last name at the time she made her false identification of Brinkert.

His Majesty's Acting Consul General, Edward H. Gerald Shepherd, at New York, studied the records, sent a long report to the Foreign office of his Government, and absolved the New Jersey police from all charges of the super-brutality that had been charged against them. He also attended the maid's funeral, in a touching gesture of loyalty to a fellow citizen who had died tragically in a foreign land.

From his cell in the Hunterdon County jail, John Hughes Curtis took occasion to have another fling at the police. He had been languishing there, unable for a time to raise the $10,000 bond required for his release pending his trial.

"Personally," he said, "I can deeply sympathize with Miss Sharpe's family and think it perfectly justified in the English press in raising a howl. Beatings, as I noticed, evidently are a common practice with the New Jersey police in gaining their ends, but are not always necessary. Lying promises often work just as well."

Violet Sharpe was not the only major character in the drama to pass from the stage before the last curtain. Fourteen months after the kidnaping, Ollie Whately, the genial Lindbergh butler, died. He had been a loyal servitor, devoted to the Lindberghs. From the first few weeks after the kidnaping his health suffered and his illness was aggravated by worry. He died, "from natural causes," at Trenton, New Jersey, in May, 1933.

CHAPTER TEN

"THE LINDBERGH CASE," SAID MR. JUSTICE JAMES M. PROCTOR, "brought out all the best in the hearts of men, but also gave opportunity to some to display the weakness and wickedness of human nature."

Before him, as he delivered his philosophic summation of the case, stood Gaston B. Means, his arms akimbo and a broad grin on his dimpled face. The date was June 15, 1932, and Means, a former operative for the Department of Justice, had just been convicted of swindling Mrs. Evalyn Walsh McLean out of $104,000 on the pretense that he could obtain the return of the kidnaped child.

The Means case, fantastic to the point of utter absurdity, formed another tragic chapter in the epic of criminality. Justice Proctor's words wrote "Finis" to the career of America's most extraordinary liar.

Gaston Bullock Means was well-born. He came of a highly respectable family in Concord, North Carolina, where for generations the male members of the Means clan had held positions of high trust in the community and state. His great-grandfather had been governor of North Carolina. His father had been mayor of Concord. His uncle had been chief of police. He was well educated at the University of North Carolina, and later achieved considerable commercial success as a salesman for the Cannon Mills.

Means was the salesman type. He was big, bland and

breezy, and if his open-handed ways and his appearance of honesty impressed the business men with whom he came in contact, his charming smile and his dimples were no less effective with women. He had a glib, persuasive tongue, the imagination of a Munchausen and the reputation of a jovial Ananias.

The first *cause celebre* involving his veracity came to public attention in 1912, when he sued the Pullman company for an "accident" that had caused him much physical suffering and mental anguish. The chain supporting an upper berth had given way, precipitating him into the aisle and producing multiple contusions and abrasions on his bullet-like head. An insurance company, investigating the matter, was annoyed to discover that the chain had been filed half-way through, and considered it highly possible that with this assistance, Means's 200 pounds of flesh and bones contributed the extra pressure sufficient to provoke the downfall.

There was, however, no way of proving that this cheerful salesman had rasped the chain, and in the absence of such proof the company made a settlement. This, together with a previously successful defense against a breach of promise suit brought by a convent graduate who said he had lied to her about many things, constituted the beginning of a long series of battles with the law.

The World War presented admirable opportunities for his peculiar talents. In 1914 he had talked himself into the confidence of William J. Burns, joined the detective agency, and worked—on his own boasting admissions—for German interests. He was, he asserted, the confidential agent of

Count von Bernstorff and the notorious Captain Karl Boy-Ed. As Operative No. E-13, he related, he was paid as high as $100 a day, and through his hands passed the millions of dollars spent in America for German propaganda and espionage. He related how, upon one occasion, he hid $1,000,000 in a suitcase and left it for Captain Boy-Ed in Trinity churchyard. And he discovered that Charles M. Schwab and the House of Morgan were violating the neutrality laws by favoring the Allies, at the same time warning this country—in a burst of patriotic confidence—that his German employers were planning to stir up a war between Mexico and the United States. In the hysteria of the moment, when no espionage story was too ridiculous to find credence, there were many who actually believed his tall tales.

In 1917, Means exercised his wiles on the family of Mrs. Maude A. King, a young and wealthy widow, and persuaded them that Mrs. King needed protection against the snares of a foreign fortune hunter. Within a short time, so effective was his ingratiating manner, he had the entire management of Mrs. King's estate in his hands, and was receiving from her a constant stream of money and securities for investment in the cotton market. The investments were not successful, but when it became necessary to replenish the dwindling fortune, Means "found" a second will of the late husband of Mrs. King, under which Mrs. King's sister was to receive $1,000,000.

There came, however, a tragic picnic party at Blackwelder's Spring, near Concord, N. C., where Means had been born and nurtured. Mrs. King was shot through the head. The bullet had entered behind the left ear.

To the amazement of the countryside, who believed a Means could do no wrong, he was placed on trial and the evidence against him looked convincing. But Means calmly went on the witness stand and told a story which somehow convinced the jury that he was a much maligned man. He and Mrs. King, he said, had gone to the picnic ground to practice shooting, with a revolver recently purchased for her. Becoming thirsty, he went to the spring for a drink, leaving the weapon in the crotch of a tree. When he returned, the weapon had been discharged and Mrs. King was dead. It was his theory, he said, that she must have reached for the gun, and in some inexplicable way it was discharged. The prosecution brought out the fact that Mrs. King was afraid of firearms, that the light was not propitious for target practice, and that there was decidedly sufficient motive to induce Means to cause the woman's death.

He was triumphantly acquitted, however, and thereafter he filed suit for $1,000,000 against the Northern Trust Company of Chicago, asserting there had been a plot to send him to the gallows and gain control of the $3,000,000 King estate. The suit was not pressed, however, and the "second will" was denounced as a "preposterous fraud." It became necessary for Means to go to work again.

Under the famous William J. Burns, who said he considered Means "the best investigator I ever had," he became a secret operative for the Department of Justice, in the administration of Warren G. Harding.

This was the hey-day of the Ohio gang, of national prohibition, of Teapot Dome scandals, of Veterans' Bureau swindles and various other sinister manifestations of a broken-down political morality. The era marked an all-time low in public responsibility and official rectitude, and Washington became a splendid field for Means's operations.

In his book, *The Strange Death of President Harding,* he described many of his activities, including the collection of at least $7,000,000 "for the administration" from New York bootleggers who had to be protected. He "revealed" details of the President's private life in lip-smacking phrases, and concluded his "revelations" with the insinuation that Mrs. Harding poisoned the President in 1923 because she was annoyed by her husband's flirtation and because "had he lived twenty-four hours longer he might have been impeached."

In all of these sensational "revelations," it was remarked, Means never told a story that could be disproved. He chose, for the subjects of his memoirs, persons who were in their graves or who were unable to reply to him through court action.

In May, 1923, he was indicted for conspiracy to violate the prohibition laws, and after ten postponements because of "illness," he went to trial.

Meanwhile, in the storm of scandal then breaking over the head of Harry M. Daugherty, Mr. Harding's Attorney General, he had played his usual sensational part. To a group of pop-eyed Senators he declared he had handled more than half a million dollars in bribes and graft as the agent for Jess Smith, friend and confidant of Daugherty. He said he could support his declarations with "a trunk full of evidence, including diaries that will tell every action, through every minute of my career." But, alas, when he wished to present the diaries, he found they had been "stolen" from him by persons representing themselves to be from the office of the Sergeant-at-arms of the United States Senate.

At the conclusion of that political storm, he was tried, found guilty, and sentenced to two years' imprisonment and to pay a fine of $10,000 for his share in the prohibition conspiracy. Still later, another two years and a second $10,000 fine were added for his part in a mail-order stock-swindling conspiracy involving the Glass Casket Company, and for a time he settled down comfortably to his scribbling, in the Atlanta Penitentiary, where he was apparently a model, and penitent, prisoner. Released at the end of his term, he dropped from public sight, but it was known that he was engaged in certain mysterious investigations of alleged Communist activity, which cost the National Civic Federation perhaps $200,000.

This, then, was the persuasive gentleman who, early in March of 1932, went to Mrs. McLean, who was the estranged wife of the publisher of the *Washington Post*, with an offer to restore the Lindbergh child to Hopewell, through Mrs. McLean's good offices.

Lightly waving away his past record which had taught him, he said, that honesty is the best policy, he told the good lady that with his knowledge of the underworld, he was positive he could get in touch with the kidnapers of Charles A. Lindbergh, Jr.

"I know the criminals," he declared, "and they know me. They know me as a straight-shooter. Furthermore, I already have made a start on the case. I know the head of the kidnap gang. I talked with him in a New York speakeasy, not long ago, when he told me he was planning a major kidnaping. We can have the child back in two weeks, if you say the word."

Means embellished his tale with all the imaginative trimmings of a detective fictionist. He invented a "code" with which to communicate with Mrs. McLean. He gave "numbers" to his "operatives" and to the principals in the case. Mrs. McLean's "number" was to be "11."

The chief negotiator of the kidnap gang, he revealed, was one Norman Whitaker, alias "The Fox," alias Neil Williams. He gave Mrs. McLean other names, dates, and the location of various rendezvous he had had with the criminals, and so persuaded her to deliver over to him, on March 7, 1932, $100,000 in $100 bills, plus another $4,000 "for expenses." In return for this ransom, he promised, the child would be turned over to the Reverend Francis Hurney, a Catholic priest in Washington.

Thereafter, Means reported "progress," and presently "The Fox—Number 19" himself appeared on the scene. Means, "The Fox," and Mrs. McLean drove to Aiken, South Carolina, for the concluding negotiations.

"I have even held the baby in my arms, and I know it is the Lindbergh child," Means solemnly assured Mrs. McLean. "We'll have the baby back, under heavy machine-gun protection."

The negotiations went wrong, a few days later, when the phantom kidnapers said they were afraid to deliver the child because they suspected a trap. So the operations were removed to El Paso, Texas. By that time, Mrs. McLean had added another person to her retinue, Miss Elizabeth Nelson, a trained nurse from Baltimore, to whom Means gave the code number "29." Means had said the child was sick, and would require special nursing.

At El Paso another hitch occurred. Means professed himself greatly troubled and puzzled by the delay, but "extracted a promise from the kidnapers" that they would return the child promptly, once the entire party returned to Washington.

Meanwhile, however, Colonel Lindbergh's own negotiations with the true kidnapers were proceeding through Jafsie. And when the world learned he had actually paid $50,-000—and that the ransom serial numbers had been published—the incident provided Means with further excuses for the non-delivery of the child.

"The kidnapers," he told Mrs. McLean, "say that the money they now have is useless because the serial numbers are known. They want $35,000 more to replace the useless currency."

Mrs. McLean, who had been drawn into the case through a woman's sympathy (her own son had been killed by accident while he was guarded from threatened kidnaping), found her personal resources becoming depleted. Nevertheless, in her anxiety to bring the negotiations to a successful conclusion, she prepared to sell or pledge some of her jewels to raise the $35,000 Means said he required.

At that point, however, she became suspicious of the entire transaction because of certain discrepancies in Means's lurid stories. She consulted her attorneys, and after a hurried investigation, Means was indicted on charges of larceny after trust.

Means went to trial in June, a smiling, jaunty figure who proclaimed in the corridors of the court, while he was being led from jail, that he "never took a dollar from Mrs. McLean."

United States Attorney Leo A. Rover prepared and presented the case. He showed that before approaching Mrs. McLean, the former detective had obtained an interview with Colonel M. Robert Guggenheim, to whom he told substantially the same story he had related to Mrs. McLean. From Guggenheim, it was shown, Means obtained the use of the private automobile, with a liveried chauffeur, of the Austrian Minister. This was necessary, Means told Colonel Guggenheim, in order to provide "diplomatic immunity" for the little group who would use the automobile to transport the baby.

Means's story to Colonel Guggenheim was replete with underworld verbiage and the patter of prisons. Means said he required machine-guns and automatic pistols for protection of the negotiators, and gave vivid descriptions of the desperate characters who would be met on this dangerous mission. After obtaining the ministerial automobile, however, Means never again talked with Colonel Guggenheim. By that time, he had interested Mrs. McLean in his story. She was a woman—and easier to handle.

When Mrs. McLean asked Means how he could reconcile his own negotiations with those carried out by Jafsie and the supposed Curtis maneuvers, the glib professor of chicanery never hesitated.

"The men who took the money from Jafsie, the gang with whom Curtis has been in touch, and my own men are all one and the same outfit," he declared. "They wouldn't deliver the child to Jafsie because they suspected the serial numbers of the ransom bills had been taken. They wouldn't go through with the Curtis negotiations because they were afraid of being trapped by the Navy. But they are willing to go through with me because they trust me."

Mrs. McLean told the jury her story.

"I told Means I had great sympathy for the Lindbergh family," she testified. "I told him that for five or six years my first son was the subject of kidnaping threats and I had to keep guards around him, and it made me a nervous wreck."

Means smirked and grinned and winked at the reporters as though he might tell a great deal more if he cared, but on this occasion he didn't care to make any of his famous "revelations." The defense called no witnesses, not even the loquacious Gaston, and Means was promptly convicted.

Justice Proctor, lecturing the defendant for his "clever and adroit plan" and declaring that "the verdict of the jury in this case reveals that the defendant capitalized not only on the sweetest and tenderest emotions of the human heart, but also the basest," sentenced him to serve fifteen years in the Federal penitentiary.

It was not until a year later that the Government laid hands on Means's "stooge," "The Fox—Number 19." Department of Justice agents caught him in New York and learned that at least one or two of the revelations made by the Master Mind had been true. "The Fox" actually was a convict, and he had known Means while they were prison mates under previous convictions. But that was as far as the truth went. "The Fox," whose real name was Norman Whitaker, had never laid eyes on the Lindbergh child, but he had been perfectly willing to help his old buddy out by assuming the rôle of "chief kidnaper."

The police found he was a disbarred lawyer, something of an inventor, and a convict twice imprisoned for automobile thefts. Upon his arrest he presented a pitifully bedraggled appearance, shabby, down-at-the-heels and unkempt. If he had shared in any considerable portion of Mrs. McLean's $104,000, none of it was left.

Means was brought from his prison cell to Washington, once more, and he and "The Fox" went on trial for "conspiracy to defraud Mrs. McLean out of $35,000," the additional sum they had demanded after Colonel Lindbergh had paid the kidnapers $50,000.

On this occasion, whether to delight his audience, or in the somewhat insane hope that his story would sound convincing to the jury, Means added considerable detail to his previous yarns.

His first astonishing assertion was that he actually knew the names of the kidnapers. They were, he said, "Wellington Henderson, head of the Third Internationale in this country" and one "Irving Fenton" whom he had met in the Atlanta penitentiary. He then related the circumstances of his early negotiations with this pair, and told how they came to him on March 9th, very much "up in the air."

"They wanted to know," he testified, "why Mrs. McLean was not at her country home at Farview. They said they had

gone out there with the Lindbergh baby, ready to deliver it
to her, only to find she wasn't there. They then said that
they had taken the baby to the home of M. Robert Guggenheim, Colonel Lindbergh's friend, but that Guggenheim
had turned the baby down and refused to receive it. Henderson and Fenton wanted to know to whom they were to
give the baby and whether they were going to get their
$100,000. I told them they were to deliver the baby to Mrs.
McLean, and that they would get the money all right."

Means then described his trips South, to meet the two
men at Aiken, and said he was there shown a baby "which
either was the Lindbergh child or was represented to me as
such." The baby, he said, had a knitted cap pulled close to
the head, with a ribbon tied under the chin. He wore a buff
coat, brown shoes and white stockings. His eyes were blue
and he appeared to be about seventeen or eighteen months
old. The kidnapers, he said, had no proof of identity, but
they were willing to have motion pictures taken of the child,
to be sent to relatives of the Lindberghs for identification.

On the second day of his testimony, his imagination
began to warm up, and he brought his story to a climax
with the declaration that Colonel Lindbergh had been
duped when he identified the body of the murdered infant
found near Hopewell as his own son. The baby still lived,
he said.

Thereafter, he said, "Wellington Henderson told me that
the body of the baby which was found in New Jersey was
a 'plant'—and not the Lindbergh baby at all. He said that
later I would see Communistic data in regard to it. He also
visited me at my home in Chevy Chase a year ago when I

was out on bond, and declared the autopsy performed in New Jersey proved that it was not the right child because of a marked difference in measurements. He told me the real Lindbergh baby was alive then, and in Juarez, Mexico."

Satisfied with the effect of his wild stories, Means improvised new and equally startling evidence that "a rum ring" headed by Max Hassel and Max Greenberg, beer runners, actually planned and executed the kidnaping. He had "heard," he said, that the child was dropped and killed accidentally on the night of the abduction, but "Henderson" had later assured him that this information was erroneous.

Means said Hassel and Greenberg used their own "operatives" on the night of the kidnaping, sending them ostensibly to deliver beer, but actually to seize the child. He implicated Violet Sharpe as the servant who was used as a tool of the kidnapers, but had the grace to say of the girl that "he didn't believe she knew she was revealing important information to the kidnapers."

He then explained what had happened to the $100,000 he had taken from Mrs. McLean and which he had promised—after his futile efforts to recover the baby—to return to her. It seems he was returning to Washington from his home in Concord, N. C., when three strangers stopped his car and demanded the money. Mrs. McLean, he said, had instructed them to receive it.

"My orders," he testified he told them, "are to deliver the money to Mrs. McLean." But they replied that the orders had been changed, gave him Mrs. McLean's code number— "11"—so he handed over the money to them. Imagine his annoyance to learn that Mrs. McLean never received the money!

On the following day, he presented a climax to his mystery story by declaring that the $100,000 he delivered to the mysterious strangers, together with $49,000 out of the ransom money given by Jafsie to "John," were all in a safety deposit box in the vaults of the Elizabethport Banking Co., in Hassel's name.

Although the authorities attached no credibility to this entire yarn, they did examine the vaults of the Elizabethport bank. There was, as had been presumed, no trace of any such sum, in Hassel's name or any other.

It appeared, besides, to have been Gaston B. Means's usual hard luck that the three people named by him, who could have corroborated his story, were dead. Violet Sharpe was a suicide a year before. Hassel and Greenberg had been killed by fellow gangsters in the Cartaret-Elizabeth hotel two months before.

As for the other two principals named in the "plot," the Messrs. Henderson and Fenton, there was justifiable belief that neither one would be able to come to the front, willingly or unwillingly, to support Means's story. Communist headquarters, scoffing at the tale, reported that no such characters were known either in New York or Detroit. A Detroit detective familiar with Communist comings and goings in that city said he had once heard of a shadowy Red character known as Henderson, but he had never been able to lay a finger on him, and doubted if he actually existed.

Finally, in one grand explosion, Means divulged the hair-raising "truth" that the kidnap gang were actually after much bigger game than Colonel Lindbergh's small son. The person they were actually trailing was the Colonel himself.

"And if Colonel Lindbergh had tried to enter the negotiations—as they expected him to do—he would have been captured and they would have asked a million dollars ransom for him," he concluded.

The jury laughed his story out of court, found him and his silent co-defendant, "The Fox," guilty of conspiring to wring $35,000 more out of the wealthy Washington woman, and he was sentenced to serve two years more at the expiration of his fifteen-year stretch. Whitaker was given the same sentence.

Officers of the Department of Justice, meanwhile, tried to discover where Means had hidden the $100,000 profit from his employment by Mrs. McLean. They ransacked his home. They searched his wife. They tried to trace the money through bank deposits. But it was never brought to light.

The nation's greatest Ananias appeared to take his sentence with a spirit bubbling over with good nature. There was no rancor in his soul when he went back to the penitentiary. He continued to insist, however, that he knew more about the Lindbergh case than any other man in America, and he grinned and smirked and winked some more as he insisted.

CHAPTER ELEVEN

THE OPERATIONS OF GASTON B. MEANS AND "THE FOX" HAD been carried on in federal territory as distinct from state jurisdiction, and they therefore came within the purview of the United States Department of Justice and its efficient Division of Investigation. On the other hand, since at the time of the kidnaping there was no federal law recognizing the crime as a national offense, this department of the government had no technical right to intervene, offer suggestions, run down clues, or otherwise concern itself with the Lindbergh case.

Its offer of assistance, coming from the chief executive of the nation, had been accepted courteously, it is true, but it is equally true that neither by the state police of New Jersey nor by the New York City police was there wholehearted and enthusiastic coöperation with the federal arm.

Passage by Congress of a law making kidnaping, where carried out through use of the mails or by transportation of a victim across a state line, a federal offense, gave the right, however, to the Division of Investigation to go ahead on its own responsibility, regardless of what support it might or might not have had from the other agencies.

When the so-called "Lindbergh Law" was enacted, therefore, the Division swung into action. It could never bring to trial the kidnaper of the Lindbergh child because this would have been an *ex post facto* case, and hence unconstitutional. But it could use its men to track down the criminal.

The standards of the Division of Investigation are high. Under the direction of J. Edgar Hoover it has become, within a decade, an amazingly successful organization, with a record for brains and courage not surpassed by any department for criminal investigation in the world. Its qualifications for admission to the service are rigorous. The applicant must be between the ages of twenty-five and thirty-five. He must be in sound and vigorous health. His mental requirements are that he shall have a degree from a recognized college or university, or that he shall have been graduated from a recognized law school, or (for specialized work relating to banking) that he shall have passed courses in accountancy. Certain other specialists, who have made their major life work a study of some other branches of criminology, also join the department occasionally under special rulings.

Beyond this, the moral character of the applicant must be above reproach. Before he becomes a member of the department his record is searched, back to school days. The slightest deviation from the true moral course disqualifies him.

The composite detective of this new type is vastly different from the old-time sleuth. Generally a lawyer, he knows what is evidence and what is not. He is sure of his ground, careful, and not often to be confounded by clever lawyers for the defense, when his case reaches the court. He is sound, deductive, and logical. He works scientifically, with all of the modern instruments for the detection of crime from fingerprints to X-rays. And he works silently, in an atmosphere of departmental secrecy.

To this organization was entrusted the Federal Government's interests in the Lindbergh crime. Francis Fay, in charge of the New York office, was in general command of the work, with Thomas H. Sisk in actual charge of the operations. Under Sisk were fifteen agents, devoting all or part of their time to the case.

The detective department of the metropolitan police force is entirely different in many characteristics from the federal force. Its members are no less courageous, but their methods are those of the police-schooled force rather than the college trained. Their strong forte is thorough knowledge of the underworld, the habits of criminals, and the vast experience born of close contact with miscreants. They are more at home when dealing with the gangster, the burglar, the robber, or with recognized and known bands of criminals, than in the more delicate approaches required in running down a lone amateur.

Twenty-four "aces" of the New York department, headed by a remarkable young man named James J. Finn, an acting lieutenant, and his companion, Acting Lieutenant Frank McCarthy, were assigned to the Lindbergh case, never to be relieved from duty so long as the kidnaper remained uncaught.

Lieutenant Finn had been given to the case upon the personal request of Colonel Lindbergh, who had recognized his ability when the young man was acting as a guard for him on a previous occasion. Lieutenant Finn, the Colonel felt, was a real friend. The Lieutenant repaid the compliment with an assiduous devotion to the cause that forms a new bright chapter in the police department's record.

Of the New Jersey State Police, third of the organizations at work on the case, Colonel H. Norman Schwarzkopf was the executive. His right hand man, rated as the best detective on the force, was Captain John J. Lamb. Under Captain Lamb there were sixteen men, detectives and troopers, also engaged solely in an attempt to trap the Lindbergh kidnapers.

Between these organizations there was not always the coöperation that would have been desirable. It is known, for example, that never once did the agents of the Federal Division of Investigation lay eyes on the ransom notes or know their contents until they were revealed to the public by the New Jersey State Police—and even then, they did not see the originals. But in the end, when the trail became warmer, the coöperation, such as it was, became a little more actual.

There were few material clues on which to work. In the order of their importance, they may be listed as:

The ransom money, to be traced if possible to its possessor.

The three-piece ladder, to be traced, if possible, to its maker.

The chisel, left behind by the kidnapers in the Lindbergh grounds.

The automobile, green or blue, that witnesses believed they had seen near the Lindbergh home.

There were no fingerprints, or if there were they were so blurred as to be useless.

On these slender clues, now that the Curtis and Means hoaxes had been exposed and their perpetrators punished, the separate crime-detecting organizations set to work.

Widespread publication of the serial numbers of the ransom bills lent some fear to the officials that the extortioners would hesitate to pass any of the notes at all. Many detectives argued that it was a mistake to make public the long list of bills with accompanying publicity that might warn the ransom-receiver that he was being watched. But if it were a mistake, it was now too late to rectify it. Every large newspaper in the country had devoted columns to the subject.

The vast machinery of the nation's banking system was turned into a potential trap. A booklet, containing the serial numbers of the ransom notes in handy form, was sent to every financial institution in the country. Secretary of the Treasury William H. Woodin ordered an extra force of girls into duty in the Federal Reserve Banks, for the sole purpose of checking all bills of the denominations contained in the $50,000 turned over to the extortioner. In the course of two years, more than forty million bills were thus to be examined.

To inspire bank clerks and tellers to make thorough examinations of incoming deposits, the Department of Justice agents made fortnightly visits to all banks in their territory, urging officials to familiarize themselves with the numbers, and imploring for the most rapid action if one of the notes should appear.

Within a week after the date of the transfer of the ransom from Jafsie's hands to those of the man who admitted the kidnaping, the first note was turned up in a bank in the north of Manhattan.

Agents rushed to the bank. Confused tellers were unable to say from which depositor the money had come. Hundreds of deposits had been made that day. Thousands of depositors' names were on the bank's books. The department checked every deposit and every depositor—and learned nothing.

From that time on there was a continuous trickle of ransom bills into the central banks. They did not come in any flood, but singly or in twos and threes. A majority of them were of the smaller denominations—$5 and $10 bills.

Yet from this flow the detectives began, after many painful and discouraging experiences, to learn something. The possessor of the ransom money was a cautious individual, not given to heavy spending, making no display of his cash, and using it apparently only for immediate living expenses.

As more experience was gained in checking the money, more rapidity was the rule in tracing it. So the detectives learned, after the flow was well begun, that the spender apparently was operating in small shops along the line of the Lexington Avenue Subway, in northern New York City. In a number of cases, they were able to trace the bills directly to the tills of the shopkeepers and occasionally, though rarely, they obtained a fleeting description of the passer.

The criminal's trail, it appeared from analysis of the locations where money appeared, originated somewhere in the

Bronx, passed through the Morris Park and Fordham sections, and thence southward, through Yorkville, center of New York's largest German community. Thence it ran through the City Hall and Wall Street sections and crossed under the river to Brooklyn, to reappear there in the Borough Park, Williamsburg, Brownsville and Flatbush sections.

Of these various scenes of operation, those most frequently used appeared to be the Bronx and Yorkville, and the theory naturally grew that the ransom distributor was not only an habitué of resorts in those zones, but probably a resident of the northern section of New York City. This theory, too, checked well with the supposition that the man to whom Jafsie had given the money lived in the Bronx, since he was familiar with the *Bronx Home News,* and since the negotiations had taken place in that county.

With this knowledge, the agents were able, within a year after the kidnaping, to build up a vague picture of the man who was operating. With each succeeding month this picture was to grow clearer, through the corroborative evidence of shopkeepers.

Of one characteristic they were sure and agreed. The bills were all folded the same way—once across their length and once across their width. The creases were inevitable. In each case, too, the passer took the creased bill from the watch pocket of his trousers and threw it carelessly down on the counter or through the cashier's wicket.

Finally, piecing together the facial characteristics of the man as hazily described by various cashiers, they arrived at this "photograph" of the person:

He was a man about five feet, nine inches in height, wearing a low-crowned felt hat which was usually pulled well down over his forehead. He had high cheek bones and flat cheeks, with a distinctly pointed chin. His eyes were blue and he spoke with a decided German accent.

At 9:30 o'clock on the evening of November 26, 1933, such a man passed a Federal Reserve $5 note at Loew's Sheridan Theatre in Greenwich Village. Mrs. Cecile M. Barr, the cashier, noticed the strangely folded bill and took mental note of the man who "drew it from his watch pocket and tossed it carelessly through the window." She even remembered the motion picture that was being shown that night.

"It was a gangster film," she said, "Broadway Through a Keyhole."

Mrs. Barr's description of the man who changed the bill was identical with that of others who had come in fleeting contact with him. She noticed the same characteristics of eyes, high cheek bones and flat cheeks, and she told the detectives that she would never forget him.

The mysteries of chemistry were then called upon. A number of the bills were taken to Dr. Alexander O. Gettler, the New York City official toxicologist, for examination. It is impossible, or next to impossible, to find fingerprints on paper currency. But Dr. Gettler found some interesting things.

The bills were musty and had a faint, earthy odor which indicated they had been buried, perhaps in a cellar. Beyond that, they revealed "glycerine esters," and traces of emery

dust "which might have come from the grinding of tools
by some mechanic."

Fifteen of the bills bore small blood stains, which might
have come from a small wound in the finger or hand of the
man who passed them.

Not long after the incident at the Sheridan Theatre, a
man appeared at the lumber yard of Cross, Austin & Ire-
land, and purchased forty cents worth of wood. In payment,
he offered a $10 gold certificate. William J. Reilly, yard
superintendent, and Miss Alice Murphy, the cashier, began
to write down the serial number of the bill. The customer
seized the note from Miss Murphy's hands, and found forty
cents in his pockets to pay for his wood.

At the very instant of this occurrence, government agents
were in the same lumber yard, at work on the clue afforded
by the ladder used in the kidnaping. The forty-cent customer went rapidly away.

In the two years succeeding the kidnaping a little more
than $4,000 passed through trade channels, into banks, and
thence to the Federal Reserve Bank. With each transaction
the chase became hotter and the federal, state and city detectives worked closer to the man they wanted. But there
were a thousand disappointments. The public hue and cry
had died down. Cashiers lost or mislaid the booklets containing the ransom numbers, or failed to check each note
carefully, and by the time the agents reached the shop at
which the bills had been tendered, the trail was cold.

While one branch of the detective force concerned itself
almost entirely with running down clues afforded by the

currency, another was engaged in an attempt to trace the origin and manufacture of the ladder.

In many respects, this ladder was more important evidence, as definitely linking the kidnaper to the scene of the crime, than were the ransom notes. It was obviously possible that the person now passing the ransom money might *not* have been the person who received it from Jafsie. It was also possible that the ransom passer might have been an innocent victim of circumstances.

On the other hand, the man who used the ladder and left it so carelessly in the Lindbergh grounds was indubitably the actual kidnaper.

Sections of the wood were therefore given into the hands of Arthur Koehler, of the United States Forest Products Laboratory, under the Department of Agriculture. Koehler was recognized as one of the most brilliant scientists attached to the laboratory. He undertook the painstaking research required to trace the wood to its source—to the very forest from which it came.

Koehler's research was slow but fruitful. Microscopic examination of the wood proved to him that it could have come from one section of the United States and one only. That was in the Carolinas. Agents traveled to 1500 planing mills to pursue their investigations. There, they were surprisingly successful in their quest. They found that only one lumbering concern had cut timber of the kind found in the ladder, and that it had shipped only a small quantity of it, chiefly to the Great National Millwork & Lumber company, in the Bronx, New York.

Nevertheless, every customer of the southern lumber firm

was thoroughly checked, even where there seemed little likelihood that a worth-while clue would be developed, and eventually the sleuths were able to eliminate all but the Bronx lumber yard as the source of the material.

The Great National, however, had many customers, and it was next to impossible to trace a small transaction, involving some two-by-four wood, occurring many months before. Patiently, the officers spread their investigations throughout the area, visiting every lumber yard, and assuring themselves that there was no possibility that some small quantity of the wood had been distributed through some other agency. There was none.

The known customers of the Great National were then thoroughly investigated and one by one eliminated from the case. At this point it appeared the detectives had come to a dead end. Unless and until there should come new developments, perhaps an arrest, progress along this line was at a full stop. But it had established another conclusive fact—that the ladder, by whomever it was built, was constructed by a person who lived or had his business transactions in the Bronx.

The third important phase of detective work, jealously guarded by the New Jersey State Police and those of the New York department who were permitted to participate in the secret, related to the ransom notes, a fertile source for deduction regarding the characteristics of the writer. In addition to handwriting experts, called in to analyze each word and letter, each dot and cross—primarily to prove that they were written by one and the same hand—the agents called upon psychologists to delve into the phraseology and attempt to determine the mental reactions of their writer.

That the person who wrote them was of German origin was unquestioned. His phrases abounded with Germanic spellings and construction. But the notes also revealed something of the man's nature, particularly when coupled with his actions during the Jafsie transactions.

He was "extremely cautious and of a suspicious nature." He had run away in the cemetery at the approach of a stranger. He had insisted that Colonel Lindbergh "take not one serial number" from the ransom bills.

He was "very reticent" and probably "shy," according to the psychiatrists. His notes said no more than was necessary to convey his directions.

He was methodical but not clever in deceit. Throughout his notes, as throughout his conversation with Jafsie, he had sought to throw pursuit off his track by one method—by relating the *exact opposite* of the truth. He had said "the baby is in gut care" when in fact the child was dead. He had told Jafsie he was of Scandinavian birth, when he was actually and provably German. Everything he said, therefore, had its opposite implication in the minds of the detectives. When he said a "gang" was involved in the kidnaping, the theory was established that he was actually alone. To that theory a majority of the detectives clung throughout their investigations.

He was an immigrant German. He had been taught to read and write in his native language, and English had been acquired. He wrote in the foreign tongue exactly as he would have translated from original thoughts. He could not, therefore, have been educated in the United States.

He owned an automobile, of a moderately priced manufacture, and in its operation he would necessarily have had to have a license. To procure a license, he would have had to fill out and sign an application blank. And at this point in the chain of conjecture, Leigh Matteson, a newspaper man who had interested himself in the case from the beginning, made the logical suggestion to the authorities that every one of the automobile license applications from within a certain well-defined zone be examined for comparison with the ransom notes. His suggestion was received with interest by Lieutenant Finn, and such a search was conducted.

Of the thousands of such documents on file, all but 480 were eliminated, according to Mr. Matteson, and within a year there remained only forty-eight possible suspects, all of whom were closely shadowed by Lieutenant Finn's men.

By the closing months of 1933, the three bureaus of investigation were agreed in presenting a definite "portrait" of the criminal. During a year and a half of intensive work they had piled up an amazing documentary history of the case. On file in New York and Washington, on the shelves of the Department of Justice, were some 50,000 cards, each of them representing the result of a separate, individual investigation. Reports of the agents, more voluminous, filled filing cabinets by the score. At intervals a "summary" was compiled of all progress. It grew into a thousand-page booklet—a "condensed" history of the department's work on one crime.

It is not far-fetched to say that these agents, at the beginning of 1934, "knew" the person they would confront when they should capture the ransom distributor. They had not only the mental portrait but they had a black-and-white sketch, drawn carefully by an excellent artist who created the face out of the descriptions given by those who had carefully observed his features.

The man wanted lived in the Upper Bronx and was a German, who spoke with a decided Teutonic accent. His blue eyes were shifty—unable to look another man in the face. His chin was pointed and the general lines of the face were triangular. He was about five feet, nine inches in height and of wiry rather than heavy build. He was a mechanic, presumably a carpenter, who was tiding over a workless depression by spending the ransom hoard for his weekly living and for mild entertainment in beer gardens. He would be found driving a small automobile. He would be reserved, uncommunicative about business, and one who shunned new or dangerous companionships. He would be thrifty, not given to lavish display and not of extravagant tastes. He would have a common school (German) education, but he would not be an educated man. He would have a knowledge of cubic contents, as witnessed by the fact that he had drawn with dotted lines, indicating its interior dimensions, a picture of the package in which he ordered the ransom money delivered. And he would be ruthless, conscienceless and devoid of the commonest of human emotions.

This picture, however, would apply only if certain theories were correct, the first being that the man who kidnaped the child was the same man who extorted the ransom money, and further that he who received the ransom was the man who was spending it.

Against all other theories the investigators of the Division of Investigation clung to the belief that the entire crime was plotted, engineered and executed, from beginning to end, by one man. While their minds were necessarily open to other possibilities, the indications that their theory was correct continued to multiply in almost overwhelming proportions.

CHAPTER TWELVE

BY MARCH OF 1934, THE JOINT BOARD OF DETECTIVE STRATEGY, including representatives of federal, state and city forces, began to feel their efforts were producing results. The trail was becoming warmer. Each successive ransom bill that fell into their hands provided another strand in the web whose center was "somewhere in the Bronx."

It was in that month that a Department of Justice official, speaking out of turn in an up-state New York city, revealed a belief that the case would "break" within a few months at most. And it was shortly after that admission—which, incidentally, was promptly denied by his associates—that considerable activity by government agents was noted in Massachusetts and New Hampshire. The newspaper men who had been assigned to the case, particularly those who, in the two years that had passed since the abduction, had been given roving assignments with but one object in view, realized a solution was near.

At about this time certain officials of the Department of Justice decided to make an appeal to the press for more coöperation. News editors of the nation's press associations and managing editors of the larger newspapers were taken into the department's confidence.

It was admitted, first of all, that the Lindbergh ransom notes were coming in, in increasing numbers, and that nearly $5,000 worth of them had been recovered. But it was also explained that whenever a news story relating a single instance of such a recovery appeared, the immediate effect was to frighten the ransom spender. It was evident that the man, or woman, engaged in disposing of the notes carefully watched the newspapers. The mere appearance of an item telling of such an occurrence produced a stoppage, sometimes for weeks, in the flow of "hot" money.

Therefore the newspaper men were asked, in the interests of justice and a spirit of coöperation, if they would agree not to print further articles on that particular subject.

A specific instance was cited. A Long Island filling station employee had taken in one of the bills and reported his discovery to the police. Either the employee or some police official had disclosed it to a local reporter. The story already had gone out over some wires, and was in print in a few metropolitan editions. By this simple slip, the chase might have been set back for months.

The newspaper chiefs instantly agreed. Press associations sent confidential messages to their clients explaining the situation. Letters went out to editors requesting the holding out of any future stories dealing with that phase of the case. There was a unanimity of acquiescence that spoke well for the fairness and common sense of the newspaper profession.

Lieutenant James Finn, of the New York Bureau of Criminal Investigation, had one obsession throughout the case. He believed the criminal would be trapped only by passage of the ransom money, but he narrowed down the probable transactions by which the notes would be "cashed" to the purchase of gasoline. The kidnaper undoubtedly owned an automobile. Ergo, he would have to buy fuel for it.

On that supposition, Lieutenant Finn had devised a system that appeared to be air tight. The owners of filling stations from coast to coast, chain dealers and independents, were enlisted in the scheme. Every man engaged in the selling of gasoline or oil was asked to take down the serial numbers of every $5, $10, and $20 bill received in the course of business, and with it the license number of the car to which the fuel was delivered.

In forty-eight states of the union this system was in operation, and to this public army of "detectives" were added thousands of collectors for gas and electric companies in New York City. The early results were slow and disappointing. A few of the bills turned up, here and there, but their source had been lost because of the many hands through which they already had passed.

Early in 1934, however, the flow of Lindbergh money began to increase, and reports of its passage became more frequent. It was also noted that the man, or men, passing the money had reached the $10 and $20 denominations. The $5 horde, perhaps, had been exhausted.

There was another fortunate phase in the money angle. When, early in his administration, President Roosevelt took the country off the gold standard and ordered all bullion and gold notes turned in to the Treasury, he unwittingly provided the agency through which the case was to be solved.

By his act of 1933, he "outlawed" gold notes. And because a greater part of the ransom was in such notes, easily distinguishable from the usual Federal Reserve notes issued in their stead, the money still in the hands of the criminals became even "hotter." Gold notes became a rarity. Everybody in the country knew—or should have known—they were illegal.

Yet here, upon the very occasion when an alert department might have earned the glory of solving the crime at one stroke, the Treasury, or the Federal Reserve Bank of New York, or its clerks and agents, missed their grandest opportunity. They were too busy to look—until it was too late—for the gold notes that had been given into the hands of Jafsie's contact man.

On May 1, 1933, the last day of grace allowed gold holders for the conversion of their money, a man carrying a package of certificates arrived early at the Federal Reserve Bank. He was not waited upon at once, for the customers were being lined up three abreast and it took hours to reach the windows where tellers, too rushed to give more than a casual glance at the huge stacks of currency they were handling, were hurrying through the exchanges without paying particular attention to individuals.

The man finally reached the cage and passed in his package. The bills were rapidly counted and $2,980 in silver certificates were thrust into his hand. He started to leave, but was called back and ordered to fill out a record. He hesitated a moment and then wrote down his name as "J. J. Faulkner," giving his address as 537 West 149th street, New York.

Three days later, when the overworked officials of the

bank had time to check over the flood of gold notes taken in during the course of that day, they discovered the serial numbers of bills in that single transaction corresponded to the ransom numbers. Attempts to find "J. J. Faulkner" failed, although the authorities did locate a "Jane" Faulkner, married in 1921 to a Carl O. Giesler, florist, who had once lived at that address. Investigation of this "clue" came to a dead end when the Giesler family proved they had no association whatsoever with the money. The criminal's use of the name and address had been pure coincidence.

Lieutenant Finn went back to his patient tracing of individual ransom bills. At headquarters there was a large map of New York. On it there began to grow a forest of little pins—colored pins like those with which patriotic citizens used to trace the operations of the armies in France during the World War. From these pins a series of lines were drawn, something like a complicated geometrical problem. They were designed to show the focal point from which the criminal was operating, and to provide boundaries for the zone in which he lived and did his business. The radiating lines pointed unmistakably to the Bronx. And it was in the Bronx that the Jafsie transaction had taken place.

Only a few of the bills—except for the one parcel of $2,980—had appeared in lower New York. For the most part the passer had operated in upper Manhattan, particularly through Yorkville, and in the Bronx itself. Shops, cafeterias and cabarets along Second and Third Avenues reported receiving many of them. And on each occasion when one of them turned up, Lieutenant Finn leaped in his car and drove post haste to the spot. Time after time he met with bitter disappointment. The trail was cold. The cashier had not discovered the significance of the bill until the man who presented it was far away. No adequate description of the passer was available.

On Saturday, September 15, 1934, a man who spoke with a decided Teutonic accent drove his Dodge sedan up to the Warner-Quinlan filling station at 2115 Lexington Avenue and stopped before one of the pumps.

"Fill 'er up?" asked Walter Lyle, pleasantly.

"No," the customer answered. "Just five gallons of ethyl."

From his pocket he drew an envelope and extracted a $10 gold note. Lyle replaced the cap on the gasoline tank and reached for the bill.

"You don't see many of these any more," he remarked, fingering the paper hesitantly.

"No," said the customer. "I guess you don't. I've only got a few of them left myself—about a hundred."

During the brief conversation, Lyle was studying the man. He would never forget him. Particularly, he would never forget his distinguishing characteristic—a pointed chin. Nor would he forget his voice, with its trace of foreign accent. The customer pocketed his change, $9 and two cents, and drove away. But as he went, Lyle jotted down, on the bill itself, the license number of the sedan. It was 4U-13-41, New York.

"There's something screwy about this business," Lyle told his assistant, John Lyons. "Maybe the bank ought to have a look at it."

Lyons agreed that the peculiar circumstances were worth enquiring into. Their own list of Lindbergh ransom notes, ordinarily carefully preserved, had been thrown away only a few weeks before.

Lyons put the bill in his pocket, and walked to the Corn Exchange Bank Trust Company's branch at 125th Street and Park Avenue. Teller William R. Strong examined the note, jotted down the automobile license number written on it by Lyle, and held a whispered conversation with the bank manager. Lyons went back to the filling station no wiser than he had been.

Immediately after Lyons had left the bank, however, important events occurred. Thomas Sisk at the Division of Investigation received a telephone message from the bank.

"We are holding a $10 gold certificate with the Serial Number A73976634A," he was told. "Our records show this is one of the Lindbergh ransom bills. Can you verify it? The bill also has, written on it by the man who received it in trade, the automobile license number of the man who tendered it. The number is 4U-13-41."

Sisk leaped into action. He called his fellow worker, Jimmy Finn, and Colonel Schwarzkopf, of the New Jersey Police. While the number of the automobile was being checked for ownership, they drove to the filling station and interviewed the now-astonished attendants. As they left the station, one of the investigators turned and said, warningly, "Don't tell anybody about this, not even your wives, but it looks as though you guys might split the $25,000 New Jersey wants to pay for the Lindbergh kidnapers."

Lieutenant Finn and his trusty men then set forth on a quest for Bruno Richard Hauptmann, German carpenter, living at 1279 East 222nd Street, in the Wakefield section of the Bronx.

The detectives found him, riding blithely in his Dodge sedan, unconscious that the hue and cry had reached home. Constantly, day and night, they remained in his company, "tailing" him, watching his every activity, following him into shops and cafés, observing every transaction in which money appeared.

They were allowing him only a little more rope—a little more opportunity to dispose of further ransom notes, each of which was neatly picked up and docketed for future evidence. Then, at nine o'clock on the morning of Tuesday, September 18th, they struck.

Bruno Richard Hauptmann left the small frame house in the Bronx where he had lived so modestly with his wife Anna, and their infant son, Mannfried. As he turned from the driveway into the street, a police car casually drew up and gently eased him to the curb. From it leaped, with startling rapidity, Lieutenant Finn and his good and true men, Detectives John McNamara, Timothy Clune, Joseph Petrosino, James Cashman, Bernard Dolan, and Frederick Itschner.

Before Hauptmann quite realized what had happened, his arms were pinioned and he was a prisoner.

"We want you at headquarters," said Lieutenant Finn.

It was not to headquarters, however, that the police led their suspect. Instead he was taken to the old bastille in Greenwich Street, an abandoned police station that had been converted into a bureau for the licensing of taxicabs and cabarets. A search of his pockets revealed another $20 note—one of the Lindbergh bills.

While this was occurring, other detectives burst in upon Mrs. Pauline Rauch, landlady who owned the home in which Hauptmann and his family occupied the upper floor, and over her astonished protests and the wringing of hands, began to make a thorough search of the premises. For a time they found nothing at all—just the few simple belongings of a German carpenter who had suffered, like everybody else, from the depression.

And still other detectives, interviewing Hauptmann's known acquaintances, piecing together the incidents of two years, tracing this and that lead back to its dim source, began their reconstruction of Bruno Richard Hauptmann's life history. They discovered some interesting and pertinent facts, chief among them that the prisoner was in America illegally, and that he had been charged with crime in Germany.

Hauptmann was born on November 26, 1899, in the town of Kamenz, Germany. In his fifteenth year when the World War began, he was old enough, before Germany had exhausted her last human resources, to serve with her armies as a machine-gunner. Two of his brothers were killed in battle. As for Bruno, he was more fortunate. Some of his German associates said he came through the ordeal unscathed. But another, Frank Talksdorf, to whom Hauptmann had related many of the incidents of his career, insisted that the young machine-gunner, not then nineteen, had been wounded in the leg by a shot that ripped to pieces his veins and left him with a slight limp.

In 1923, Talksdorf said, Hauptmann smuggled himself aboard the *S.S. George Washington,* and lay in bilge water all the way across the Atlantic, only to be discovered before he could land. He was returned to Germany, "promising" the liner's captain at Hamburg that he would return with him on the next trip.

He did attempt to stow away, but the crew found him again, and he escaped only by leaping overboard and swimming to the pilings of a pier, where he clung for hours until he was rescued.

His third attempt was successful because he had disguised himself and stolen a landing card, and he walked ashore with two cents as his sole capital.

There was ample reason for Hauptmann's decision to reach the United States at all costs. Germany was too hot for him. When the war was over, the young man became the official bad boy of Kamenz, served one term in jail for theft, and escaped a second by breaking jail. It was therefore as an escaped convict that he desired to shake the dust of his native land from his boots.

Officials of Saxony, Germany, outlined the prisoner's career to the attentive American police.

They described him as "exceptionally sly and clever," and as bearing an alias—Karl Pellmeier or Cellmeier. His most daring exploit had been to break into the home of the Mayor of Penbruch, Germany, and steal 1,000 marks from the burgomaster. For this burglary he was sentenced to a term of two and a half years. Implicated later in a street holdup, he received an additional sentence of two and a half years.

He had begun to serve the second term when he made his daring jail break.

In the United States his "luck" was comparatively steady. His first job was with a chemical plant in New Jersey, but after a brief engagement as an unskilled laborer, he moved to the Bronx, which was thereafter to be the scene of his quiet home life.

Business was flourishing during those years. The United States was recovering from the effects of war, and the Great Boom had started. Building construction was lively, and Hauptmann was handy with a carpenter's tools. He saved his money, met and married Anna Schoeffler, who was a salesgirl in a Bronx bakery, and "settled down" to an eminently respectable life.

Never was there anything over-spectacular about Bruno Hauptmann. He lived neither riotously nor noisily, but in keeping with the moderate income becoming to a young journeyman carpenter. There was a strain of thriftiness to his nature that forbade him both extravagance and display. When he played cards—pinochle—it was for small stakes only, two and a half cents a thousand. He was not a drunkard. He drank beer, not schnapps.

There was a lighter side to his nature, too. On picnics at Hunter Island, which he frequented, he was vigorous, athletic, inclined to horse-play. During such occasions, when he relaxed and gave himself over to what the Germans call *ein bummel,* he was a ringleader in outdoor activity. His friends on these sunny picnics—Anita Lutzenberg, the dress fitter for a New York department store, and John Braue, counter man in a doughnut shop—thought him a good sport. He owned a canoe and was considered "a good man" at inshore sailing.

When autumn came, his neighbors said, it was not unusual for him to go hunting and bring home a well-loaded bag of game. But he never gave away any of it, even after a certain hunting trip in Maine with his friend, Carl Henkel. Quantities of ransom notes appeared in Maine about that time.

On warm summer evenings, like any good German family man, he enjoyed strolling out to a café and remaining, over a seidel or two of beer, until closing time.

But when it came to his personal affairs, his friends found him secretive. Even the most casual of questions appeared to put him on his guard. By 1934, it was known that the building trade was poor; that he hadn't done a day's work at carpentering for many a month. Where, then, did the cash *come from* for such moderate expenses as were entailed in the keeping of a family of three, even in the far from luxurious conditions of the Bronx home?

Hauptmann's answer, curtly given, was that (at a time when nearly all others were losing money in Wall Street) he had found a system of making profitable speculations.

But how did he get the money with which he first entered the market? Again a simple and logical reply. He had saved it from his high wages when business was good. And the tone of his replies would choke off any further prying curiosity regarding his own business. The subject of conversation would be changed abruptly.

The police turned their attention to Anna Hauptmann. How much did she know of her husband's business? Her hysterical responses to their questions left them with alternate impressions. Either she was a courageous and magnificent prevaricator, or she was an innocent German *hausfrau* who had faithfully accepted what little her husband had told her about money affairs. A majority of the police were inclined to the second theory.

She admitted having gone to Germany in 1933 on money supplied by Bruno Hauptmann. The purpose of this trip, she was forced to admit, was to cast up her husband's accounts with the German police, in an attempt to wipe the slate clean. Bruno wanted to go home, with his family. He could not, so long as a prison sentence was hanging over him. Anna's mission failed on that occasion; but only two months before his arrest, Bruno's aged mother succeeded in quashing the case through the statute of limitations.

Over and over Anna Hauptmann repeated her story to the detectives. When the kidnaping occurred she was working as a waitress, and it was a woman customer who first told her of the terrible deed.

"It made me sick," she said. "I have a baby of my own. I prayed it would be brought back to them."

The inquisition into her knowledge of Hauptmann's financial affairs brought no results. When times were good, she said, her husband could make $70, $80, perhaps $90 a week. He was not a lavish spender. Naturally, he had saved much. Also, he played the stock market a little, making an occasional extra dollar through his investments. He was a good husband, and he loved his baby, Mannfried, devotedly.

For twenty-four hours—while detectives were fever-

ishly ransacking the home in the Bronx and tearing to pieces
the garage Hauptmann had built to house his sedan—the
police interrogated her with that type of insistent questioning that seldom fails to trap a suspect. Then they let her go
back home. As evidence, Anna Hauptmann was a blank.

The search in Hauptmann's living apartments was as disappointing as Anna's inquisition. It yielded nothing more
than a few old photographs of the man in holiday mood,
and a small amount of petty cash. But the garage was a gold
mine. When the axes of the detectives crashed through the
flooring they struck pay dirt.

Secreted in canvas bags, buried beneath the planking, and
hidden in the window casings, $13,750 in gold certificates
were found snugly tucked away. A hurried check of the
serial numbers identified it as part of the $50,000 ransom
money.

The detectives were jubilant. "When Hauptmann is confronted with this, he is sure to break," they thought. But
Hauptmann did not break. Physically exhausted from the
long strain, he maintained his stolid composure and hoarsely
offered a new explanation for his possession of the incriminating money.

"There was a man named Isidor Fisch. . . ."

Hauptmann's story, without embellishment, was this:

Fisch and he had engaged in a little dealing in furs and,
over the course of several years, their partnership had been
profitable to the extent of, say, $10,000. But Fisch had lost
his money, while Hauptmann, ever thrifty, had saved
enough to lend the furrier $7,500 in a time of financial
trouble.

Fisch was a sick man. He knew he had tuberculosis, and wanted to go home to Germany. In December of 1933, knowing his days were numbered, he departed, leaving in Hauptmann's care certain of his belongings, including a large package of what appeared, from the outside wrappings, to be letters or papers.

Curiosity, said Hauptmann, led him to open the package long after Fisch had sailed away on the liner *Manhattan*. Out of it tumbled these heaps of bills.

Well, Fisch owed him $7,500, didn't he? So where would be the harm in dipping into this treasure and taking what belonged to him? Since that day Hauptmann had used the money as his own, dipping into it for his daily requirements.

And where, the detectives asked with infinite sarcasm, might this Isidor Fisch be at the present moment?

He died at Leipzig, Germany, on March 29, 1934.

CHAPTER THIRTEEN

TO A PERSON OF DELICATE SENSIBILITIES THERE IS SOMETHING shocking about a police "lineup," although there is nothing new in the general principles upon which the authorities operate upon such important occasions. The lineup is designed to acquaint the detective force with the characteristics of criminals or suspects, in the hope that the detectives' camera-brains will thereafter recall the man should they have occasion to do future business with him.

The principle is old, but the methods have changed greatly since Mr. Pickwick "sat for his portrait" in the old English debtors' prison, under the scrutiny of a few unwashed turnkeys.

Today there are brilliant lights on the stage, beneath which the blinking prisoner is paraded. There is an audience of 250 alert detectives in front, taking written or mental notes of everything the man says or does. On the stage with the prisoner, a microphone before him, sits the officer of the day. Merciless in his description of the subject, he lectures—as a scientist might lecture about a germ—upon the attributes of the man on show. Then he asks the prisoner a series of pitiless questions, searching his mind and probing his soul.

They paraded Bruno Hauptmann before such an audience. They prodded him up the stairs, clinging to a brass rail, and forced him beneath the hot lights, fumbling his frayed hat nervously. The audience of detectives straightened in their chairs and listened attentively.

First, Hauptmann was backed against a measuring board. His height was recorded as five feet, nine and one-half inches. Inspector John J. Sullivan sat at the pulpit-like lecture-desk and told Hauptmann and the assemblage that he was accused of the extortion of the Lindbergh ransom money.

"How long have you been in this country?" the Inspector asked, and the loud speakers filled the hall with his booming voice.

"Thirteen years," said Hauptmann. His tone was guttural and hoarse. But he had been answering questions for days.

"How did you get in?"

"As a stowaway."

"What boat?"

"The *Portia.*"

"What is your business?"

"Carpenter."

The duel continued, the Inspector's short questions bringing even shorter, more staccato replies, until Hauptmann was asked:

"Where did you get the money found at your house, nearly $14,000?"

Hauptmann shifted his weight from one foot to the other and twisted his body nervously. There was perspiration on his forehead.

"From a friend of mine," he said at last, "a friend who is not coming back. He died in Germany."

To the Inspector's continued pressing he answered that he didn't know the package his friend gave him was money —not, that is, until recently, when he spent from $150 to $200 of it. The Inspector changed his line of questioning abruptly.

"As a matter of fact," he said, "you haven't worked a day since 1932, in April, have you?"

"Not steady," was Hauptmann's reply. But he couldn't remember how many days, if any, he had actually worked.

He admitted hiding the money in his garage "about three weeks back," and repeated his story of playing the market in Wall Street ("sometimes successful but later I was losing") and of dealing with "a friend" in furs. As for the customers who purchased from that partnership, he couldn't remember any names. His friend, it appeared, kept all the books.

"And did you own an automobile?"

"Since 1931."

The question concerning Hauptmann's automobile was the last of the inquisition. Then Inspector Sullivan straightened himself before the microphone.

"I might say," he told the audience, "that there is no doubt in my mind about this man being the right man. We have a perfect case of extortion, and the other case, a far more serious case, is developing rapidly." Then he added an unusual compliment to another profession.

"I want to pay my respects," he said, "to a number of men who have had information about the case. They are the newspaper men around this building. There were two or three of them who came to me and said they had the information about Hauptmann, but they wouldn't use it until we had the case. That's an outstanding thing for them to have done. I respect them for their coöperation."

He snapped off the light over his desk and Hauptmann was led away, swaying unsteadily in his baggy clothes. There were black circles deeply carved below his blue eyes.

Events moved rapidly for the prisoner—and for the newspaper editors who found fantastic, flamboyant headlines ready made for them, with each succeeding hour. Before noon arrived, Hauptmann was arraigned in the Bronx County Courthouse at Third Avenue and 161st Street, on a short affidavit accusing him of having extorted $50,000 from Colonel Charles A. Lindbergh. The court had been turned into a motion picture lot. Again there were the bright lights, the movie cameras, sound cables, newspaper reporters, court attachés and "extras," swarming through the room until it lost all semblance of a court and became a theatrical spectacle.

Hauptmann pleaded not guilty and said he didn't care to have any counsel. Magistrate Richard McKinery held him for a hearing on Monday, September 24th, without bail.

As Hauptmann was taken away, shackled to his guard of detectives, reporters hurled questions at him. "Did you do it?"

"It ain't me, it ain't me!" he repeated in a monotone.

Despite the confident assurances of the New York police that Hauptmann was definitely and completely linked to the receipt of the extortion money, and the more reserved statement that progress was being made in the attempt to associate him with the actual kidnaping, the authorities were still far from placing Hauptmann at the Lindbergh home on the night of March 1st—or even in New Jersey.

Dr. Condon, zealous as he was and eager to solve the mystery, had such regard for his reputation and his word that he refused to make a positive identification of the prisoner as the man to whom he had passed the $50,000 in the deep shadows of St. Raymond's cemetery more than seventeen months before.

"He resembles the man," was the limit of his identification. "I can see a resemblance, but I cannot swear to it." Nor could they make him swear to it, although they kept him, all through one hectic evening, in the office of District Attorney Samuel J. Foley, showing him this and that view of Hauptmann, "refreshing his memory," almost imploring him to say definitely and finally, "Yes, this is the man!"

On the other hand, there was Joseph Perrone, the taxi-cab driver who, on Saturday evening, March 12, 1932, delivered a note to Dr. Condon hot from the hands of the extortioner. Long before he had repeated, over and over, his description of the man who sent him to Jafsie with that letter.

"He had a pronounced German or Scandinavian accent. He was about five feet, ten inches tall, perhaps thirty-five years old, and had a fair complexion and blue eyes."

When Perrone was taken to see Hauptmann, he said without hesitation, "That is the man. I will swear to it."

Nevertheless, even Joseph Perrone's identification would not place Hauptmann in New Jersey at the time of the kidnaping. Furthermore, there was this puzzling matter of Isidor Fisch, the furrier, who had so inconveniently died in

Germany. Hauptmann had told the truth in respect to part, at least, of their relationship. His story that Fisch had left certain of his personal belongings in his care when he went to Germany was confirmed when the officers of the law found some of these effects in Hauptmann's home. There was some truth in their business relationship, and certainly a whole lot of fact in the story of their friendship.

So, while the authorities on this side of the Atlantic were blasting away at Fisch's history here, other detectives were at work in Germany. By a piece of strange good luck, a New York detective was in Europe at the time on another case. Detective Arthur Johnson, a linguist of ability, had been sent to Europe several weeks before to bring back, if possible, one Captain Ivan Poderjay. The New York police wanted to ask the captain a few questions about the disappearance of Miss Agnes Tufverson. Arthur Johnson was therefore hauled away from his immediate task, and set about the business of probing into the last days of the tubercular Isidor Fisch.

On this side of the water, the police unearthed Harry Uhlig, a friend of both Fisch and Hauptmann. It was he who had accompanied Fisch on his last trip to Germany, and it was he who had been present in Leipzig when Fisch died. As Uhlig unfolded his story to the police more coincidences appeared. His story, corroborated by police details and elaborated by State Department and steamship records, was this:

Fisch, who was forty-six, realized he had not long to live. He obtained a passport from the State Department on May 12, 1932, the very day the body of the Lindbergh baby was discovered in the Sourland hills. A few weeks later, he appeared at the Adriatic Steamship Agency, in Yorkville, and booked passage for the July sailing of the *Leviathan*. Then perhaps because he felt better, or because he lacked funds, he cancelled the booking and for a year appeared to have abandoned his intention to go home.

On August 18, 1933, Fisch and Uhlig went to the same agency and deposited $300 toward passage for both of them, on the liner *Manhattan*. In November, Fisch again went to the agency and bought $600 worth of Reichsmarks and two tourist-class tickets—the best in that class on the ship—for $210 each. He paid for the currency and tickets with gold certificates of $10 and $20 denominations.

George Steinweg, the steamship agent, remembered the transaction perfectly for many reasons. First, he had been rather surprised at seeing so much cash come out of the pockets of a fur cutter who had never appeared to be over-prosperous. Second, he remembered the gold certificates. Third, it appeared to him that Fisch was financing his friend Uhlig's trip abroad.

When Steinweg, therefore, read in the newspapers that Fisch's name had been brought into the case, he went to the police and divulged what he knew about the transaction. And after that, his mind going back to the flutter of gold notes over his agency counter, he went to his own bankers and asked if they had a record of a $1,000 deposit in such certificates, on or about November 14, 1933.

The bank officials also remembered the matter very well. They had discovered, upon checking over the certificates, that they were a part of the Lindbergh ransom money. But at that time they had no means of tracing them back to the depositor, and although the Federal Government was notified, the trail was lost.

Fisch and Uhlig sailed on the *Manhattan* on December 9th, and Bruno Hauptmann was at the pier to bid them goodbye.

The little furrier lived only three months after reaching the home of his brother, Pinkas Fisch, in Leipzig. Uhlig remained for the funeral and then returned to New York to settle up the dead man's affairs and to transmit whatever was left of the estate, if any, to the brother in Germany. He found no assets, he said. In fact there was an indebtness against Isidor Fisch.

Hauptmann claimed he had lent Fisch $7,500.

Uhlig's story was straightforward and convincing. Apparently he had nothing to conceal, and the police released him, told him to go home and say nothing, and publicly exonerated him from all complicity or knowledge of the kidnaping or the extortion plot. Meanwhile, they interviewed the furrier's old neighbors.

"A nice little fellow, quiet, harmless, couldn't have had a thing to do with a crime," the neighbors said.

"He had no money—once in a while he would borrow a dollar," said others.

"A nice man—the nicest fellow I ever knew," said a fellow roomer at his East Side boarding house.

Over in Germany, Arthur Johnson was busy. He found Pinkas Fisch, the furrier's brother, and Pinkas talked readily and volubly, going deeply into Isidor's past, describing his sickness and his poverty, and informing the New York detective that Isidor had not even been able to have the expert care he needed at the last, for lack of funds. His story dovetailed in every particular with that of Uhlig.

For the present, that was the end of the Fisch investigation. The police, having tried vainly for a week to sweat the truth—or what they conceived to be the truth—out of Hauptmann, developed a new and dramatic line of attack, looking to the prisoner's positive identification as the misty figure "John" who took $50,000 from Jafsie in St. Raymond's cemetery, and handed him in return the false information that the baby was on "the boad *Nelly.*"

They called Colonel Lindbergh himself to the jail. They disguised him as well as they could, in a cap and horn-rimmed glasses, and sat him in a chair in District Attorney Foley's office while Hauptmann, unconscious of the identity of the lone spectator, was paraded back and forth.

"Now, Hauptmann," said Foley, "I want you to repeat these words: 'Hey, Doctor! Over here, Doctor!'"

Without hesitation, Hauptmann gave the responses. The action was repeated, at varying distances and in different degrees of tone, and the prisoner was taken out. He never looked at the seated figure of the Colonel.

As Hauptmann disappeared, Colonel Lindbergh rose. He was satisfied with the test. It was his belief, he told the District Attorney, that the voice of the man he had just heard belonged to the man who, from behind the cemetery fence, called out the words, "Hey, Doctor!" to Dr. Condon and thereafter received the ransom money.

While the detectives were thus building up a circumstantial case against Hauptmann and attempting to convict him out of his own mouth, the authorities were unearthing more substantial evidence out of the very timbers of the little house in the Bronx. The garage itself was carefully demolished. Every piece of timber was put through a microscopic examination. Its wood was compared to the wood used in the kidnap ladder. Nails found in it were matched against the nails used in the ladder. Then, when the garage had been levelled and the ground beneath which it had stood had been plowed and churned, the police turned their axes upon the house itself. And this physical labor produced some astonishing results.

In the garage, built solidly into the wall, they had found a block of wood, smooth-surfaced on the outside, but honeycombed within. The holes, cleanly drilled, were the cache for more ransom money, and $840 in hidden gold certificates were added to the $13,750 in the possession of the District Attorney.

At one end of this ingenious wooden "safe" another hollow had been made. In it police found a small pistol, made in Germany and designed for bullets of an extremely small calibre. The weapon itself, in fact, was so small it could easily be concealed in the palm of the average man.

Ripping away at the furnishings within the house, and inspecting every square inch of woodwork of the Hauptmann's apartments, flashing their lights in the dim closet of a bedroom, they came upon some scribbled words and figures which proved to be—2974 Decatur . . . Sedgwick 3-7154.

Dr. John F. Condon, "Jafsie" of the ransom payment,

lived at 2974 Decatur Avenue. His telephone number, before he had it changed to a private line, was Sedgwick 3-7154.

When he was confronted with this material evidence, Hauptmann was ready with an explanation. He admitted having bored the holes in the block of wood for the better concealment of the currency "given" him by Isidor Fisch. As for the concealing of the pistol, he had realized he had no permit to carry a gun, and thought he might get into trouble if it were found in his house.

Regarding the address and telephone number of Dr. Condon, he "wasn't sure" even that he had written them in the closet, but if he had, it was at the request of his friend, Fisch.

Thereupon the police placed two questions before him more difficult to explain away.

"If you were afraid to have that little pistol in your house, what about the shotgun when you went hunting?" was the first.

"You didn't meet Fisch until long after Dr. Condon's telephone number had been changed. Why then, did you write down the *old* telephone number?" was the second.

To both of these questions Hauptmann remained mute.

With their material evidence and physical exhibits in hand, the authorities prepared for the indictment of the prisoner on charges of extortion in Bronx County. The indictment would serve to hold him in jail until the New Jersey police might build a substantial murder case against him.

At nine o'clock in the morning of September 26th, platoons of police tramped out of the ward-rooms of Bronx precinct stations and marched to the county court house to form a solid, protective line around the building. The patrolmen cleared the corridors of visitors. A "pigeon patrol" was established on neighboring rooftops. Automobile traffic was diverted from nearby streets. Opposite the building, on the open square formed by the intersection of Walton Avenue and 161st Street, a crowd of more than a thousand spectators were held straining against the police lines. Colonel Charles A. Lindbergh was on his way to give evidence before the Grand Jury.

At eleven o'clock he arrived in an automobile with Colonel H. Norman Schwarzkopf and the doors of the Grand Jury room closed behind him. Before the day was over, on the strength of what he told the twenty-three jurymen, together with the corroborative evidence of detectives and the material exhibits, "Richard Hauptmann, alias Bruno Richard Hauptmann, alias Karl Pellmeier" was indicted for extortion.

The indictment accused him of receiving the entire $50,000 from the hands of Dr. Condon, after having made threats to Colonel Lindbergh. It had been necessary to prove that the ransom-payers were actually motivated by fear occasioned by these threats, and it was to that effect that the Colonel testified.

Bail was set at $100,000. It might as well have been a million. If Bruno Hauptmann had been able to raise the lower amount, additional indictments and increased bail would have been established at once.

By this time, the uncommunicative prisoner had obtained counsel. James M. Fawcett undertook the defense, announcing that he had been retained by Anna Hauptmann and that friends of the suspect, whom he did not name, had provided the necessary funds.

On the day after his indictment, Hauptmann appeared to have sunk to the depths of despondency. The days and nights of merciless questioning had sapped his high vitality and he sat dejectedly, his head buried in his hands, on the edge of his cell cot, refusing to speak even to his guards. Occasionally he sobbed and muttered a few words in German.

Early on the morning of September 28th he was brought the usual prison breakfast of prunes, bread and butter, and coffee. When he had finished breakfast, the utensils were removed. An hour later the kitchen employee whose duty it is to check on the return of dishes, knives and forks, reported in agitation that a pewter spoon was missing from Hauptmann's tray.

Guards entered the cell and demanded to know what had become of the spoon. Hauptmann blinked and remained silent. The guards began a systematic search of the cell. They stripped the prisoner and found nothing. Then they turned their attention to the primitive plumbing that exists in the antiquated Bronx jail. The prison plumbers worked for three hours, and finally retrieved the missing spoon.

It had been broken into four parts. One piece was found in the wash basin drain and the others in the pipes below the toilet bowl, where they had been tossed, perhaps in fear of detection.

All four pieces had been sharpened, in that brief hour,

to knife-like edges, evidently by friction against the metal of Hauptmann's cot. One of the pieces of the handle had been bent into the form of a hook.

To the mind of Sheriff John J. Hanley the incident could mean but one thing. Hauptmann was contemplating suicide. From that moment on, the guard over Cell Number Nineteen was doubled, and every movement of the prisoner was watched. His leather belt was taken from him. His necktie and shoe strings were removed, and thereafter he ate on paper plates, used paper forks, and drank from paper cups.

Interwoven with the New York efforts to pin a conclusive case on the German carpenter were even more painstaking labors on the part of the New Jersey authorities who naturally wanted to prefer the more serious charges of abduction and murder against him.

The State of New Jersey already had served notice that it would ask for Hauptmann's extradition, and Colonel Schwarzkopf had told District Attorney Foley of the Bronx that he expected, within a few days, to present a positive case. There was no desire on the part of New York officials to try Hauptmann for extortion, provided there was justification for the belief that New Jersey had a sufficiently strong case to warrant trial on the capital charge.

"If we feel the New Jersey authorities have sufficient evidence against Hauptmann on a murder charge, we won't hesitate for a moment to turn him over to them," said Foley.

In the afternoon press conference at which, by agreement, the newspaper reporters were permitted to submit written questions to the District Attorney, Foley made a number of significant replies.

"Is there any other person, man or woman, against whom any of the evidence points?" was one question.

The answer was: "No."

"How many people," he was asked, "actually participated in the kidnaping of the Lindbergh baby on March 1, 1932?"

"I haven't any idea. I can't say whether one or more."

But to the persistent prodding of the news writers who wanted a definite answer to the question of the day, which was whether Hauptmann was believed to have worked with accomplices, his repeated response was:

"So far as I know, no other individual is under suspicion."

It was on that day that the authorities discovered that Hauptmann, far from making a living out of Wall Street over the eighteen months he had not done a day's work, actually lost $7,000 in speculation.

It was true, the police discovered, that Hauptmann had dabbled in the market before the Lindbergh kidnaping. What was apparently his first account with a brokerage concern was opened on November 1, 1929, with the firm of Carleton, Mott & Co., at 170 Broadway, since defunct. This account, which ranged from $500 to $1,000, never exceeding the latter amount, was closed on May 25, 1932, at a slight profit.

In April of 1932, however, he began his heavier operations, when he opened an account with the firm of Steiner, Rouse & Co. with $10,000. This was in the same month that the ransom money had been delivered to the Lindbergh extortioner. The account itself was carried in the maiden name of Hauptmann's wife, Anna Schoeffler.

Subsequently, the account was replenished by more than one $2,500 deposit.

On September 27, 1934, the books of Steiner, Rouse & Co. showed a balance to Hauptmann's credit of $886, of which $111 was in cash. His wife's account showed a credit balance of $5,017, of which $1,242 was in cash.

Also on deposit, in the Central Savings Bank, he had $2,578. A thorough check of the "buy" and "sell" orders on his brokers' books indicated that he had lost nearly half of approximately $15,000 he had put into his own and his wife's accounts.

CHAPTER FOURTEEN

New York's official interest in Prisoner Bruno Richard Hauptmann ended with his indictment and arraignment on charges of having extorted $50,000 from Colonel Charles A. Lindbergh. The indictment itself was merely a gesture, a legal pretext to keep the man locked up until the neighboring State of New Jersey could go through the formality of finding "probable cause" to believe Hauptmann was guilty of the actual kidnaping or murder of the Lindbergh child.

Early in October, 1934, therefore, the Hunterdon Grand Jury was convened, to listen to the evidence of the detectives and a notable array of witnesses gathered by the authorities to support their suspicions that Hauptmann was the "right man."

Grand Jury proceedings are, by law, wholly secret. In New Jersey, as elsewhere, no man or woman enters the Grand Jury room unless to give evidence. What the witness says within that room is said under the seal. To reveal Grand Jury testimony is an offense against the law. Yet, when it became noised around that this October Grand Jury, of twenty men and three embarrassed women, were to gather to consider the Lindbergh case, the small town of Flemington, Hunterdon County seat, gathered as though for a state fair. The court house steps were packed with jostling townspeople, farmers, and farmers' wives. The jurors were greeted

with applause and neighborly cheers, but the arrival of
Colonel Lindbergh was marked by no demonstration. He
walked up the steps of the century-old building, guards
closed in about him, and the doors were closed.

There was laughter in the little Grand Jury room when
Colonel Lindbergh entered to give his brief testimony. The
jurors had been exploring the musty records of the past, to
find vast amusement in the quaint legal phraseology that
has been, through a hundred and fifty years, a part of the
civil and criminal jurisprudence of Hunterdon County.
They read the Colonel a passage from an ancient indictment:

> . . . that the accused did not have before his eyes
> the fear of God, but was moved and seduced by the
> instigation of the Devil. . . .

The Colonel smiled, was sworn, and then told his story.
When the ordeal was over, he shook hands with the jurors
and left the court house. In deference to his position, the
crowd was silent as he passed.

To the waiting throng outside the little court there was
no question about what this farmer-jury would do. Decidedly there was no question after the charge of Supreme
Court Justice Thomas W. Trenchard, who had gravely reminded them of the law and their duty. He had said:

> The State's representatives . . . have stated to
> the Court that the evidence to be presented will
> tend to show that Hauptmann, the accused, in the
> course of a burglary in the dwelling house of the
> Lindberghs, done for the purpose of committing a
> battery upon the person of the Lindbergh child,

caused such child to be stricken and injured, as a result of which he died; or else the evidence will show that the child was killed as the result of a blow or stroke closely connected with the burglary, the stroke being caused by the accused.

If you find that the stroke was not inflicted in the course of a burglary, but that the evidence reasonably tends to show that the stroke that caused death was delivered by accident in Hunterdon County with intent to do bodily harm while the child was being carried from the home, you should find him guilty regardless of whether the stroke was accidentally or intentionally inflicted. . . .

Burglary, in the form that we are now concerned with, is defined by the statute as the willful or deliberate entering or breaking into any house by night, with intention to commit a battery.

If the evidence shows that the child was feloniously stricken in Hunterdon County by Hauptmann, and afterwards died as a result thereof, a stroke causing death struck in pursuance of the burglarly either on the premises or while the child was being carried away, you should return an indictment for murder.

If you do return an indictment for murder, the degree of the penalty, if the defendant is found guilty, rests with the Court.

The witnesses in this short session were few. One of the first was Dr. Charles Mitchell, who had performed the autopsy on the child. His evidence was presumed to have dealt with the supposed cause of death, as deduced from the condition of the body. Handwriting experts came, capable of pointing out similarities between Hauptmann's scrawls and the irregular script of the ransom notes. Neighbors of the Lindberghs, who had seen, or thought they had seen, a man lurking about Hopewell who answered to Hauptmann's description, gave their testimony. The government agents who had watched and waited and planned and investigated false clews for two patient years went before the jury to tell their stories.

The discussion within the jury room was brief. Within an hour after the last witness had quietly given his testimony and as quietly slipped away, an indictment was handed down—a short to-the-point charge of murder. It said:

> HUNTERDON COUNTY, OYER AND
>   TERMINER
>
> Hunterdon County SS.
>
> The Grand Jurors of the County of Hunterdon, being sworn and empaneled, do present that Bruno Richard Hauptmann, late of the Township of East Amwell, in the County of Hunterdon and the State of New Jersey, on March 1, A.D. 1932, did willfully, feloniously and of his own malice aforethought, kill and murder Charles A. Lindbergh, Jr., contrary to the statute in such cases made and provided, against the peace of this State, the government and dignity of the same.
>
> GEORGE N. ROBINSON, Foreman
> ANTHONY M. HAUCK, Prosecutor.

A number of unusual circumstances were remarked when the indictment was read. In the first place, Hauptmann was charged solely with the capital offense—with murder. There was no related charge and no second count alleging kidnaping. Consideration of the legal position in which the authorities found themselves, however, brought the obvious conclusion first, that the prosecution believed they had a stronger case for murder than for kidnaping and, second, that they were not so sure they could place the prisoner, except by vague circumstantial evidence, at the scene of the kidnaping.

Let it be supposed, they argued, that Bruno Hauptmann himself had no physical hand in the abduction. Failure to produce any co-conspirators would result automatically in a breakdown of the case, for no "conspiracy" could be proved. On the other hand, even though Bruno Hauptmann had no guilty knowledge, at the beginning, of the conspiracy to kidnap the child, his alleged profiting by it made him the participant in a felony which resulted in the child's death and hence laid him open to a charge of murder in the first degree.

Furthermore, once Hauptmann could be brought, on any charge, within the jurisdiction of Hunterdon County, it would be a matter of days only to draw a superseding indictment, and the main purpose of the Grand Jury action as of October 8th was to accomplish his extradition from New York.

The formalities of the extradition, however, had to be met, for it was known the prisoner would go to the last possible legal recourse to prevent his removal to New Jersey. First, Governor A. Harry Moore had to sign the extradition warrant and send it by officers, in due form, to Governor Herbert Lehman, of New York. Thereafter, following the New York Executive's granting of the request, there had to be a formal trial, at which the State of New Jersey would be required to disclose sufficient of its evidence to prove reasonable grounds for trying Hauptmann, before New York would relinquish its prior right to try him for extortion.

The preliminary skirmish was soon over. Governor Lehman signed the State's release of its prisoner, and Hauptmann's attorney at once instituted habeas corpus proceedings which acted as a stay of execution of New Jersey's warrant. Justice Ernest E. L. Hammer, in the Bronx County Supreme Court, heard the case.

Under the peculiarities of the legal system, it devolved upon the prisoner to show that he was not in New Jersey at the time of the kidnaping or murder. Burden of proof, in such cases, rests with the defendant, not with the state. And although the state was required to give a skeleton presentment of its evidence, it needed only to show (a) that the crime was committed, and (b) that it possessed circumstantial evidence which would link the prisoner to the crime, and (c) that the prisoner was a fugitive from justice, properly indicted under the laws of the State of New Jersey.

Hauptmann, on the other hand, was required to demonstrate, through credible witnesses, that he could not possibly have been in the State of New Jersey, or at least within striking distance of the Lindbergh home on the night of the crime. And it would be difficult, even for a man wholly innocent of wrong-doing, to prove exactly where he might have been on a night more than nine hundred days before.

On the afternoon of October 15th, the prisoner was taken before Judge Hammer and placed on the witness stand in his own defense. It was his first prolonged exposure to the public gaze since his arrest, nearly a month before. He was calm both under the direct and cross-examinations, and coldly contemptuous of the staring crowds that greeted his appearance and strained to hear every word of his alibi.

His story of the events of March 1, 1932, followed the normal routine of a jobless carpenter. On the morning of that day, he said, he took his wife to work at Christian Fredericksen's bakery, left her there, and then proceeded either to an employment agency to look for work, or else to a building where he "thought" he had temporary employment. In the evening, at seven o'clock, he called again at the bakery, ate supper with his wife in the little shop, and then went directly home where they spent the night.

His explanation of how he came to possess the Lindbergh ransom hoard differed in many respects from the version he originally gave the police, but he insisted that he found it in a cardboard box entrusted to him by his late friend, Isidor Fisch. He was forced to abandon his first tale of finding the money only three weeks before his arrest, and admitted that on March 18, 1933, he made three deposits of gold certificates, one in his own bank, the Central Savings Bank, and two in the Federal Reserve Bank.

"But that was all Isidor Fisch's money," he declared firmly. "I did it as a favor to Fisch."

"You told the police," he was reminded, "that the $20 bill found on you when you were arrested was part of $300 you had saved in gold certificates, and then that you had received those certificates from your friends or the bank. Was that the truth?"

"No," said Hauptmann stolidly. "I lied. I was trying to hide the money."

Then he was questioned about the clever hiding place he had constructed for the $840 in bills discovered by the police when they ripped apart the garage at his home—the two-by-four plank bored with holes into which the bills (and his little revolver) neatly fitted.

He had made the holes as long ago as October, 1931, he said, to keep certain of his smaller tools. Later, when he "found" the money in Isidor Fisch's amazing shoe box, he recollected the plank and decided it would be an excellent place to hide the money, lest he be accused of hoarding.

Here, again, there was conflict. He had told the police, when they discovered the strange cache, that he had bored the holes only two weeks before!

Attorney General David T. Wilentz of the State of New Jersey rose to his feet. His voice rose through a now silent court room.

"Didn't you build a ladder," he shouted, "and put it up against the Lindbergh house, and didn't you go up that ladder into the house and murder the child?"

Hauptmann strained forward in his chair. His usually pale face was flushed.

"No," he declared, in tones as loud and vehement as those of the prosecutor. "No, I did not!"

Hauptmann's counsel presented only a few witnesses to support his alibi. The first, and most important, was his wife, Anna. Faithfully, she recounted her "best recollection" that "if March 1, 1932, fell on a Tuesday," then her husband must have called for her that evening at the bakery, "because that was the regular thing."

"But there were some Tuesdays on which he didn't call for you," the prosecutor suggested.

"But he was usually there," Mrs. Hauptmann insisted, "and I know it was his day to call for me when I worked late. I am positively sure that he called for me that night."

"But didn't he ever leave you for a few days?"

"Yes, when he went hunting."

Christian Fredericksen and his wife, proprietors of the little bakery where Anna worked, gave feeble substantiation to the belief that "if it was a Tuesday, then Hauptmann must have called for his wife on the night of March 1st." But counsel tried in vain to make their recollection more positive—to obtain an unequivocal declaration that they were sure, of their own knowledge, that the prisoner had called at the shop on the date at issue.

Neither from the employment agency, where he might have gone during the day of March 1, 1932, nor from the Majestic Apartment building, where he might have been employed as a part-time carpenter, did Hauptmann produce verbal or documentary evidence supporting his story. There remained little for the State to do except to add a few words of testimony which would give grounds for a plausible belief that Hauptmann could have been at the scene of the kidnaping, and thus could have taken part in the tragedy.

That little was provided by a handwriting expert, Albert S. Osborn, internationally famed and universally respected by all courts wherein conflict over the authorship of script becomes involved.

Osborn, dignified and elderly, and listening to the questions through an ear trumpet, provided the State's first material link in the chain of evidence that would bind the man from the Bronx to the scene of the crime at Hopewell. Osborn carried Hauptmann directly into the sleeping room of the Lindbergh infant through the medium of the ransom note.

He swore that, to his belief, the note left in the child's room was written by the man who wrote the subsequent ransom notes received by Jafsie. And he pointed to the fact that one of the series of later ransom notes asked pointedly why the Lindberghs had ignored the note left in the nursery.

"Our contention," said Attorney General Wilentz, "is that these various notes are Hauptmann's admission and confession of his presence in the nursery the night of the kidnaping."

Pressed for an explanation of his belief that the notes were written by the same person, Osborn told the court:

"The writing was that of a man who had originally learned to write in German, also a writer who was somewhat illiterate, and also a writer who wrote what is known as the Latin script in an imperfect way. I call attention to various expressions in the letters and to certain peculiarities which would serve to identify the actual writer.

"I observe on this one [an exhibit of Hauptmann's application for an automobile license for 1931], one of the characteristic errors of the writer. That is his answer to the question: 'Were you ever convicted of a violation?' and the answer: 'Past red lihgt.'

"Compare this application form with the alleged ransom

notes and in Exhibit F-1 the word is spelled lihgt. On Ransom letter 4-KK we have the word 'right' spelled 'rigth.' The same thing occurs in other connections—a peculiar error of arranging the letters in the wrong order. In Exhibit L-1 we have it, the word 'the' spelled 'hte.'"

Other similarities, Osborn said, occurred throughout the notes in the State's possession. One of the outstanding peculiarities was the writer's method of writing the letter "x," which appeared like a double "e." Never, said the witness, had he seen the letter made similarly before.

The State of New Jersey then produced a gaunt, weatherbeaten woodsman, owner of a small farm adjacent to the Lindbergh estate, who swore he actually saw the prisoner on two occasions during the month before the kidnaping, in the vicinity of the manor. Millard Whited, describing himself as a "logger," and described by others who followed him to the stand as not the most trustworthy of witnesses, said that "sometime between the 18th and 20th of February" he saw the accused man standing in the road about a mile from the Lindbergh home, and that later in the month he saw him emerge from a piece of woodland not far from his own farm.

Whited was certain the stranger was Hauptmann. Strangers were few, he declared, in those parts. He knew everybody in the township, and he wasn't likely to forget a face, he averred. And he claimed to have told his story to the police in the early morning hours of March 2nd, when the hue and cry for the kidnapers began to spread through the neighborhood.

"He had a look as though he was surprised or something

on his mind," Whited said solemnly. "A person if they haven't anything on their mind generally has a smile of some sort on their face when you meet them. I saw him standing on that there cross-road, that right-hand turn off the Hopewell road, just the same as you or I would be, if a car was coming."

William Geltz, Millard's cousin, went to the witness chair.

"What is Millard Whited's reputation in Hopewell?" he was asked.

"Not much," said Geltz genially.

"Good or bad?"

"Bad."

William Diehl, another farmer, told the court Whited's reputation was "bad, yes, sir!"

George J. Lentz, another of Whited's neighbors, shouted "bad!" when he was asked about the witness's credibility.

That appeared to dispose of Whited's testimony, and at any rate it disposed of the day's court session, and with it the evidence that was to determine whether Hauptmann would be taken to New Jersey to stand trial for murder in the first degree, or be held in New York to answer to the charges of extortion.

Judge Hammer reviewed the evidence of both sides in the following digest:

"On behalf of the respondent (the State of New Jersey) after testimony of Albert S. Osborn, handwriting expert, that in his opinion they were written by relator (Hauptmann), there were placed in evidence writings which in the record are exhibits H, I, J, and K. Previously, exhibit G was received with motion to strike out reserved unless connection was shown.

"This also, in the opinion of the witness, Osborn, was written by the relator. Exhibit G is the note found in the Lindbergh home on March 1, 1932, upon the discovery of the kidnaping. It contains the demand for ransom.

"Exhibit H asks: 'Why did you ignore our letter which we left in the room?' Exhibit K states: 'We will send you the sleeping suit from the baby.' Exhibit J asks: 'Did you send the letter package to Mr. Lindbergh?' and states: 'It contains the sleeping suit from the baby.'

"The witness Millard Whited testified he lived in East Amwell township, N. J., about a mile from the Lindbergh estate and that between Feb. 18 and 20, 1932, he saw the relator about a mile from the Lindberghs' driveway. He testified he again saw the relator between Feb. 25 and 27. He identified the relator in court by leaving the witness stand and placing his hand on the relator's shoulder.

"The relator denied this testimony and also that he wrote exhibits G, H, I, J and K. The general credibility of the witness Whited was also attacked by two rebuttal witnesses.

"Bearing in mind the rule that evidence should be construed liberally in favor of the demanding State, the exhibits G, H, I, J and K in my opinion, for the purpose of this hearing, constitute admissions of the presence of the relator in New Jersey at the time of the commission of the crime.

"The testimony of the witness Whited may be weakened by the attack made on his credibility, but, considered by the same rule, it adds to the weight of the admissions showing presence.

"I do not regard this statement as setting forth a rule of evidence for the guidance of a trial court which later may consider the same evidence. My conclusion is that relator has not conclusively established that he was not in the demanding State at the time it is charged the crime was committed.

"Writ dismissed and relator remanded to custody."

As a matter of form, Attorney James M. Fawcett carried an instant appeal to the New York Appellate Division, and three days later, on Friday, October 19th, the high court ordered Hauptmann turned over to the New Jersey authorities for extradition to Flemington.

At eight o'clock that evening, Hauptmann, manacled to two detectives, was taken by automobile over the eastern marshlands of New Jersey and through the rolling countyside to the thoroughly excited Hunterdon County seat. Preceding the prison car were three automobiles loaded with police. Trailing it were three more. Motorcycle policemen, armed with rifles, rode at the side. Hauptmann was more closely guarded than any prisoner in the history of the United States.

Shortly after ten o'clock in the evening the roaring motorcade rushed into Flemington. On ordinary nights the entire village would have been abed. On that night Flemington's main street was ablaze with light and its streets jammed with citizens and visitors. Flares, planted at the corners of the jail, made the night bright. Camera and news men dominated every vantage point, and the repeated explosion of flash bulbs contributed fireworks.

Hauptmann, handcuffed to a state trooper, was hurried into the jail.

In Trenton, at his Capitol, Governor Harry Moore issued an official statement.

"The New Jersey State Police, working with other agencies," he said, "have arrested a suspect after two and a half years of tireless effort.

"They have been diligent in their search and have traced down every lead. New Jersey will be diligent in its prosecution of the man charged with the commission of the crime.

"There is an old maxim in law that a man is innocent until he is proven guilty. New Jersey will see that Bruno Hauptmann gets a fair trial."

Sheriff John Curtiss, spelling his name meticulously with two "s's" lest there be confusion and possible identification of himself with the other John Curtis, of Norfolk fame, became the trustee of the prisoner and the custodian of the court house in which he was to be tried. Within a week he found the second task more sleep-destroying than the first. More than one hundred and thirty applications for seats at the forthcoming performance came to him by telephone and telegraph, by letter and personal appeal, from newspapers, press associations, news reel companies, news picture associations, psychologists, investigators, fiction writers and magazine editors.

"Looks like the whole United States is comin' here for the trial," said Sheriff John Curtiss.

CHAPTER FIFTEEN

THE CASE AGAINST BRUNO RICHARD HAUPTMANN, AS IT appeared when the sullen German carpenter was locked in his cell at Flemington, was constructed purely on circumstantial evidence. No man had seen him erect his three-piece ladder against the walls of the Lindbergh home. No man had seen him fleeing with the kidnaped child. No man had traced, save by deduction, his supposed wanderings between Hopewell and the Bronx. Yet he was indicted on a charge which was the most difficult to prove in any court of law—murder. He was not charged with kidnaping. He was not charged with being an accessory either before or after the fact.

To prove this charge, therefore, it was necessary to show a great deal more than the mere possession of ransom money, or to prove that he participated in the profits of the crime. The State set for itself the task of showing that Hauptmann actually took part in the events which led to the death of the child.

Circumstantial evidence, at its best and most convincing uses, can never do more than indicate guilt beyond a reasonable doubt. It can do little more, in fact, than set before a jury a certain set of questions, answerable according to logic and experience in human behavior, in only one way.

The State's task, therefore, became one of piling up such

overwhelming, such crushing testimony that its weight would overcome any doubts in the jury's minds. To that end, it had the services of the finest legal and police talent afforded by three police and juridical bodies—the police and prosecutors of the State of New Jersey, the police of New York City, and the Division of Investigation of the United States Department of Justice.

First of all, Hauptmann's possession of $30 of the Lindbergh ransom money was provable. He had changed a $10 bill at a Warner-Quinlan gasoline station, on September 15, 1934. A $20 note was found on his person when he was arrested three days later.

Thereafter came the discovery of $13,750 of Lindbergh's gold certificates, buried in careful wrappings in various hiding places within Hauptmann's garage, followed by the finding of $840 more of the ransom money still more cleverly concealed in holes drilled into a plank.

The question propounded by the State therefore became this: Why does a man conceal a large amount of money (particularly when he has a brokerage account and had dealt with banks), hiding it so securely that not even his wife suspects his possession of it?

The State's second duty was to tear down, if possible, the credibility of Hauptmann's explanation of how he came to have possession of this money. Hauptmann said it was left him "in a shoe box," by his friend, Isidor Fisch, and that he did not discover the package contained money until long after Fisch had departed for Germany, where he died.

The explanation in turn presented a host of questions to be answered by the defendant. If Fisch possessed $15,000 and was going on his last journey to Germany—there to die of tuberculosis—why didn't Fisch pay Hauptmann the $7,500 he owed him? Why, if Fisch owed him money, did Hauptmann "cash" gold notes at the Federal Reserve bank in Fisch's behalf, without collecting at least some of the money due him? Would a man, leaving another man a shoe box full of money, not warn his friend what it contained, lest it be lost?

The Hauptmann-Fisch association, as related by the prisoner, began in a joint fur business, in which "Fisch kept the books" and "we made about $10,000." The next set of questions aroused by this declaration are these: If the fur business was profitable (and Fisch never showed any indication to his friends and neighbors of being anything but a poor fur cutter) why did Fisch need to borrow from Hauptmann? Where did Hauptmann get the $7,500 to lend Fisch? Why did Fisch die in poverty? If Hauptmann lent Fisch $7,500 in "good" money, why was it necessary for Fisch to pay for his passage to Germany in Lindbergh ransom notes?

Investigation of the defendant's financial affairs, again, led into another tangle of discrepancies, conflicting statements, and unanswered questions. It will be recalled that Hauptmann and his wife made, separately, several explanations of the sudden wealth that appeared to have descended upon the modest artisan's home at a time when nearly all other Americans were hard put to it to make both ends meet, when unemployment was rife, and the average worker, however thrifty and industrious, faced financial disaster.

Hauptmann's explanation of his comfortable living—

without work—was that he had been playing the stock market, and that it had become a sure source of income.

Anna Hauptmann's explanation was that he had been thrifty and had saved his normally high wages during good times.

And out of these savings, to be sure, Hauptmann had:

Sent his wife on a trip to Europe;

Lent Fisch $7,500;

Lived a life of ease, with summer vacation parties at the seashore and autumn hunting parties in Maine;

Owned and operated an automobile;

Maintained a brokerage account;

Held two real estate mortgages;

Enjoyed a brokerage account *in his wife's maiden name!*

All this, the State set forth, was done during the lean years, when Hauptmann could not prove by so much as a pay voucher that he had been engaged in any gainful occupation over a period of two years.

The questions naturally asked of the prisoner, in the light of the foregoing, were these: Why did Hauptmann claim to be making money on the stock exchange, when as a matter of record, he was losing some $7,000? Why did he lend Fisch $7,500—and keep his wife on a strict allowance of $10 a week? In less than ten years, had this carpenter, however thrifty, been able to save an *average* of $60 a week? Or could he show investments or speculations, perhaps during the boom days, which would indicate how at least $30,000 passed through his hands in the two years before his arrest? Granted such a theory were true, would he not be able to show records of such investments?

From the field of pure theory, the State then passed to more material facts, foremost among them the various ransom notes, the first of which was left in the Lindbergh baby's room, with subsequent communications delivered into the hand of Dr. John F. Condon.

Inspection and analysis of the notes could not possibly lead any logical man to any other conclusion than that the writer was:

A man of German antecedent, of Teutonic habits of thought and expression, and one who translated literally from his native tongue into English;

A man of meager education;

A resident in or near the Bronx;

A craftsman who knew "cubic contents," as witness the drawing of a picture of the "box" in which the ransom bills were to be delivered;

A man of extreme caution, crafty, reserved, and silent;

A man of dogged determination, of steel nerves.

He would be a thrifty man, because the ransom money was spent, not lavishly, but at an approximate rate of $40 a week. He would be a frequenter of Yorkville and the Bronx, because it was in those localities that much of the ransom money was distributed.

The man who wrote the notes to Dr. Condon would be the *same* man who wrote the original ransom note, left in the baby's room. Why? Because the notes received by Jafsie spoke definitely of the first message. And because *each of the notes bore the imprint of the same symbol,* that peculiar system of interlocking circles, with the three indentations, that marked the first note.

Again, taking up the known facts as opposed to conjecture, there was definite proof that the writer of the ransom notes actually had access to the child or had participated in the abduction. The proof there rested in the fact that the extortioner, whoever he might have been, was able to produce the garment worn by Charles A. Lindbergh, Jr., on the night he was kidnaped. Of that there was no doubt, and there would be plenty of witnesses to swear to it.

How, then, to link the prisoner to the notes? By handwriting, of course. All men, however they may seek to disguise their script, are unable to deviate from certain peculiarities. The authorities obtained specimens of Hauptmann's handwriting. In them they found peculiarities of chirography, of spelling, of the transposition of letters, common to all the documents they were able to collect. Handwriting experts were ready to swear that the man who filled out Bruno Richard Hauptmann's application for an automobile license in 1932 was the same man who wrote the ransom notes, also in 1932.

Handwriting evidence, even from such a distinguished and honorable expert as Albert S. Osborn is, however, entirely circumstantial. Only if one person actually sees another person write a signature, a phrase, a sentence, can he swear that, of his own knowledge, he knows who did the writing. The best he can do, in the absence of such visible proof, is to swear that he "believes" certain things to be facts, and to explain the reasons underlying his belief. The credibility of such testimony depends upon the reputation of the expert. Its effectiveness depends upon how firmly he can convince a jury.

If, however, the State could show that Bruno Hauptmann wrote the series of ransom notes, it would thereby prove Bruno Hauptmann's presence at Hopewell, his guilty knowledge of the kidnaping, and his active participation in the crime out of which grew the murder.

Another important phase of the State's attempt to prove that the man now known to have passed several of the ransom bills was the man who actually received them from Dr. Condon involved the question of physical identification of the shadowy figure in St. Raymond's cemetery into whose clutching hands Jafsie delivered the package. Of three such identifications, one was positive, one was open to question, and the third was identification of the voice only.

Joseph Perrone, the taxicab driver who delivered a note from the extortioner to Dr. Condon, had made positive identification of Hauptmann as the man who paid him one dollar to carry the message. Previously, he had given the police a description of the man—of his pointed chin, his flat cheeks, his blue eyes. That description tallied with other descriptions given by shopkeepers who had changed ransom bills for one whom the police insisted must be Hauptmann. But Perrone had gone further. He had picked Hauptmann from a lineup and said, "This is the man who paid me to take the note to Dr. Condon."

The second identification, by Dr. Condon himself, had been less satisfactory from the police point of view. Jafsie looked carefully at Hauptmann shortly after he was captured, and said, "I can't be sure this is the man." Later, when some of the first excitement had died down and Hauptmann was visited by the good doctor in his cell at

Flemington, Jafsie was more willing to swear that this was the cemetery negotiator. It was explained that in the interval between his arrest and his removal to New Jersey, the prisoner had lost thirty pounds. The man Jafsie saw in March, 1932, was about thirty pounds lighter than the Hauptmann he saw in the Bronx County jail. There was a question, therefore, in the minds both of the police and public, as to what Dr. Condon would say if and when he should go to the witness stand.

The third identification, as has been related, was that of Colonel Lindbergh, who had sat in an automobile near the cemetery fence, and had heard the negotiator cry out, "Doctor! Over here, Doctor!" The Colonel had listened to Hauptmann's voice, repeating similar words, and had declared his belief that the voice was the same voice he heard thirty months previously. He never, however, had seen the man's face.

The abductor of the Lindbergh child had left behind him, not far from the home from which he was fleeing, one of the most important physical clues to his identity in the abandoned ladder sections.

This ladder, as has also been related, was of "home-made" construction, and showed evidences of having been built by an experienced carpenter. Its joints were made by no amateur. Its only weakness was where one rung—made from second-hand wood—had split.

Research in which the United States Bureau of Standards had been called into action afforded definite proof that the wood had originated in a certain section of the southern states. Detective work had traced shipments of this wood to New York, to the Bronx, and to the very lumber yard to which Hauptmann had access and where he had previously obtained materials—if not this very wood. The long trail had ended there, because it could not be proved that Hauptmann had bought any of the two-by-fours with which the sides of the ladder were constructed. Therefore the ladder and lumber clues became the sheerest of circumstantial evidence, and could be offered only on that basis, for whatever corroborative effect they might have.

The ladder was built with nails similar to nails found in the Hauptmann garage. But they were nails widely used in many forms of carpentry and by many craftsmen. Again, they would provide only circumstantial evidence, valuable only when taken in conjunction with supporting facts.

If, however, it was easy for Hauptmann to enter a disclaimer to all knowledge of the ladder, another piece of wood rose to plague him—a strip of paneling from his closet, on which were written in pencil the address and telephone number of Dr. John F. Condon.

Hauptmann had professed an inability to understand how those figures came to be written there. He could not, he said, remember having placed them there himself. He did not "think" they were in his handwriting. They might have been placed there some time before, by Fisch—or for Fisch's convenience.

Here, again, was circumstantial evidence. No living person could be found who saw Hauptmann write those figures in the closet or say what was their purpose. But they might indicate to a jury the possibility that they consisted of a reminder that one desiring to communicate with Jafsie might do so readily—by calling Sedgwick 3-7154.

In the absence of other evidence tending to show that the abductor had accomplices in his plot, the State became interested in demonstrating its theory that Hauptmann accomplished the deed single-handed and profited from it alone. To have admitted that he had associates in the crime would have confused the issue and would have created further questions as to the degree of guilt, if he were guilty at all, of the man in custody. Evidence on this point was intangible —negative. The police attempted to work out a solution by deduction.

First, they asked, why had the ladder, potential source of devastating evidence, been abandoned in the flight? Men cool enough, thorough enough, to have planned the monstrous crime, could never have been guilty of such an error in judgment as to leave behind so tangible a clue. But if there had been two men in the abduction gang, one of them could have carried the ladder with ease, while the other carried the child. One man would have found the double burden too great, and naturally would have discarded the ladder rather than the object of his raid.

Another logical reason for limiting the number of criminals to one—and only one—was found in an analysis of the money involved. The government's check of the ransom money accounted for at Hauptmann's home, paid into banks, spent in various shops, cafés and movies, and turned into the Federal Reserve bank in exchange for new currency, showed a total surprisingly close to the $50,000 that had been demanded and received by the extortioner. A substantial proportion of this, of course, had been traced directly to Hauptmann's hands.

Had there been more than one man in such a desperate feat, it was argued, the demanded sum would have been far larger. It was regarded as unthinkable that a man, however criminal and daring, would in his right mind take such chances for a mere $10,000 or $20,000.

The psychologists of the three investigating forces were also agreed that had there been more than one man in the crime, detection would have come long before the denouement of September, 1934. A gang, for example, of five men stands a chance of self-betrayal, through inadvertent slips, through mistakes, or through the weakness of an individual, five times as great as does a "lone wolf."

Beliefs, however, are not evidence. Sometimes it is easier to prove that a criminal has operated with associates—even though the associates may not be apprehended—than it is to prove that he was alone in his crime. The only supporting testimony that could be offered, to show that Hauptmann alone was guilty of the crime, was of a general nature, wholly circumstantial, and consisting principally of an "accounting" of the ransom money as made by the federal authorities. If Hauptmann were able to prove that Fisch placed the money in his hands, such an accounting would be valueless.

In many courts and under many circumstances, it is impossible to introduce evidence of previous criminality on the part of a defendant as having any bearing on his guilt or innocence in the case at trial. The world realizes, however, the effect upon a jury when testimony to previous convictions is permitted in the record. Is a man capable of committing a fiendish crime? Look into his record and see if he has lived an exemplary life. Find out his reputation. Search for his character. The plausibility of his story may hang on the result.

Detective Johnson did a thorough job of exploring into Hauptmann's record, and discovered that from March, 1919, until June, 1923, when he disappeared over the Atlantic horizon, life for the young machine-gunner had consisted of a long series of clashes with the provincial police, in which Hauptmann, as a rule, had emerged victorious, though a fugitive.

The picture of Bruno Hauptmann, at the age of nineteen, was far from prepossessing. In company with a young reprobate named Fritz Petzold, he appeared to have terrorized the peaceful countryside of Kamenz in a thorough and workmanlike manner.

On the night of March 15-16, 1919, Hauptmann and Petzold broke the window in the living room of a burgher in the town of Bernbruch, jimmied their way into the house, and stole 300 marks in cash and a silver watch. The victim who bemoaned the loss of his silver timepiece was none other than the Herr Burgomeister Schierach. Hauptmann and Petzold divided the money, but Hauptmann kept the Mayor's watch.

On the following night, the same pair burglarized the home of Eduard Scheumann, a leather tanner, in Kamenz, stealing 200 marks in cash, a quantity of postage stamps, and a watch and chain. In this robbery they calmly lighted a gas lamp, the better to conduct their unholy business.

These two robberies were preceded by one at Rackelwitz, in which they used a crow bar to gain entrance to a house which they robbed of 400 marks and another watch and chain.

Hauptmann's fourth escapade of that month was to hold up two women on the road between Wiesa and Nebelschutz. Petzold, on that occasion, waggled a revolver at the women (Hautpmann's revolver, it was afterwards shown) and took away from them a quantity of food stuffs and several food cards, such as were issued to all families during and after the war. When the women refused to stop, the police related, Hauptmann urged his companion to "shoot, and waste no time."

"We're radicals," the ex-soldiers shouted at the two females, "and we're ready to shoot."

The frightened women ran away from their babyless baby-carriages, in which they had been carrying home the family provender, and left the loot to the young men.

The police lost little time in tracking down the pair, and Hauptmann and Petzold were arrested on March 26, 1919, in Kamenz. While they were being transported to a safer jail at Bautzen in the following month, however, Hauptmann escaped from the prison van, only to surrender later to the Kamenz police.

Hauptmann was convicted by the first district court at Bautzen on June 3, 1919, on three charges of grand larceny, one charge of petty larceny, and as a receiver of stolen goods. He was sentenced to two years, six months and one week in jail. In a subsequent court case at Bautzen, dealing with the highway robbery, he was sentenced to an additional two years and six months, making a total of five years and one week.

He began serving the sentence in the jail at Bautzen, but was paroled in March, 1923. Within a month a series of petty depradations in Kamenz pointed in his direction, and he was arrested on June 7th of that year, charged with having stolen valuable leather belting from a pottery, a saw mill, and a machine shop.

No disposition of these cases was ever obtained. Before he could be brought to trial he had escaped, in leisurely fashion, while exercising in the jail yard, and the harrassed authorities never saw him again.

So Hauptmann was in the United States illegally. A determined man, he had twice stowed away before he was able to effect an entrance to the country. The occasion of his flight from Germany was to escape punishment for previous crimes. He was a burglar and a thief, and a jail breaker into the bargain. Little in such a record to inspire confidence in the prisoner. Yet nothing in the record, either, to prove decisively that Bruno Hauptmann committed the Lindbergh crime.

Against this array of circumstantial evidence, what could Hauptmann bring forth by way of rebuttal?

First there was, according to his story, the physical impossibility of being in Hopewell on the night of the kidnaping because he had called at the bakeshop where his wife was employed at seven o'clock on the evening of March 1, 1932, had remained there with her for supper, and had returned with her to their home. This evidence was, of course, corroborated by Anna Hauptmann, and had a partial corroboration from Mrs. Hauptmann's employers, who "believed" Hauptmann called for his wife each Tuesday night when she was working at the bakery. If the defendant could convince the jury of this circumstance, he would be saved.

Hauptmann's next task was to prove the innocent sources of the money upon which he lived, without working, from April, 1932, until the time of his arrest. He had two explanations—to which his wife added a third—for this. He had made considerable money in association with Isidor Fisch in the fur business—a fact which Fisch could not dispute, since he was dead—and he had had considerable success in the stock market. Anna Hauptmann, defending her husband, already had said that in more prosperous times, her husband had saved a greater part of his earnings.

Possession of the ransom money, of course, would have to be admitted. On the other hand, there had to be an explanation of that possession. Again Hauptmann had to rely upon the dead man, Isidor Fisch, who could not be summoned from the grave. Hauptmann's defense therefore was that Fisch had left the money with him, without telling him what the package contained, and that it was not until long afterwards that, purely by chance, he discovered the bills. To the natural question as to why he hid the money with such caution, his reply would be that he feared running afoul of the hoarding laws. Proof that Fisch actually gave him the money would be circumstantial proof that Fisch, rather than Hauptmann, committed the crime. In partial support of such a theory, Hauptmann was able to point to several other objects left in his care by the departing traveler, when he went abroad on the journey that was to be his last. In further support would be Hauptmann's claim for $7,500 against Fisch's "estate," the sum Hauptmann claimed he lent the furrier long before Fisch went to Germany.

Regarding the ransom notes, Hauptmann's only defense could be a positive denial that he ever wrote or saw them, that he knew nothing about the secret symbol which stamped their genuineness, and that the handwriting experts were mistaken in their judgment.

The identifications, likewise, were a matter of one man's word against another's. A straight denial that he had ever seen Dr. Condon, that he had ever dispatched a note by the taxicab driver, Perrone, and that he had ever conferred with Jafsie at any time or any place whatsoever was Hauptmann's answer to the State's declaration.

There were certain questions which the prisoner, in turn, might propound to the authorities. They had released Anna Hauptmann with a public announcement that not only was she not concerned in the case, but that she knew absolutely nothing about it. And her attitude and actions since her husband's arrest bore out that belief. Yet was it possible for a guilty husband to conceal, for two years and a half, the dreadful truth from a wife? Was it possible, even if he had been able to commit the initial crime without his wife's knowledge, to have kept her in complete ignorance thereafter, never betraying anything of the secret shadowing his whole life?

The defense to charges of previous criminality was that the earlier transgressions in Germany were merely the peccadilloes of youth—that Hauptmann had grown older, steadier, wiser. One answer was that, as a boy, his life nearly blasted by the World War, he had returned to his home town to find a disrupted social scene, in which the wildness of youth ran riot. Another answer was that in the ten years of his illegal residence in the United States, he had never once behaved in any fashion that would give rise to the belief that he was anything other than an honest German workman, steady and conscientious, thrifty and home-loving.

Anna Hauptmann's testimony to his character was that of a kind husband and a fond father. The defense would ask the psychologists if such a man would be likely to devise and execute the most amazing crime in American annals.

As the time approached for the trial of the case—the date having been set for January 2, 1935—the preliminary skirmishes between State and defense developed into a battle of publicity and propaganda.

CHAPTER SIXTEEN

"ANY STATEMENTS ON THIS CASE," SAID ATTORNEY JAMES Mark Fawcett pleasantly, "will have to come from Mr. Whitney. You'll have to see Mr. Whitney."

Then he bowed courteously and departed through a door marked "private," leaving a group of news hounds to wonder who "Mr. Whitney" might be and in what official capacity, if any, he was serving the interests of the defense forces. He was not an attorney, nor was he a member of Fawcett's legal staff. He was variously described, for the moment, as Fawcett's contact man, as a private investigator, as a defense detective, and as Anna Schoeffler Hauptmann's "business representative."

"Mr. Whitney" failed to classify himself and parried adroitly all questions relating to his own status. He did, however, "speak for Mrs. Hauptmann" upon occasion, emphasizing to the press her splendid devotion to her husband and her belief in his innocence. In Flemington, he busied himself finding a humble dwelling place for Anna and her baby, Mannfried, arranging a birthday anniversary for the child (duly recorded by the sob-sisters of the tabloids and sympathetic news reels) and in many other ways endeavoring to "sell" the Hauptmann family to the great American public as pathetic humans unjustly trapped in the toils of circumstance.

The burden of the publicity emanating from the defense, late in October, revolved around the New Jersey State Police, who were pictured alternately as bunglers and as unconscionable and wicked conspirators, seeking to railroad an innocent man to the electric chair. Unable to charge that the defendant had been subjected to the "third degree" (as a matter of fact the police both of New York and of New Jersey so feared any repercussion from brutality that they had been unusually gentle with the prisoner), they did charge the authorities with a new form of "torture."

Hauptmann's cell, and the corridor upon which it abutted, was brightly lighted, day and night, twenty-four hours a day. Guards of state police and sheriff's deputies sat with Hauptmann, inside and outside the cell, in his waking and sleeping moments. They were forbidden to converse with him unless the prisoner directly addressed them, although many of the better natured guardians ignored the admonition.

The close watch and, particularly, the illumination, became the subject of bitter attacks by the defense, who described it as a deliberate attack on Hauptmann's morale comparable to the Chinese "sleepless torture."

"It is an attempt to break him down physically," they declared. "The State is murdering his sleep."

As for Hauptmann, if his spirit were crushed by surroundings he never showed it. He ate well and heartily, complained little, and even hummed an occasional tune as he paced up and down in the narrow cage. Weekly physical examinations indicated no change in his health. His phlegmatic disposition appeared to be upset only occasionally, and then when Baby Mannfried was brought to visit him.

Attorney General David T. Wilentz, to whom the subject of Hauptmann's "torture" was referred, in turn referred the matter to Sheriff John H. Curtiss.

"We propose to guard the prisoner against any contingency," the sheriff replied. "Hauptmann has not complained to us." So the guard was maintained.

If "Mr. Whitney" proved a diligent press agent for the defense, he was no less diligent in protecting his own interests—whatever they may have been. Emissaries purporting to come from him appeared at the editorial offices of some metropolitan newspapers with broad hints that the services of Mrs. Hauptmann—or even of Hauptmann himself— might be obtained, for a price, to "cover" the forthcoming trial. It also suggested that radio, news-reel, or even vaudeville engagements were being considered.

"Mr. Whitney's" sartorial appearance had undergone revision since his early days in the outer offices of James M. Fawcett, back in New York. His raiment, of subdued tone and careless disarray upon his début as "Mrs. Hauptmann's manager," took on an elegance approaching that of the fastidious James M. Fawcett, whose taste runs to delicate purple ensembles.

In his pocket, Harry Whitney—who had revealed his first name to the newspaper correspondents in an unusual burst of confidence—carried two mortgages, for $3,750 each, on property in Brooklyn and Queens, transferred to his name by Anna Hauptmann. But the transfer had not been made to "Harry Whitney." The name on the document was "Weisensee."

Presently there arose rumors of dissension within the defense forces. Fawcett had not yet chosen the New Jersey counsel to be associated with him, as attorneys of record, in the coming trial. Statements from him regarding the case became less frequent. The entire management of Hauptmann's affairs appeared to be vested in Whitney—or Weisensee.

On November 2nd, Edward J. Reilly, of Brooklyn, announced that he had been retained as chief counsel for Bruno Richard Hauptmann, to succeed James M. Fawcett, "who will retire from the case." Fawcett professed to be extremely surprised at the suggested retirement.

"It is news to me," he said. "Of course, if Mrs. Hauptmann wishes me to withdraw and wants to engage Mr. Reilly, she has a perfect right to act."

Whitney—or Weisensee—confirmed the change of lawyers. Mrs. Hauptmann confirmed the change. Neither would advance any reason for discharging Fawcett, nor would Fawcett or Reilly discuss the move.

One theory was advanced, however, that gained wide credence among observers and that, at least for the time being, was not denied. It was that Attorney Fawcett had decided to plead his client "not guilty by reason of insanity." It was known that Fawcett's alienists had examined the prisoner and made a secret report to the lawyer. What, if any, conclusions they had reached were securely hidden in Fawcett's filing cabinets. But Fawcett, under the ethics involved, was estopped from making any explanations. If

236 The Lindbergh Crime

he had said, "I am out of the case because I could no longer conscientiously defend him," the harm would have been incalculable. If he had said merely, "I am withdrawing from the case," without offering any explanation for his action, the effect upon the public would have been equally severe on the defendant. Therefore, it had to be made to appear, not that Fawcett was himself surrendering his client, but that he had been ousted. So Mr. Fawcett said nothing, and Mr. Reilly set to work.

Two days after his appointment as chief defense attorney, the news reels spread before the public views of Mr. Reilly in action. Mr. Reilly had had no opportunity to study the case, and his first address to the public, via the sound-pictures, was necessarily platitudinous. From behind a neat array of calfskin bindings, Mr. Reilly told the American people that "a man must be considered innocent until he has been proven guilty"; that it is a recognized principle of American jurisprudence that "a mere accusation of guilt is not proof of guilt"; that his examination of the case, brief though it necessarily was, had convinced him beyond a doubt of "the innocence of my client."

Mr. Reilly's tones and undertones were those of a skilled pleader. He had force. The phrases that rolled from his lips were occasionally the time-worn expressions that could be found in rhetorical flights of long-forgotten forensic giants, but with them went a certain sweet persuasiveness common to those happy individuals who become known as "very good men with a jury."

A new flood of "interviews" was loosed upon the world, shortly thereafter, some hinting at "new evidence" which would clear Hauptmann unmistakably of the crime with which he was charged. Witnesses—fifty of them at least—were promised, all of whom would present alibis for the prisoner.

"Dr. Condon," said an associate for the defense, "knows that at least five persons were associated in the kidnaping. Why doesn't the State find the other four criminals?"

The question would have been pertinent, had it been based on an accurate premise. Dr. Condon did not "know" that five people had been members of the kidnap gang. He was told so—by the lone negotiator to whom he surrendered Colonel Lindbergh's $50,000 in St. Raymond's cemetery. He had never seen any suspect other than the extortioner. He had no reason to believe—other than the word of a criminal who took $50,000 in return for the murdered child's sleeping suit—that any other person was concerned with the crime.

Reilly, the impressive chief counsel who boasted an amazing record of acquitting clients indicted for various capital crimes, did not delay as long as his predecessor in choosing his New Jersey associates. He asked Frederick A. Pope, Egbert Rosecrans, and C. Lloyd Fisher of Flemington, whose weather-beaten sign hung opposite the century-old court house, to join with him in the action. Fisher had unsuccessfully defended John Hughes Curtis of Norfolk in the matter of the seafaring hoax and had finally succeeded in getting his client off with a $1,000 fine and a suspended sentence.

Together, the attorneys compiled an embarrassing list of questions to ask the prosecution.

The indictment, it was obvious to them, was too general

in nature and too vague in terms to give the defense an idea of the charges they would have to meet when the case went to trial. It recited, merely, that the defendant was accused of causing the death of Charles A. Lindbergh, Jr., by some means as yet undisclosed, but during the commission of a felony.

What they demanded to know, "in order to set up a defense," was the manner and method by which the State contended the kidnaping and murder were carried out, and by what means the State intended to prove that Bruno Hauptmann was actually responsible for the death of the child. They also sought to pin upon the State the responsibility for naming the exact place and hour of the killing.

A defendant is, under all judicial decisions, entitled to know the accusations against which he must defend himself. This axiom is used, from time to time, to force the prosecution into showing its hand, and the request of the Hauptmann defense for a "bill of particulars" was not unexpected. After weeks of consideration, Reilly and Fisher presented a demand that the State answer twelve questions, to elaborate on the indictment and determine what the prosecution hoped to prove.

In brief summary, the defense asked:

"Does the State contend that Bruno Hauptmann alone committed the crime against the Lindberghs, or did he have associates?"

The question was designed to drag into the open the prosecution's contention that Hauptmann had no associates.

"Where and when did the actual murder of Charles A. Lindbergh, Jr., occur?"

The question was asked to force the prosecution to reveal its theory regarding the events of the night of March 1, 1932.

"By what method does the State contend Charles A. Lindbergh, Jr., met his death?" was the twelfth question.

There was a conference of attorneys. The Messrs. Reilly and Fisher talked the matter over with the Messrs. Wilentz and Anthony Hauck, Jr. The two leading State attorneys refused to elaborate on the indictment. Reilly and Fisher went into court with a formal demand.

Justice Thomas W. Trenchard, of the New Jersey Supreme Court, listened to the twelve questions and discarded the first eleven, as being fully answered by the indictment. Then he came to the twelfth, which concerned the actual manner in which Colonel Lindbergh's son died.

Ruling that the indictment answered every one of the first eleven questions, he declared that the prosecution must advise the defense by what instrument—if they knew—the infant had been put to death.

Justice Trenchard made it plain that the prosecution was required to advise the defense by what lethal instrument the infant had been killed, only if it could identify the weapon with a degree of certainty. His order appeared to emphasize that the manner of death, rather than the means, was the important factor.

The prosecutors, therefore, regarded the order as a complete victory. They needed to turn only to the official verdict of the medical examiner of Trenton to give the defense a theory, and that verdict was broad enough to admit of any number of variations. It said:

"Death was caused by a fracture of the skull, due to external violence."

External violence may consist of any number of things. It may be an accident, in which the violence is done by a wholly innocent force. A person who falls down stairs and fractures his skull thereby is a victim of external violence. External violence might mean any action, consciously undertaken or otherwise, originating outside the person of the victim. It might be the impact of a locomotive, an automobile, or a baseball. It might be the lethally designed blow of a knife, a hammer, a hatchet, or a bullet from a gun.

To the twelfth question propounded by the defense, therefore, Attorney General Wilentz responded only in the words of the medical examiner—that the State would contend Charles A. Lindbergh, Jr. met his death "as the result of a fractured skull, due to external violence." He did not say how, or with what instrument, the death blow was inflicted.

Attorney Reilly nevertheless appeared to be satisfied with the response. He announced that the State's replies to his questionnaire had been "satisfactory" and that he would neither ask more questions nor file further motions. The demand for the bill of particulars, however, had clarified the State's position to a certain extent. In standing on the indictment, and in arguments opposing Reilly's demands, it had made plain a certain course of action by which it was, in theory, bound when the trial started. The details of this plan were:

1. Bruno Hauptmann, and Hauptmann alone, was accused of having killed Charles A. Lindbergh, Jr.

2. The State would oppose the introduction of any contrary theory setting up the hypothesis that other criminals participated in the crime.

3. While the State stood on the law—that a death resulting from the commission of a felony was indictable as murder—it would attempt to show that Hauptmann was the physical as well as the legal murderer of the child.

4. The State regarded Hauptmann as solely responsible for the deliberate execution of the crime, from its conception to its completion.

When the State's response to the defense questions became known, the news correspondents crowded around Joseph Lanigan, David Wilentz's chief assistant, and pressed innumerable questions at him. Did this mean the State had evidence to show exactly how the baby died? Did it mean that witnesses or material evidence would be offered to prove that Hauptmann was at the scene of the murder and that he participated in it?

"I am sorry, gentlemen," said Lanigan, "but I cannot reveal our case."

But it became known, not long afterwards, that the authorities had reconstructed, to their own satisfaction, what they considered the true story of the night of March 1, 1932. It was this:

The kidnaper climbed to the nursery window by means of his three-section ladder. He left the ransom note, picked up the sleeping child, and began the descent to the ground. The ladder gave way at its weakest point, and he fell to the ground with his burden. Limping, he took the time to remove the ladder from the wall, and began his flight. His first 100 yards of progress, under the double burden of the ladder and the child, who was perhaps struggling and crying, proved to him that he could not continue with both. So he abandoned the ladder on the lawn, and proceeded to his automobile, parked in the lane nearby.

The kidnaper then drove over the dirt roads to a clearing high above the Lindbergh manor, from which he had, on many occasions, observed activities within the house, by means of his high-powered field glasses. It should be remembered that in the note he left behind, he warned Colonel Lindbergh against notifying the police. It had been his intent, up to that moment, to kidnap, and not to kill, the infant.

But reaching this clearing, he turned to survey the dark scene below. Through his binoculars he could see that the house was brilliantly lighted. There was no question in his mind but that the abduction of the baby had been discovered. The hurrying figures, discernible even at that distance, through his magnifying glasses, told him that the police had been called. Within half an hour, he knew, word would have gone out to all police, and every means of egress from the desolate territory would have been blocked. To have attempted to make his way for miles out of New Jersey, over roads which were being watched, would have been suicidal so long as he had in his possession the most incriminating burden of all—the kidnaped child.

He hesitated, perhaps, for a few moments. Then——

"Death was caused by a fractured skull, due to external violence."

The child's body was taken into the underbrush, and

placed in a hurriedly scraped grave. The kidnaper brushed the dirt from his hands and drove on, passing innocently through the recurring cordons of police that were, even then, being established at strategic points along the New Jersey highways.

It was a sensational theory, but it was no more sensational than the Lindbergh case in its bizarre entirety.

"The defense," said Lloyd Fisher, "will bring fifty witnesses to prove that Hauptmann was not in New Jersey at any time on or about March 1, 1932."

"The prosecution," retorted Anthony Hauck, Jr., "will bring a hundred witnesses who will link Bruno Hauptmann unmistakably to the crime."

During the month of December, as time for the trial approached, new clues were discovered almost daily by the press, which had grown somewhat bored waiting for the main event. That the "clues" were abandoned almost from one edition to the next made little difference. The correspondents had to have something to write about, and the suppositions, guesses, theories and imaginings helped to fill space.

Jafsie himself seemed imbued, at that moment, with the spirit of new investigation. Disappearing from New York, he bobbed up in Florida, to admit genially that he was "running down certain clues" that had come to him in some of the twenty-five hundred letters he received after Hauptmann's arrest.

In an interview at Palm Beach, Jafsie was quoted as saying: "The State of New Jersey will never convict Hauptmann of murder. It would have been better to have tried him for extortion."

In an interview at Miami, he said, "I never told anybody I thought the State of New Jersey couldn't convict Hauptmann of murder. I never discussed my own beliefs with anybody."

Attorney Reilly caused a brief flurry of excitement when he filed suit in New York Supreme Court to force Attorney Fawcett to deliver over to him all papers, documents and other material gathered by him to aid the defense. Attorney Fawcett replied that he would gladly turn over the papers as soon as he had been paid for the services he performed before he was discharged. The Hauptmanns, he set forth, still owed him $4,200. He asked, in a counter-action, that the mortgages held by Whitney—or Weisensee—be impounded by the court until he should receive his fee.

Justice Frank F. Adel ruled on one issue—that "a defendant has the right to change his counsel, and the counsel he selects must be given all the information at the disposal of any previous counsel," regardless of unpaid fees or impounded mortgages.

Meanwhile, the populace of Flemington settled down to somewhat self-conscious appreciation of their importance to the world in view of the impending trial. They deplored notoriety which had come to upset the even tenor of the little town, but they could not be blamed for desiring, secretly, to profit a little by an event of such magnitude.

The normal population of the county seat was about three thousand. More than one thousand "foreigners" were to pour into Hunterdon County in January, and demand lodging and refreshment. The little brick hotel whose fifty rooms had housed comfortably the wayfarers who customarily dropped into town, could not accommodate such a crowd. So the housewives dusted out their spare rooms and became temporarily innkeepers.

Before January, the quest for living quarters became a frantic race. One New York newspaper leased a country club on the outskirts of Flemington, and in it housed and fed its staff of reporters, special writers and telegraph operators. Another rented two unfurnished apartments, stocked them with a dozen cot beds, and installed its special telegraph lines so close to these couches that a reporter might easily dictate his account in delightful recumbence.

From the Hunterdon County court house, which was built in 1828, the two major communications companies prepared to send one million words a day. Obviously, the court house had not been built with an eye to 1935, and accommodations for forty telegraph lines—and forty operators—had not been in the architect's mind when he designed its chaste, church-like interior. But festoons of black cable twisted their way up its walls and disappeared into the ancient garret where forty operators were to sit arm-to-arm and send out the thousands of words that had been scribbled on yellow paper in the court room far below.

If the good people of Flemington were interested, and perhaps a little shocked, by these preparations, they showed at least one universal trait. They were agreed that Bruno Richard Hauptmann was entitled to a fair trial, and that he would get one. Fearing they would be charged with prejudice, first because of the nature of the crime and, second, because of the prominence of the principals, they indicated strongly a determination to try the case on its merits.

"No Hunterdon County jury can be stampeded into railroading an innocent man to the electric chair," they declared.

CHAPTER SEVENTEEN

WHEN, ON THE MORNING OF JANUARY 2ND, 1935, HUNTERDON County's ancient court of Oyer and Terminer was called into session, its high-ceilinged judgment room was crowded to suffocation and a thousand would-be spectators clamored for admission.

Throughout the previous night a seemingly endless procession of automobiles had brought more and still more of the morbidly curious to the scene of the drama. A heavy detail of State Police, resplendent in their horizon-blue uniforms and flaring yellow-striped riding breeches, guarded the entrances and held back the mob.

The news correspondents, prospective witnesses, court attachés, telegraph operators and talesmen were admitted through small lanes, upon presentation of their red, blue, yellow and white tickets.

Simple pine boards, squared off in eighteen-inch spaces, formed the writing tables for one hundred and fifty newspaper reporters, who sat wedged together and almost incapable of movement on hard benches, eight inches wide. The gallery was given over entirely to the press. The talesmen occupied the rear of the court room.

Hauptmann was led into court at 9:45 o'clock, by Lieutenant Allan C. Smith and Deputy Sheriff Hovey Low, each of whom had a wrestler's grip on one of the prisoner's wrists.

He was seated, with his back to the rail forming the lawyers' enclosure, directly at the center of the room. Squarely in front of him was the defense counsel table. To his right was the prosecution table, where Attorney General Wilentz, his chief assistant, Judge George K. Large, Prosecutor Anthony M. Hauck, Jr., and Assistant Attorney General Joseph Lanigan were already seated.

Hauptmann's own attorneys, Edward J. Reilly, C. Lloyd Fisher, Egbert Rosecrans, and Frederick A. Pope, gathered in front of him. The prisoner seemed cheerful as they talked to him—alert, occasionally smiling, rather welcoming than fearing his ordeal.

The babel in the court room was hushed when Justice Thomas W. Trenchard, gowned in a black silk robe, took his seat at the bench, and the court crier droned his age-old formula—"hear ye, hear ye, all manner of persons having business before this court of Oyer and Terminer"—declaring the session open.

The court settled down to the tedious business of selecting a jury. When darkness came, four women and six men had been admitted to the jury box, and only two more remained to be chosen from the fifty remaining talesmen.

Charles Walton, first to be seated, was a man of forty-four, unsmiling, slight of build and quick of movement, with graying hair and a sharp profile. He was married, and had four children.

"One of my best friends," Defense Counsel C. Lloyd Fisher thought with satisfaction as Walton, who was to become foreman of the jury, took his seat.

Both sides appeared satisfied with Mrs. Rosie Pill, fifty-eight years old and a grandmother. Mrs. Pill looked as one would have a grandmother look, kindly, gentle, understanding. She became Juror Number Two.

Mrs. Verna Snyder was the wife of a cross-roads blacksmith at Centerville, New Jersey. Sleepily, she said she "wasn't sure" she had scruples about capital punishment, but she was willing to determine the case on the evidence. She weighed two hundred and sixty-one pounds when she took her seat as Juror Number Three and surveyed the audience through somnolent eyes. She was to gain thirty pounds more during her incarceration as a juror.

Charles F. Snyder, a grave-faced farmer from Clinton, New Jersey, was another unsmiling citizen to pass the inquisition of the lawyers and join the first three in the jury box. He seemed fascinated by his nearness to the prisoner, and gazed intently upon him as he took his seat.

Mrs. Ethel Stockton, brown haired and dimpled, a woman of twenty-nine who had had considerable experience in the law as clerk to a Clinton attorney, was accepted as Juror Number Five. Her face grew grave and white as she was sworn in.

Elmer Smith, a breezy insurance agent, dapper and versed in city ways, was seated next to Mrs. Stockton as Juror Number Six.

He was followed by a younger man who appeared to be his antithesis. While Smith was smiling, Robert Cravatt, a youth of twenty-five, was scowling. He seemed depressed by the turn of fate that brought him into the case as a juror. He was an educational advisor at a Civilian Conservation Corps camp, and a somewhat lonesome young man.

Philip Hockenbury, a sixty-year-old farmer from Clinton township, whose frosty moustache gave his lean and tanned face a somewhat bedraggled appearance, and who admitted to being "very poor," was accepted as Juror Number Eight.

George Voorhees, another farmer, of sentimental nature, fond of playing old-time melodies on a wheezy gramophone, and despising publicity, became the ninth juror in the box.

Mrs. May F. Brelsford, the only native of Flemington to be chosen for the solemn duty, was well and favorably known for her intellectual attainments. She was a civic leader, interested in women's clubs, interested in social research, alert and capable. She became Juror Number Ten.

On the following morning, January 3rd, the jury was completed with the selection of two more.

Liscom C. Case, a retired farmer, widower, and sufferer from chronic heart attacks—he was later to give Mr. Justice Trenchard grave concern because of his ill health—was chosen without long questioning by either side.

And finally, Howard V. Biggs, a one-time bookkeeper, slight, colorless in countenance, and prone to smile upon occasion, completed the jury as Number Twelve.

It was a substantial jury, a cross-section of the life of Hunterdon County, where there are more farmers than bookkeepers, and more housewives than women law clerks.

Clerk of Court Lloyd Fell announced to the court the completion of the jury. Attorney General David T. Wilentz rose to make the opening address for the State of New Jersey.

Lean, ascetic, olive-complexioned, a touch of the Savonarola in his vivid pronouncements, the Attorney General presented a marked contrast to his opponent, the rotund and florid Edward J. Reilly. Bitter where his adversary was suave, sneering where Reilly was bland, sarcastic where his enemy would have been naïve and ingenuous, Wilentz put fire into that opening.

"It was more of a summation than an opening," Reilly declared afterward. But at any rate, while the reporters were sending out startling bulletins, based on the more spectacular declarations of the Attorney General, the contentions of the State were placed before the jury in their most dramatic form.

"This is the first prosecution I have ever undertaken in any criminal case," Wilentz told the jury. "I came here because it was my duty as Attorney General, not because I wanted to prosecute a man for murder."

"This child," he declared, "was killed by a crushing blow, delivered almost at the very instant of the abduction."

That statement provided Bulletin Number One for the newspapers. It was followed by even more sensational statements, delivered in a mixture of bombast and bathos.

Wilentz said the kidnaper had entered the Lindbergh nursery by means of a ladder discovered later, some seventy feet away from the house; that the ladder had broken under the combined weight of the abductor and the thirty-pound infant, perhaps throwing the kidnaper and his burden against the wall of the house.

He pictured the kidnaper, attempting to flee from the estate, finding the ladder and the child—"now dead"—too difficult to carry, and abandoning the less important burden. He described how the criminal "ripped and tore away the baby's sleeping suit, even before he had left the Lindbergh grounds," and then, in the darkness of the Sourlands, "hastily scraped a grave and buried the body."

"We will prove to you, beyond a reasonable doubt," he declared, "that the man who committed this crime was Bruno Richard Hauptmann, and that it was Hauptmann alone."

There ensued a brief and uninteresting interlude, in which Walter E. Roberts, a county engineer, identified and described maps he had drawn of the Lindbergh home, the estate, the Hopewell region, and the entire state. The jury appeared little interested. During Wilentz's address it had been entranced.

Mrs. Anne Morrow Lindbergh's name was called. Immediately, from the long press benches in front, there came a snow-storm of white copy-paper, passed from hand to hand by rows of messenger boys, and thence to fleet runners outside who rushed, three steps at a time, up the stairs to the wire rooms. Mrs. Lindbergh took the oath and seated herself in the ancient witness chair, which had been ironed securely to its base to prevent desecration by souvenir hunters.

She made a pathetic picture as she sat there, awaiting the questioning, and the Attorney General's voice was very low as he asked her about her domestic life at the Hopewell manor. She replied in firm but not loud tones, and in the silent court room her well-modulated voice and its cultured accent rose to the last seat in the gallery. She folded her small, gloved hands in her lap and watched the Attorney General through unblinking brown eyes.

She related the scenes at Hopewell on the day of the kidnaping, and explained her unfortunate decision not to take the baby to his grandmother's home in Englewood because of his illness. She told of her telephone message to Nursemaid Betty Gow, advising her of her change in plans, and bidding her return to the Hopewell residence.

Then, in a lower voice, she recalled how she and Betty Gow had put Charles to bed, rubbing his chest with oil and dressing him in an extra undergarment, hastily made by the nurse from an old petticoat.

The next four hours, she said, were uneventful. The Colonel made his unexpected arrival. There was dinner. Betty Gow moved about the house in her usual pursuits. Mrs. Lindbergh prepared for bed, while the Colonel retired to his study, just beneath the nursery.

Twice, during the recital of the scenes that followed, Mrs. Lindbergh appeared close to tears. The first occasion was when she described how Betty Gow called to her and asked her, at ten o'clock, whether the Colonel had the baby, and the subsequent discovery of the empty crib. The second occasion was when Attorney General Wilentz placed in her hands the baby's sleeping garment, which had become such a material piece of evidence in the State's case, and asked her if she could identify it.

She appeared to fondle the garment for a moment. She passed her hands over it and hesitated. Then she looked straight at the Attorney General and said, "Yes, that is the sleeping garment in which he was put to bed." Her eyes were moist but she did not cry.

"There will be no cross-examination, Mrs. Lindbergh," said the chief defense counsel courteously, and the witness returned to him a look of gratitude.

At the outset of the trial, Wilentz had made it plain that the State would pursue an orderly, chronological course in the presentation of its case. Its plan was to place a sequence of pictures before the jury which would begin with the day of the kidnaping and end with the completed investigation of the prisoner, after his arrest in the Bronx.

Thus far, the fact of the kidnaping had been established, and that was all. The State now proposed to go a step further and show by what means the crime was accomplished. Colonel Charles A. Lindbergh was called to the stand.

The first chapter of the Colonel's story, told in a firm crisp voice while the witness leaned forward in his chair and gazed only at his questioner, was mainly corroborative only of his wife's evidence. But from the moment he told how he rushed, fear-stricken, out of doors with his rifle, the tempo of his story changed, becoming more breathless and dramatic with each succeeding incident.

Hauptmann, too, from his seat between his two guards, was leaning far forward and watching the Colonel. His back was motionless and his eyes were stolid, far sunken in their hollow sockets. Only a quickening of the pulse, a little spasmodic jerking in the muscles around his lips, and a slight reddening of his neck above the neckband of his shirt indicated any deep emotion.

When court recessed for the night, Colonel Lindbergh had reached the moment of his first negotiations, through "Jafsie," with the supposed kidnapers of his child.

The trial reached its first real climax on Friday, January 4th, when Colonel Lindbergh, resuming the witness stand, told of his authorization to Dr. Condon to pay the extor-

tioner $50,000. He told how clerks at the banking firm of
J. P. Morgan and Company had counted out the ransom
money, with an extra $20,000 for good measure in case the
kidnaper insisted upon the extra payment. He told how Dr.
Condon persisted in his belief that the extortioner would be
satisfied with the $50,000 he had first demanded, and how
—after the package had been made up—$20,000 of it was
taken out and set aside.

"We took out all the $50 bills," he said. Then came his
story of the ride to St. Raymond's cemetery in the Bronx,
alone with Dr. Condon after the protestations of the police
had been overruled. He told how he parked his automobile
while Dr. Condon went across the street to the cemetery
fence, for his fateful meeting with the kidnaper. He related
the moment of brief delay and his own disappointment, and
then told of the strange voice from over the cemetery fence—

"Doctor—over here, Doctor!"

The spectators leaned forward in their seats expectantly,
and a deep flush spread over Hauptmann's ordinarily pale
face.

"Have you heard that voice since?" the Attorney General
asked.

"I have."

"Whose voice was it?"

"It was the voice of Bruno Richard Hauptmann!"

Thus dramatically, almost at the outset of the trial, came
the first of a series of identifications that, some tenuously and
some directly, were to associate the former German machine-
gunner with the extortion plot and, afterward, with the kidnaping and murder.

Through Colonel Lindbergh the State laid the entire foundation for its case—a skeleton which was to be provided with flesh and clothes by Dr. Condon and scores of others, and finally emerge as the complete, living figure of Bruno Hauptmann.

Through the Colonel's testimony, the prosecution proved there were blurred, muddy footprints in the nursery—proof that the kidnaping was not an "inside job," as insinuated by the defense. Through him it proved that the kidnap ladder was alien to his property, that it was brought to his estate from outside. Through him it placed in evidence the wrappings of a package in which his child's sleeping suit had been returned, with handwriting which experts were later to testify was that of the defendant. And finally, through him, the State established the *corpus delicti,* proof that the child had been murdered and that it was the child of Colonel Lindbergh and none other.

At a press conference held the evening before, in the crowded, smoke-filled offices of C. Lloyd Fisher, Edward J. Reilly had announced his intention of "sparing no one—not even Colonel Lindbergh—in any future cross-examination."

"He, like every other witness, will be made the subject of the most searching investigation," he said. "There are many things in his story that require examination, and I'm not going to handle him with kid gloves, as I did Mrs. Lindbergh."

The "Bull of Brooklyn" made good his promise. But in doing so, he gave the prosecution its first knowledge of the line of defense along which the legal battle was to be fought. His defense was to throw before the jury the inference that everybody and anybody in the world save Hauptmann committed the crime, a defense intended, if not to clear Hauptmann, then to cast suspicion on every major figure in the drama, including Dr. Condon, Betty Gow, Violet Sharpe, Henry ("Red") Johnson, Oliver Whately, and a host of other persons, now dead, who could not be summoned from the grave to bear witness.

So Reilly's questioning resolved itself into the following interrogations:

"Didn't you ever, Colonel, suspect that someone in your employment participated in this kidnaping?"

"Didn't you ever realize that the child could have been carried downstairs and out the front door?"

"Did you ever have any personal enemies?"

"Didn't you at one time believe this was the work of a gang?"

"Didn't you think it peculiar that an outsider should have known the baby would be in Hopewell on March 1, 1932?"

"Don't you know that the police blundered from the outset?"

The barrage of questions failed to shake the equanimity of the Colonel. He leaned forward, the better to deliver his replies, and answered with a smile on his lips. He gave a contemptuous "no!" to each question.

Reilly launched his first broadside against Dr. Condon and was stopped short. He had been referring to Jafsie's insertion of advertisements in the *Bronx Home News*.

"Did it ever occur to you, Colonel?" the chief defense counsel asked, "that a master mind in the crime could have both written and answered those advertisements himself?"

Colonel Lindbergh appeared to consider the question thoughtfully for a moment. He looked across the court room and out the window. Then his gaze returned to the cross-examiner, and he said in a crisp voice with a twist of scorn to his lips:

"The thought is—inconceivable!"

Reilly pursued his questioning little further. He did enquire whether the Colonel knew Dr. Condon had made a hobby of studying "theosophical cults." Colonel Lindbergh denied knowing any such thing, and was released. But before he left the witness chair, the prosecution asked him one more question.

"Do you believe Bruno Richard Hauptmann kidnaped your son?"

"I do," he said. Both the question and answer were made in such a low voice that only a few of the scribes sitting in the front rows heard him.

Mrs. Elsie Whately, widow of the late estimable butler, Oliver Whately, was then called to the stand and afforded a momentary lightening of the tragic scene. There was a gleam of righteous indignation in her eyes as she sat herself on the edge of the witness chair, for in her mind was the innuendo planted a little while before, by Edward J. Reilly, when he made the suggestion that Ollie Whately might have been friendly with Violet Sharpe.

"You are the widow of the late Oliver Whately?" the prosecutor asked.

"Yes," she said, lifting her voice until its shrill tones rebounded from the high ceiling, "I am, and I'd like to say further, if I may be permitted, that my husband *never* went out with Violet Sharpe!"

Laughter swept the court room. Justice Trenchard pounded for order. The answer was ordered stricken from the record as "unresponsive." But Mrs. Whately settled herself comfortably back in the chair with a happy smile on her countenance. The Whately honor had been vindicated.

Elsie Whately's testimony was, for the most part, corroborative of the previous evidence. She did, however, add a homely picture to the below-stairs life of the Lindbergh home, and told how Betty Gow had fashioned a crude undergarment for the baby from an old petticoat on the day of the kidnaping. The undergarment had been identified as found on the child's body.

Court was adjourned at that point for the week-end. And during that week-end, the town of Flemington was to learn something of the penalties of fame. Saturday was a quiet day, except for the busier of the newspaper correspondents who had to match rumor for rumor, rush about the county running down fantastic stories about "surprise witnesses," "new mystery witnesses," and "startling new evidence" that was bound to clear Bruno Richard Hauptmann or send him to the chair, and write long and detailed accounts of what had gone before together with predictions as to what was to follow.

Sunday found the highways leading into Flemington blocked by a parade of vehicles and a procession of pedestrians that extended almost to New York City, moving at the rate of three miles an hour and producing a traffic snarl that a hundred State Police were unable to untangle. The sight-

seers came from New York and Philadelphia, from Trenton
and Camden, from every large and small city within a radius
of seventy-five miles. They swarmed through the Union
Hotel and formed an immovable mass in front of the court
house. Nearly five thousand of them penetrated to the actual
court room.

They tramped up the stairs and through the telegraph
wire rooms, where guards had to restrain them from cutting
away strands of cable "to take home as souvenirs."

They marched down the aisles of the court, plumped
themselves down in Rosie Pill's chair, sat for a brief instant
in the seat that had been honored by Bruno Hauptmann,
squatted a moment in the witness chair, and then moved out
to the packed street again, in an endless chain. It was after
midnight before the last of the spectators had departed and
the town was quiet, save for the clattering of the telegraph
instruments sending out the Monday morning stories of the
correspondents.

The episode was significant of the public's hysterical re-
action to the Hauptmann trial. It was the first indication that
dignity was in flight and that the circus was coming to town.

Yet those who drove into Flemington that Sunday and
went home with the glow of satisfaction they derived from
having sat in Hauptmann's, or Justice Trenchard's, or
Charles A. Lindbergh's chair, were little different from many
of their brothers and sisters of the so-called upper, and presumably more restrained, classes.

For during the week-end Sheriff John H. Curtiss was
swamped with applications for tickets. The applications
came from state and United States Senators, from Broadway

actresses and Hollywood stars, from night club owners and New York men-about-town, from society women, social reformers and ministers, from professors and prostitutes, from preachers and publicans, and from radio artists ranging from concert singers down to crooners.

Unfortunately for the working press, it appeared, most of these celebrities managed, in one way or another, to obtain their tickets. All Broadway arrived early Monday morning, to witness a drama such as was never conceived or produced in New York or Hollywood.

CHAPTER EIGHTEEN

BETTY GOW WAS SOMETHING OF A SPITFIRE. HER SCOTTISH DE-
termination not to be browbeaten by Edward J. Reilly—or
anybody else—had been fired by the repeated insinuations of
the chief defense counsel that she had had a hand in spread-
ing knowledge that made it easy for the kidnaper to make
his raid on the Lindbergh nursery and escape unscathed.

Miss Gow, patterning her voice and accents after the culti-
vated tones of Anne Morrow Lindbergh, responded politely
to the questions of Attorney General Wilentz. She reviewed
the events of March 1, 1932, corroborated Mrs. Lindbergh's
story of the evening of the kidnaping, and repeated, in detail, her story of finding the vacant crib.

Her testimony reached a climax when she was asked:
"And then, after the child could not be found, what did
Colonel Lindbergh do?"

"He said, 'Anne, they have stolen our baby!'" A hush fell
over the court room, and Colonel Lindbergh's face flushed.

The torn and stained garments that were clinging to the
child's body when it was found were passed to her, one by
one, and one by one identified as having been worn by the
infant on the night Betty Gow and Mrs. Lindbergh tucked
him in his crib and fastened the blankets down with two
large safety pins. She told about attaching the thumb guards
to the sleeping suit.

"A month later," she said, "at a short distance from the house, I picked up one of the thumb guards, lying by the side of the walk."

Her declaration was of vital importance to the State's case against Hauptmann. It afforded proof that the sleeping suit, according to Wilentz, had been "ripped from the body before the kidnaper left the Lindbergh estate."

Reilly, who rose to thunderous heights whenever he cross-examined a servant, a policeman, a menial, or any person from the humbler walks of life, undertook the cross-examination. He was in top form.

Upon her admission that she once worked in Detroit, he asked her whether she knew any members of the notorious "Purple gang." She replied with an indignant "no!" He asked her if she hadn't dropped the thumb guard herself at the place she found it. She shouted "no!" He asked her if she hadn't turned the lights in the nursery on and off "as a signal to someone outside." She uttered a scornful "no." Then he took up the issue of Henry ("Red") Johnson.

"You were very fond of "Red" Johnson, wurrent you?" (Reilly invariably pronounces "weren't" as "wurrent.")

"You mean *Mister* Johnson," Miss Gow retorted severely. "Yes, I was fond of *Mister* Johnson."

"And this 'Red' Johnson——"

"*Mister* Johnson!"

"Mr. Johnson knew you wurrent to be in Englewood that night?"

"Certainly. I had telephoned to Mr. Johnson, but I couldn't reach him, and he called me up that evening."

Betty Gow gave her inquisitor back retort after retort, and

finally, so spirited did her conduct become that the court was moved to waves of polite applause, and the bailiffs had to step in and stop the noise. She left the witness stand unscathed, and perhaps with an enhanced reputation.

There came to the stand a succession of minor characters, policemen for the most part, who reviewed the events of the night of March 1, 1932, and the following frantic days. Of these witnesses, by far the most important was Frank A. Kelly, State Police fingerprint expert, who described the shapeless footprints left in the nursery, the single footprint found beneath the nursery window, "which might have been made by a Number Nine shoe covered with a stocking," and the utter absence of fingerprints on the woodwork of the nursery or on the so-called kidnap ladder.

The soil in the blurred footprints in the nursery was like that of the ground outside. Thus the State proved that *the kidnaper had come in to the house from the outside and the child had not been passed out to him, or carried down the stairs.*

On Tuesday, January 8th, the State produced its first "surprise witness," with the calling of Amandus Hochmuth.

Amandus Hochmuth was a spry old gentleman of eighty-seven, long a resident of Hopewell, whose chief occupation in life was gazing out upon a lonely road waiting for something to happen. He was very seldom gratified by witnessing any event worth recording on the tablets of his mind, but at noontime of March 1, 1932——

"I saw a car coming around the corner, pretty good speed, and I expected it to turn over in the ditch. And as the car was about twenty-five feet away from me, the man in there looked out of the window like this . . . and he glared at me as if he saw a ghost."

"And that man you saw—is he in this room?" the Attorney General asked.

"Yes . . . alongside the trooper there."

The old man stretched a long finger in the direction of Bruno Richard Hauptmann, and as he did so, the lights in the court room dimmed and flickered out. Melodrama. Heavy black clouds above and swirling fog around the court house threw the room into semi-darkness.

"Is there any reason for extinguishing the lights?" Wilentz shouted. "At any rate, do you mind stepping down and showing us the man?"

Hochmuth eased his rheumatic limbs from the witness chair and groped his way past the prosecution table, to lay a hand on the prisoner.

"Right here," he said.

Upstairs, working with candlelight, the operators were sending frantic bulletins signaling the first positive identification of Bruno Hauptmann in Hopewell on the day of the crime.

Hauptmann's tall frame bent over his guardian trooper toward his wife, and made his first comment on the evidence.

"*Der Alter ist Verrückt!*" he said. "The old man is crazy."

But cross-examination failed to shake the old man in any essential of his story, and attempts by Reilly to make him admit that his eyesight was poor, that he had a weak memory, that he was subject to hallucinations, that his health was failing and with it his mind, could not beat from him any

damaging admission as to his credibility. The State then
turned to the home-made, three-section ladder found on the
Lindbergh premises several hours after the kidnaping.

Frederick A. Pope, associate defense counsel, fought well
and ably to keep the ladder out of evidence. He pointed out
that the ladder had been taken apart, piece by piece, for
examination in Washington and elsewhere; that nails had
been drawn from it and put back—without proof that the
same nails were replaced—and that the State had not traced
its possession through many hands, since the day of its discovery in the dewy grass of the Lindbergh estate.

"And finally," he declared, "there is absolutely no connection either by circumstance or by direct evidence between
this ladder and the accused."

Attorney General Wilentz, angry at the temporary block-
ing of his program, responded indignantly.

"Why, we will run this ladder right into Hauptmann," he
shouted. But he was forced to retrace all the steps taken by
the investigating officers, from the moment it was found
until the moment it was brought into court and placed
against the wall behind the witness chair.

Lieutenant John J. Sweeney of the Newark police offered
the most important testimony in this phase. He told how the
rails of the bottom section fitted exactly into two depressions
in the turf beneath the nursery window. Of still more significance was his story of the various experiments he conducted,
first with the three sections of the ladder joined together,
and then with the lower two sections. When three sections
were joined by the dowel pins and the completed ladder was
placed against the wall, it reached a point above the window.

But when only the lower two sections were used, the ladder reached to within thirty inches of the window sill.

And at that point, he found two marks on the wall, corresponding exactly to the tops of the ladder rails. The ladder had slipped, perhaps when it broke, and had scraped away the paint. Microscopic examination of these marks *showed they contained fragments of wood.*

Abruptly, Wilentz turned away from the ladder and called to the stand Joseph A. Perrone, Bronx taxicab driver. When Perrone settled himself in the witness chair, the prisoner's muscles seemed to stiffen. Seated within eight inches of Hauptmann—I could have touched him—I saw the color mount from beneath his collar, and rise to flush his normally pale, flat cheeks. He twisted in his seat. He appeared to be struggling with his emotions.

Perrone testified he had been stopped on the night of March 12, 1932, by a man who appeared beneath an arc light in Mosholu Parkway, the Bronx, and that the man who stopped him gave him a dollar and a letter to carry to Dr. John F. Condon's home.

"Who is the man that gave you that envelope?" Wilentz demanded.

"Bruno Richard Hauptmann," the taxicab driver swore.

"Come down and point him out, please."

Perrone leaped from the stand, strode past the prosecution table, and clapped his hand—hard—on the prisoner's shoulder. "This is the man," he said.

Hauptmann's hollow eyes blazed with anger. He leaned forward, as though to meet a blow, and spat out the words, "You're a liar!" His guards seized his wrists. In the uproar, the official stenographers failed to set down the interruption in their transcript. Reilly insisted the words should go into the record.

"I didn't hear them," said Justice Trenchard.

"Five or six people heard it," Reilly expostulated. "The press heard it. It should be in the record."

The justice accorded the chief defense counsel permission to bring the press as witnesses, if he cared to correct the transcript, and Reilly pressed the issue no further.

When Perrone had been dismissed, after a searching cross-examination, James J. O'Brien, another Bronx taxicab driver was called. He related how, on the evening of March 12, 1932, Perrone showed him the letter and the dollar, and told him he was taking it to Dr. Condon's home.

The letter, of course, was one of the fourteen ransom notes that reached Colonel Lindbergh or Dr. Condon between March 1st and April 2nd.

Gradually, the State had been entering into the second phase of its case—the Bronx extortion. It was laying the groundwork for the appearance of its star witness, the grizzled Jafsie, who was in court already, sitting next to Colonel Lindbergh and awaiting in pleasant anticipation his day in the limelight.

The two friends, who had driven with Dr. Condon to Hopewell on the night the Doctor received his first communication accepting him as a go-between, testified briefly. They were P. Milton Gaglio, a tailor, and Max Rosenhain, a restaurant proprietor from whose establishment the fateful telephone call to the Lindbergh home had been made. Then Al Reich was called.

Reich, once called "The Adonis of the Prize Ring," a retired boxer who long ago became devoted to Dr. Condon as a squire to his knight, testified to Jafsie's first meeting with the Bronx extortioner in the gloom of Van Cortlandt park, near Woodlawn cemetery.

Reich described the "paper chase" that led himself and Condon to Woodlawn cemetery, and told how he saw a man "come down off the cemetery gate——"

"And when you say you saw a man come down off the gate, what do you mean?" asked Wilentz.

"He came down after coming up on it from the inside, to come out over the gate."

"Did you see him jump off?"

"Yes, I saw him jump off."

The witness told how the mysterious visitor ran away, and how Dr. Condon gave chase, and finally how he watched the two sit down on a park bench and engage in conversation for more than an hour.

It was in that conversation that the first outline of how the ransom money was to be delivered was given to Colonel Lindbergh's emissary.

At dawn, on the morning after Reich had paved the way for introduction of the State's star witness, there were a thousand would-be spectators massed around the Hunterdon County court house, held in restraint by a new detail of State Police. Many of the visitors had been there for hours, wrapped in blankets against the cold, and stamping their numbed feet on the ground. One, a woman, proudly announced she had come all the way from California to see Jafsie on the witness stand. By common consent it was recognized that this day might mark the turning point in the case of Bruno Richard Hauptmann and that upon Jafsie's testimony might depend his death or freedom.

That Dr. Condon had enjoyed his prominence and reveled in his fame was unquestioned. That he believed he was doing his duty "as a patriotic American citizen" also was not open to contradiction. But he had told so many different stories, particularly to the inquisitive press, that when he went to the witness stand, not even some members of the prosecuting staff knew exactly what his testimony would be.

Hauptmann, meanwhile, had begun to show signs of the mental strain he was undergoing. Each day his eyes appeared a little more sunken. Where he had sat stolidly, motionless, without a quiver, through much of the testimony, it was evident that he was beginning to dread each day's appearance in court. On the night before Condon was called to testify against him, he spent restless hours pacing his cell. He was white when the officers led him in, on the morning of March 9th, to listen to the evidence of the Patriarch of the Bronx.

Dr. Condon, expansive, voluble almost to the point of being garrulous, recited the long list of his accomplishments and his college degrees as a prelude to his testimony. Then he told of the early negotiations—how, in the interest of justice and to see the kidnaped child "returned to his mother's arms," he had offered his services.

The Doctor related, in dime novel fashion, the events that led up to his meeting at Woodlawn cemetery with the extortioner. He told of the ransom notes he had received and identified them. He described his journey to the cemetery with his body-guard, Al Reich, and graphically portrayed how "like an athlete in a German turner society," the man he went to meet came swinging down from the cemetery gate and then ran away at the approach of the guard.

"I ran after him and caught him," he said, with evident pride in his wind and speed—at seventy-four years of age.

Separated only by the length of the park bench, he recounted, the extortioner and he talked about the case. Nor could the good doctor refrain, he said, from reading the man a little homily on the virtue of honesty, and a brief lecture on "what his mother would think."

Jafsie reiterated his previous statement that the man called himself "John," that he had a bad cough, that he seemed to be shivering in the March cold, and that his chief concern was only for immediate payment—cash.

"And who was the man, this 'John,' to whom you talked?" the Attorney General asked.

"He was Bruno Richard Hauptmann," Dr. Condon declared firmly.

Hauptmann's body stiffened again, but he made no movement. I saw his neck muscles grow taut, and color creep up his neck and into his sallow cheeks. He was restraining himself with difficulty. Once more the snow-storm of copy swept through the court room to the runners, and the newspapers had their evening headlines—"Jafsie Identifies Hauptmann."

Through that day and on into the next day's session of court, Dr. Condon continued his story. He described the return of the sleeping suit and how the final arrangements were made for payment of the ransom money. He told how, at the last moment, he had insisted that $20,000 be taken

from the $70,000 prepared by the House of Morgan for
Colonel Lindbergh, on the chance that he could talk the extortioner into reducing his price.

The melodramatic recitation of the ride to St. Raymond's
cemetery, broken at intervals by the discovery of new directions for finding the extortioner, was received by a hushed
and breathless court room. While the prisoner stirred un-
easily, Dr. Condon filled in the outline of the shadowy figure
he had met at the cemetery fence, told how he passed the
$50,000 to the swindler—after a ten minute delay while the
extortioner "went to get a receipt"—and once more identified the negotiator as Bruno Richard Hauptmann.

His story paralleled that of Colonel Lindbergh in every essential, including the opening of the final note containing
what he supposed were directions for finding the kidnaped
child on the "boad Nelly," and the futile flight to Vineyard
Sound with Colonel Lindbergh that ended with the unmistakable conclusion that they had been swindled.

The old man concluded his story and was released to the
ungentle examination of Edward J. Reilly—Reilly who had
more than once proclaimed openly his belief that Condon
was "part and parcel of the conspiracy to defraud the Colonel out of his money."

Condon was not afraid of the empurpled chief defense
counsel. At the outset of his testimony he joked and swapped
badinage with him.

"Would you say I am a heavyweight?" Reilly asked, during the Doctor's discussion of athletes and athletics.

Condon hopped down from the stand, felt of Reilly's arms,

sized him up and said, "Yes, you are a heavyweight—so physically, at least, we start on even terms."

The chief defense counsel carried the old man back over his story and at intervals hurled new insinuations at him. He was particularly insistent upon knowing whether the Doctor had ever known Henry ("Red") Johnson, whether he had been associated with a vague "City Island gang," whether he had ever been interested in a theosophical cult— which Condon laughed to scorn—and whether he was the "John Condon who took from the New York Public library, shortly before the kidnaping, a book on mystic symbols."

Reilly was shooting in the dark, for the most part. He had been told that such a book, possibly containing the symbol used at the bottom of the ransom notes, had been taken from the library by one "John Condon." He had not been told, however, that the name of the man who had taken the book was not Condon but "Condax," and that Condax lived in Philadelphia. Naturally, his arrow, shot so blindly in the air, fell to earth harmless. Condon left the witness chair without a dent in his story.

It remained for Colonel Henry C. Breckinridge, Colonel Lindbergh's friend and legal advisor, to end forever any thought, suggestion or whisper that Dr. Condon was himself involved on the criminal side of the case.

Colonel Breckinridge revealed, for the first time, that he had been a guest at Dr. Condon's Bronx home, from the day Jafsie returned from Hopewell after his first mission to Colonel Lindbergh, until after the ransom had been paid—that he had counseled with Condon, participated in the negotiations, advised him as to procedure, and in fact taken a major rôle in all the strange activities that followed receipt of the first Condon note.

His most striking evidence, evidence that tore to pieces any defense theory that Dr. Condon himself received any of the money or was the man who instigated its payment, was that——

"Dr. Condon was opposed to payment of the ransom money except on a C.O.D. basis—upon return of the baby. He did not want us to take the chance. He was overruled by the rest of us."

He also testified that the police had wanted to surround St. Raymond's cemetery, to go with Colonel Lindbergh and Jafsie and seize the extortioner, but that they, too, had been required to keep their hands off "in the interest of the safe return of the child."

When, on cross-examination, Colonel Breckinridge was asked why, "as an officer of the court and the law of New York," he had not insisted that the police "do their duty," with Reilly's insinuation that he was violating the law and perhaps compounding a felony, Breckinridge straightened himself in the witness chair and declared, firmly:

"I considered I had a higher duty."

When Colonel Breckinridge stepped down, he had completely vindicated the old man of the Bronx who, through a strange set of circumstances, had entered the case and become one of its principal characters. He had settled, it was hoped, for all time, the questioning and suspicions, the insinuations and innuendoes, some printed and some spoken, that had plagued the patriarch for nearly three years. It was Jafsie's day of triumph.

He was a remarkable old man, eccentric it is true, but with an eccentricity that was born of ingenuous, child-like honesty and a patriotic courage that is rare in a sophisticated age.

When he emerged from the court house, accompanied by a State trooper, there were cheers from the throng outside, to which snatches of his testimony had been relayed, and he beamed his appreciation, waving his hands cheerily to his applauders. If there had been an American flag handy, he would have waved that, too.

Inside the court house, the State prepared to enter the next most damaging phase of its evidence against Bruno Richard Hauptmann. Great black and white charts, like magnified school slates, were being unrolled in front of the jury. Thick books of photographs were stacked on the counsel table. Fourteen letters, on cheap notepaper, the writing protected by celluloid covering, were placed in front of Attorney General Wilentz.

These were the ransom notes, and it was the government's intention to place them in the powerful hands of Bruno Hauptmann—to prove that his crude fist penned them all, from the note found in the nursery on the night of the kidnaping down to the very last communication which gave the false information that the child was on the "boad Nelly."

To trace these notes to the hand of Hauptmann, the State of New Jersey had gathered from East, South and West, eight of the most noted handwriting experts in the United States. Each of these experts, given ample time to examine the ransom notes, had been required to arrive at his conclusions independently. There was no collusion. Each was to weigh his decisions by the measure of his own experience. They had been instructed particularly not to communicate their findings to others than the Attorney General and members of the prosecuting staff.

It was Friday, January 11th, before the first of these experts went to the stand, and with a pointer such as might be used by a singing master, began reading a lecture to the jury on handwriting and "the unconscious habits that inevitably will betray a man."

CHAPTER NINETEEN

WHEN ALBERT S. OSBORN, WHITE-HAIRED AND SOMEWHAT DEAF, went to the witness chair to begin his long explanation of the peculiarities of handwriting that, in his opinion, proved Bruno Richard Hauptmann wrote the ransom notes, Edward J. Reilly turned to his colleagues and whispered, "this isn't the battle of the century, but the battle of the centenarians."

Osborn was no centenarian, but at seventy-four he was well up with Dr. Condon, Amandus Hochmuth and others advanced in years who had testified against the prisoner. His deafness he overcame by using an electrical apparatus with a small microphone, held in front of him when he was questioned. He testified in the loud voice common to those who cannot measure the strength of their own tones, and what he had to say was delivered with a positive accent that left a strong impression on the jury. And he read one of the most engrossing lectures ever heard in a court of law on the art and science of identifying disputed writings.

Before him he had thirty pieces of script, including fourteen ransom notes and sixteen acknowledged specimens from the hand of Hauptmann. The script was divided into three classifications—the disputed ransom notes, the "conceded writings," such as Hauptmann's automobile license applications, and the "request writings," *i.e.,* writing done in the police station by the prisoner, under the dictation of the authorities.

"My opinion," said Osborn at the beginning of his testimony, "is that the ransom notes were all written by the writer of the various papers signed 'Bruno Richard Hauptmann.'"

The elderly handwriting expert then went on to explain how he linked the ransom notes, the "conceded" writing and the "request" writing done by Hauptmann to the same origin.

"I found," he said, "that they were connected with each other in a large number of ways, seven or eight different ways. A number of these ways were outside of the question of handwriting."

The crude symbol, the red and blue interlocking circles with the three holes found at the bottom of each ransom note, unmistakably proved a common origin, Osborn said. Then he demonstrated how, if these symbols were superimposed one upon the other, the three holes matched exactly, and that when these superimposed symbols were held to the light, "you can see right through the holes."

He left the inference that the symbol had been made by some crude instrument which punched the holes through a pad of paper, one sheet of which was torn off whenever the extortioner wanted to send a new communication.

The second connecting link was the misspelling of many words. Some of the more glaring mistakes appeared commonly in the "request" writings, the expert pointed out. Among these misspellings were:

"Note" for "not"; "gut" for "good"; "mony" for "money";

"singnature" for "signature"; "boad" for "boat"; and "anyding" for "anything."

Osborn called particular attention to the writing of the letter "t" and the letter "x," both in the conceded script and the ransom notes. He showed there were 391 small "t's" in the ransom notes, all but three of which were left uncrossed, and that in Hauptmann's writings nearly every "t" was uncrossed.

Of the tell-tale letter "x," Osborn said Hauptmann had invented a form of writing the letter which was wholly individual and highly characteristic. No other man in the world ever made an "x" like it. It was formed by writing a peculiar symbol that resembled a double "e."

Another habitual error made by the prisoner, both in the ransom notes and the "request" and "conceded" writings, was the formation of the letter "y," which appeared generally like an un-dotted "j."

Hauptmann was again linked—by a hyphen—to the writing of the ransom notes. It was his custom, both in the writing he did under the direction, or compulsion, of the New York police, to write the name of the city "New-York." The hyphen appeared not only on the ransom notes, but on his automobile license application and in the script dictated to him for comparison.

It was evident, too, that Hauptmann had trouble with the letters "th" and "gh," whenever they occur together in the English language. Invariably he wrote "hte" for "the," and in such words as "right" or "light," he ended with the transposed letters, thus—"ihgt." He had once received a summons for "passing red lihgt," he had naively informed the authorities when he applied for his license to drive an automobile.

Osborn concluded his testimony, on Monday, January 14th, with the declaration that the physical evidence proving Hauptmann wrote the ransom notes was "irresistible, unanswerable and overwhelming."

The jury's collective brain was then given a rest while Miss Hildegarde Alexander, a clothing model, was presented as another "surprise witness." Miss Alexander testified only briefly, but what she had to say was startling.

On an evening in March, 1932, she told the jury, while the ransom negotiations were in progress, she chanced to visit a Bronx railroad station to use the telephone. She saw Dr. Condon, some yards away, talking to a telegraph operator. And watching him, at the other side of the room, was— Bruno Richard Hauptmann.

Reilly's sneering inference that Miss Alexander was "looking for a movie contract" was laughed away, and the young woman, tall, languorous, and quite aware of her own beauty, clung to her story, unshaken by a terrific hammering by the cross-examiner.

The Hauptmann trial then resolved itself into a handwriting lecture room. For the remainder of the day—and for two further days—sensation was at ebb-tide. Attendance fell off, for the evidence was repetitious, dull and uninteresting except as it tied the defendant more completely to the authorship of the extortion letters—including the one found in the Lindbergh nursery, left there by the same man whose blurred footprints were found leading from the window to the crib.

Seven government experts dissected the ransom letters,

discussed the similarities, talked of the writer's peculiarities of expression and of forming individual characters, and agreed the notes came from Hauptmann. They were Elbridge W. Stein, John F. Tyrrell, Herbert H. Walter, Harry C. Cassidy, Dr. William M. Souder, Albert D. Osborn (son of the previous witness), and Clark Sellers.

Mr. Sellers concluded his testimony with the declaration that "Bruno Richard Hauptmann might as well have signed his name to them all."

With the handwriting experts happily off the stand, their work completed and their maps rolled away, the government moved to establish the finding of the ransom currency, hidden in Hauptmann's garage.

The murder trial fans flocked back to court demanding sensation and within an hour they were gratified. Thomas H. Sisk, youthful federal agent under whose direction the search of Bruno Hauptmann's home and garage in the Bronx was conducted, went to the witness chair.

When Sisk, who had had charge of the investigation in New York from the moment the national government intervened, sat calmly in the seat and began his matter-of-fact relation of the search, Hauptmann began to fidget. He twisted his long body nervously in the small chair between his two guards and began muttering. But it was very hot in the court room, and the handwriting experts had nearly put the audience—and the guards to sleep.

Sisk described how, under the eyes of the prisoner, he and his men hunted through the little Bronx flat without finding anything, until he noticed Hauptmann's frequent glances out of the window and towards the garage. It was the captive's nervous glances towards the spot where the ransom money was hidden, he said, that led him to order a search of the garage.

Sisk described how, digging down below the floor of the garage, he came across a crock in which, Hauptmann admitted, he had kept some of the money.

Hauptmann's hatred for Sisk, the one man in the world whom he blamed more than any other for his predicament, burst out in volcanic wrath. Hauptmann rose to his feet and his body lunged towards the witness. His face was distorted with rage and he thrust both hands in front of him, across the edge of the prosecution table.

"Mister, mister, you stop lying! You're telling stories!", he screamed.

In the court room there was tumult, the rattle of papers, the pounding of gavels, the shouts of sheriffs commanding "quiet, quiet!" Hauptmann's guards leaped for his wrists and dragged him back into his chair. Justice Trenchard bent over his bench and regarded the prisoner, who appeared on the point of sobbing.

"One moment," he said calmly. "Let me suggest to the defendant that he keep quiet. If he has any observations to make, let him make them quietly, through counsel."

Sisk's eyes blinked, but his expression never changed. Those who had written so many words about Hauptmann's "iron nerve" began to fear they were mistaken, that he was "cracking."

The prosecution was moving more rapidly now, binding up the loose ends of the net in which Hauptmann had been captured. On Thursday, January 17th, in addition to Sisk, who—together with a dozen police officials—told of demolishing the garage and finding $14,600 in ransom bills hidden away—the State proved the "corpus delicti" by William Allen, the Negro truck driver who had discovered the child's body, and by Dr. Charles H. Mitchell, the coroner's physician who conducted the autopsy. The testimony made Colonel Lindbergh bite his lips. It was the most poignant moment of the trial, if one excepts the instant when her baby's garments were thrust into Anne Morrow Lindbergh's hands for identification.

Dr. Mitchell established an important point for the State, however. He showed that "the fracture of the skull occurred while the child was alive" and that "death was instantaneous, or almost so." The importance of his evidence lay in the fact that the State of New Jersey was bound to prove that death of the child took place "during the commission of a felony" and before the completion of the burglary with which Hauptmann was charged.

Whether her husband's outburst inspired her to go and do likewise, or whether she was merely unable to check her temper, it was Mrs. Anna Hauptmann who, on the following day, delighted the fans by staging a demonstration against a witness.

An old neighbor—and former employer—testified against Hauptmann. She was Mrs. Ella Achenbach, another of the State's hidden squad of "surprise witnesses." Mrs. Achenbach, in heavy Teutonic accents, said that a few days after the kidnaping, Mr. and Mrs. Hauptmann visited her home. Hauptmann, she said, walked with a limp, and the matter was explained by Mrs. Hauptmann who said he had sprained his ankle. Beyond that, Mrs. Achenbach testified, the wife of the prisoner told her that she and her husband had "just returned from a trip."

The damaging evidence struck home. Mrs. Hauptmann, sitting at the left of the defense counsel table, drew her small frame up from her chair. Her rust-blonde hair was streaming down. Her face was white.

"Mrs. Achenbach, you are lying," she shrilled. Once more there was an uproar. Attorney General Wilentz made a shouted protest against "these demonstrations, staged or otherwise." C. Lloyd Fisher's voice was heard protesting against the insinuation that the defense was "staging" the Hauptmann family's outbursts. Justice Trenchard took a firm hand with the defendant's now subdued wife.

"Madam," he said, "don't you see the impropriety of your interrupting the trial with an outburst of this kind?"

"Yes, I see—" Mrs. Hauptmann began meekly.

"Now will you promise me and these gentlemen and the jury that you won't offend in that respect again?"

"Well, I will try to do so, but sometimes it is very hard."

"But I am asking you now if you will promise to keep quiet."

"Yes, I will."

The incident was closed by a proffered apology to the court both in behalf of Mrs. Hauptmann and her husband who had wanted, his counsel said, to apologize for his behavior of the previous day.

The State then called Cecile Barr to the stand. Mrs. Barr was the cashier at a Sheridan Square motion picture house where, on the night of November 26, 1933, the government says Hauptmann changed a ransom bill.

She recounted the incident, demonstrated how the bill was taken from her customer's watch pocket, folded so that it made eight creases, and tossed through her wicket. She paid especial attention to the man who gave her the bill, she said, because of his manner and appearance. And the man, she said firmly, was Bruno Richard Hauptmann.

On the following day she was advised by the authorities that a Lindbergh ransom bill had been turned in from her theater. She recognized the creases and recalled the features of the man who gave it to her—perfectly.

Before the conclusion of the day's testimony, the State had introduced another damning piece of evidence—the board taken from Hauptmann's bedroom closet, on which were written the address and telephone number of Dr. John F. Condon. And police officers had told how Hauptmann, in the Bronx before his extradition to New Jersey, had admitted writing the numbers "because he was interested in the case."

It had also introduced Hauptmann's brokerage accounts with the firm of Steiner, Rouse & Co., showing that his balance with the concern at the end of 1931 was $77.26, and at the end of 1933, $5,040.85.

On the following Monday, a cold little accountant with many large books took the jury through Hauptmann's financial transactions, carried them with him into brokerage offices and New York banks, and placed a total of $44,486 "in new money, all acquired after the date on which the $50,000 ransom was paid," in the hands of the Hauptmann family. Breaking down this amount (an amount, the Attorney General said, which definitely proved Hauptmann received *all* the ransom money and was hence alone in the crime) he showed the following figures:

Cash deposits in Hauptmann's or his wife's brokerage accounts after April 2, 1932,—$16,942.75.

Cash deposits in Hauptmann's or his wife's bank accounts after the same date—$9,073.25.

Mortgage which the Hauptmanns bought in 1933—$3,750.

Gold certificates identified as part of the Lindbergh ransom, found in Hauptmann's garage—$14,600.

Gold coins found in his home—$120.

The total was $44,486.

The State brought to the witness stand on the following day eleven witnesses, all of minor importance save two, who were to testify to having seen the long-legged Bronx carpenter, with his ladder, in or near Hopewell in February and on March 1, of 1932.

Millard Whited, the grizzled lumber man from the Sourlands, who had once before testified he watched Hauptmann twice, late in February, in the vicinity of the Lindbergh home, repeated his evidence and was excused after cross-examination brought out the fact that he "couldn't read enough to get much out of the newspapers."

Charles B. Rossiter, a salesman, swore he saw Hauptmann, fixing a tire, on the Princeton road at 8 o'clock in the evening before the kidnaping. He was unshaken on cross-examination. Then Attorney General Wilentz prepared for his final assault—to fulfill his pledge to "run this kidnap ladder right into Hauptmann."

Max Rauch, the Hauptmann's landlord, testified that after Hauptmann's arrest, he inspected the attic of his house and discovered one of the floor boards was missing. State Senator Joseph J. Dorn, of McCormick, S. C., testified with shaking hands that he had shipped a carload of Carolina pine to a lumber firm in New York, which had in turn sent it to the National Millwork and Lumber Co., in the Bronx—the concern to which Hauptmann had access, and from which, in December, 1931, he bought a quantity of lumber.

The way was thus paved for Arthur Koehler, the State's star witness—the man who was to place the so-called kidnap ladder in the hands of Bruno Hauptmann and prove it was the Bronx carpenter's crude handiwork.

Arthur Koehler went to the stand to tell the most fascinating detective story ever unfolded before a living jury. He told it as a scientist, with calm, cold impersonality. But when he had finished he had made his inanimate blocks of wood shout to the jury their condemnation of the prisoner.

First he took the now famous "Rail Sixteen" of the kidnap ladder and matched it against a portion of a floor board from the Hauptmann attic. He showed that "someone" had sawed the attic board into almost equal lengths—and that in grain, texture, annual rings, and the distortion of the grain caused by knots, there was proof that "Rail Sixteen" was once a part of the attic board.

He pointed out four nail holes in the ladder rail, and matched them, to a minute fraction of an inch, against four nail holes found in a joist in the Hauptmann garret, from which the board had been wrenched. He showed how nails, run through the ladder rail and into the joist "fitted perfectly, although one of them had been driven in slantingly."

"The ladder rail and the attic board were originally one piece," he declared with finality.

The defense fought strenuously to keep his evidence from the jury. It succeeded in proving that one section of the board, a little more than an inch long, was missing—forming a slight gap between the ladder rail (when it was replaced on the attic joist) and the companion board from which it had been sawed. But Koehler, by drawings and photographs, and his clear explanation of wood grains, overcame the objections by demonstrating that the tell-tale lines in the ladder rail could have gone in only one direction—to join the lines in the attic floor board.

Koehler then began his discussion of certain markings he found on the ladder rails, where they had been planed down. He took from a tool chest, from Bruno Richard Hauptmann's tool chest, the prisoner's carpenter's plane, and waved it in the air.

"In examining this ladder rail," he said, "I noticed that both edges had been planed with a hand plane. The plane was not in very good condition and left little ridges . . . The ridges are of different size, and when I plane a piece of wood with that plane (Hauptmann's) it makes similar ridges, of the same size and the same distance apart, as those found on the ladder rail."

There followed one of the most amazing demonstrations of the trial. The wood expert took a piece of paper, placed it over the edge of the ladder rail, and rubbed it with a heavy crayon. "I learned to do this with coins, when I was a boy," he remarked. The result was a graphic picture of the ridges made by the defects—"nicks"—in the Hauptmann plane.

Then Koehler affixed a piece of wood to the justice's bench, clamping it tightly down. He took up Hauptmann's plane, placed blue marks on the wood to show that he would shave it to considerable depth, poised himself behind the bench, and then plunged at it, scraping off a long shaving. He took more paper, placed it on the freshly scraped wood, and applied his crayon.

The markings on the two papers, one from the wood he had planed, the other from the ladder rail, were identical!

The witness, still coldly scientific, went on to prove that chisel marks on the ladder, used to make the recesses in which the rungs were fitted, matched chisel marks made by the three-quarter inch chisel picked up in the Lindbergh grounds after the kidnaping.

Then Koehler began his engrossing story of the 18-months of labor in which, through thousands of lumber mills throughout the nation, he traced the wood used in construction of the ladder to its source—and back again to the Bronx where, the State declared, Hauptmann obtained it.

"It is a long story," said Koehler apologetically when Attorney General Wilentz asked him a question on his tracing the lumber.

"Let us have it," said the Attorney General, knowing the jury would be entranced.

Koehler told how he had examined, microscopically, the machine-plane marks on the surface of the ladder rail. He explained the mechanical principles of planing, and showed how the work was done by knives, set in revolving "cutter heads."

As the knives revolve, he said, while the board is moving along beneath them, they scoop out little ridges. If there is a nick in one of the knives, or if one of the knives is not set properly, it will leave a distinguishing mark. If there are, let us say, eight knives in the cutter head, then each eighth "ridge" in the board, visible only when magnified, would bear this mark.

By counting these ridges, Koehler was able to determine that the machine planer used in whatever lumber mill dressed the board "had eight knives in the cutter head."

"This lumber," he said, "passed through the planer at ninety-three one-hundreds of an inch for every revolution of the top and bottom cutter heads, and eighty-six one-hundredths of an inch per revolution of the side heads. This meant there were eight knives in the top and bottom cutter heads and six knives in the side head (i.e. revolving knives that dressed the edges of the board.)"

"Now," he continued, "from an investigation of planers used in this section of the country on Carolina pine, I found that comparatively few planers have eight knives in the top and bottom heads and six in the side heads. The fact is, I made a thorough canvass of all planing mills from New York to Alabama. There are 1,598 altogether, and I found only twenty-five firms that had such a planer. Two of these I could rule out because they did not dress this kind of lumber. I got samples from the other twenty-three firms, and I found that only one of those firms made revolution marks of the same spacing as on the ladder rail. All the others made wider or narrower revolution marks."

"And what was the name of that firm?" Wilentz asked.

"That was the M. G. and J. J. Dorn Company, in McCormick, S. C."

Joseph J. Dorn, it was recalled, had testified to shipping lumber to the firm by which it was sold to the National Millwork and Lumber Company, frequented by Hauptmann.

But Dorn had shipped forty-five carloads of lumber over the period in question. Koehler proceeded to trace each of those carloads over the circuitous routes, to the ultimate consumer. Because the Dorn lumber dressing machine frequently sharpened its knives, not all of the lumber bore the same markings, Koehler testified. But at last, from the lumber yard of the Bronx lumber dealers, he picked out North Carolina pine, shipped from the Dorn mill, *which had markings on it identical with the machine-plane marks on two uprights of the kidnap ladder.* The long chase was over. In December, 1931, Bruno Richard Hauptmann had bought nearly $10.00 worth of lumber of that type from the National Millwork and Lumber Company.

Koehler identified saw cuts made in sawing out the recesses for the rungs as having been made by the type of saw found in Hauptmann's tool chest, and then court recessed for the night.

On the following day, Thursday, January 24th, Koehler completed his testimony by relating how he had fitted the three-piece ladder into Hauptmann's sedan—proving it would have been possible thus to carry the instrument to

Hopewell. A searching cross-examination by Frederick A. Pope failed to drive him into changing his testimony in any detail, major or minor.

"The State rests," Attorney General David T. Wilentz announced.

There were the usual motions for a directed verdict of acquittal, argued for the defense by Egbert Rosecrans, who insisted the State had failed to prove a burglary had been committed or that Hauptmann was at the scene of the crime.

Justice Trenchard denied the motion three seconds after the arguments had been concluded.

Bruno Richard Hauptmann stirred in his chair. He was ready for his day in court.

(AUTHOR'S NOTE: In the Spring of 1932, when the police realized that their hunt for the kidnaper would be long, the ransom notes were turned over to Albert D. Osborn for analysis. After examining them, he composed a "test paragraph," which included the nine words frequently misspelled in the ransom notes. The phrases he used were, of course, unrelated to the subject of kidnaping. Every suspect captured by the police was required to write this "test paragraph." No suspect, except Hauptmann, consistently misspelled many of these words. But Hauptmann, writing under the dictation of the police, *spelled each of the words exactly as they had been spelled, erroneously, in the ransom notes.*

The words misspelled in the ransom notes were: "ouer" for "our," "note" for "not," "latter" for "later," "everyding" for "everything," "mony" for "money," "haus" for "house," "gut" for "good," "hte" for "the," and "boad" for "boat.")

CHAPTER TWENTY

MR. EDWARD J. REILLY SPOKE TO BRUNO RICHARD HAUPT-mann in a fatherly fashion, drawing from him the story of his early life in Saxony. Under the soft questioning of his chief counsel, Hauptmann dwelt on his apprenticeship, at fourteen, to a carpenter; of his entering the German army at seventeen, in a machine-gun battalion; of his being gassed and emerging from the conflict to find deprivation and starvation waiting him at home.

He slipped lightly over the "peccadilloes" of the nineteen-year old boy who had robbed the Mayor of Kamenz, stolen, burglarized the burghers, and finally committed a highway robbery, at the point of a gun, upon two females who were pushing baby carriages along the highway. It seemed, from his answers, that this was only a wayward youth.

Hauptmann told of his attempts to reach America, and of his modest success when he had entered, after two futile voyages as a stowaway. He recalled the various places he had lived, with German companions, until his marriage to the drab little waitress, Anna Schoeffler.

"I saved nearly all my money," he said, while Anna, the bakery drudge, was using the $33 a week she earned for household expenses. His own money, he said, and the money he made from an occasional flutter on the stock exchange, he kept in a trunk at home.

On the first day of March, 1932, he declared, he went to the Majestic apartments, to see if there was any work for him. He talked with the superintendent, found there was none, and left for Radio City, where he also attempted to obtain work.

On April 2nd, the day the ransom was paid in St. Raymond's cemetery, he insisted, he did work at the Majestic apartments, and arrived home about six o'clock in the evening. His friend, Hans Kloppenburg, he said, arrived at his house about eight o'clock, for their regular Saturday "music evening." He pronounced the word "moosic," to the delight of the court room.

In his high pitched voice, that sounded as though it were coming through a metal funnel, he told his reason for quitting his job as a carpenter on the Monday after Dr. Condon had paid $50,000 to the Bronx extortioner.

He discovered, he said, that instead of the $100 a month he was supposed to receive, he was getting only $80 a month. The State later was to disprove this statement by introduction of time sheets and pay checks—showing he was credited on the books at the rate of $100 a month.

The impression Hauptmann gave—wholly at ease under the guidance of Reilly—was not exactly a happy one. In those phases of his testimony touching on his domestic life, he presented perhaps unconsciously, the picture of a German who permitted his wife to labor while he enjoyed himself at Hunters Island on Sunday outings, who saved his own money and let his wife pay the household expenses, who cared little whether he worked or not so long as he could take his ease. He even excused his wife's absence from the island picnics on the grounds that she was about to have a baby—hence, of course, she could not participate. Or perhaps, he suggested, it was because she had to work on Sundays!

Haupmann's testimony was interrupted by the appearance on the stand of two friends who did their utmost to offer him an alibi for the night of the kidnaping—but who would not commit perjury, even to save him.

Christian Frederiksen and his wife, Katy, proprietors of the little pastry shop and restaurant in the Bronx which, later on, was to become peopled with a motley array of alibi witnesses, were called to testify to the events of the evening of March 1, 1932.

Mrs. Hauptmann, they said in successive testimony, habitually worked at their bakery on Tuesday nights during February and March of that year. Tuesdays and Fridays, they said, Mrs. Frederiksen had her nights off, and on those occasions Anna Hauptmann waited on the customers. They, too, knew it was Bruno Hauptmann's custom to take his wife to work and to call for her at night. On Tuesday nights, particularly, it was his custom, they said, to come to the bakeshop, have a cup of coffee or maybe something to eat, and then escort his wife home when she closed the shop.

Now, since March 1, 1932, was a Tuesday, it stood to reason, they argued, that Mrs. Hauptmann must have been working, and it was also apparent that her husband must have called for her. It must have been so because that was the custom.

The little Danish baker and his wife did want to help in

every possible way. When Mrs. Frederiksen was testifying, indeed, she tried to make her answers positive.

"Now did you have Tuesday nights out?" Reilly asked her.

"Every Tuesday—it never failed," she answered.

But their well-intentioned alibis fell to the ground under the attack of Attorney General Wilentz. Christian, it was proved, was always working in the bakery, and did not see either Mrs. Hauptmann or her husband on the disputed night. And since Mrs. Frederiksen was nowhere near the bakery on the evening of March 1, 1932, she could not say she had actually seen Hauptmann there.

Hauptmann returned to the witness chair for continued direct examination on Friday, January 25th. Again under the direction of Reilly, he began an accounting of his financial transactions—the transactions that led him out of comparative poverty into a modest fortune. He began his tale with his meeting Isidor Fisch on Hunters Island "sometime in March or April, 1932."

Thereafter he outlined a long series of vague business deals and mysterious investments "in the fur business and in a joint stock brokerage account," in which he said Fisch supplied nearly all of the cash and he—apparently—provided the brains.

The principal lines of business endeavor in which the two men were engaged, he said, were furs and securities. Isidor Fisch managed the fur business. Hauptmann ran the speculations. Apparently no books were kept in the fur business, or if they were, it was Isidor Fisch who kept them and handed Hauptmann whatever profits he thought were

his share. "Over a thousand dollars it was, one year," Hauptmann declared.

Then Hauptmann told his famous story of the "shoe box"
and the ransom money, and how he harbored the bills for
nearly a year before he discovered what they were. The
story, in Hauptmann's own words:

"Well it was he (Fisch) was throwing a party when he
left for Germany; it was at his request in our house; we
invited a couple friends and about nine o'clock or a short
while before nine o'clock, Fisch came out and got a little
bundle in his arm. I answered the doorbell, my wife was in
the baby's room. He came out and we went in the kitchen
and he said: 'I leave it, I leave it something, if you don't
mind, keep care of it and put it in a tight place.' I didn't
ask what is in it . . . I put it in the broom closet on the
upper shelf."

It was in August of 1934, eight months after the shoe box
had been tucked away on the upper shelf, that he made
his chance discovery that the box contained gold certificates.
"It was a nasty day, it had been raining," he said, "and I
went to the broom closet to get a broom. In some way I
must have hit the box with the broom handle, and I looked
up and saw it was money, all soaking wet."

He took the money out to his garage to dry, he said, and
then—strange man!—didn't count it until a week later. At
his recital of this unusual human behavior, significant
glances shot around the prosecution table.

Reilly took the witness into a series of general denials that
he ever was in Hopewell, that he ever saw the Lindbergh
baby, that he constructed the kidnap ladder, that he com-

mitted the kidnaping, that he ever met Dr. Condon, that he ever "coughed at Dr. Condon in Woodlawn cemetery," and that he ever wrote a ransom note.

Hauptmann was emphatic in his denials. And wholly at ease, he attempted, once in a while, a little heavy facetiousness.

"Did you build this ladder?" Reilly asked.

"I am a carpenter," Hauptmann retorted, swelling pridefully at the laughter that followed. And again, when Reilly asked him to look over the ladder and give an expert journeyman's opinion on it, he declared:

"It looks like a moosic instrument. To me it looks (not) like a ladder at all. I don't see how a man can step up."

Reilly turned to the question of Hauptmann's whereabouts on the night of November 26, 1933, when he was accused of passing a ransom bill at a Sheridan Square theater. That night was Hauptmann's birthday.

"I was never in Sheridan Square or Greenwich Village in my life," Hauptmann said vehemently. "And on that night we had a little party at my house, a little birthday party, a couple of friends present, Mrs. Mueller and her little daughter, my wife and a friend of my wife from her home town in Germany and I."

Reilly thrust into the steady hands of the witness a sheaf of photostatic copies of his brokerage transactions. In contrast to the hands of Joseph J. Dorn, the worthy lumber man from South Carolina whose hands had shaken as though with the palsy when he testified to a mere matter of a bill of sale, the fingers of the defendant were without a tremor. He pulled a pencil from his pocket and awaited the questions on his intricate stock market deals.

Slowly the defense counsel took him over all his purchases and sales.

"This money came from Fisch; that money came from Fisch; I got this money from Isidor" was the burden of his testimony. Yet the account was in Hauptmann's name.

"Was one cent of Lindbergh ransom money ever put into this account?" Reilly asked.

"Not one cent," he answered.

When Hauptmann put away his balance sheets, he was smiling that well known twisted smile of his, the smile that pulled one corner of his lips up and the other down. He believed he had answered fully the State's charges that his brokerage accounts had fattened on the Lindbergh ransom money.

Reilly turned to the good old Brooklyn—and New York —plea in criminal cases that the defendant had been "beaten up" by the police and that he had made his "request" writings under duress and in fear. Hauptmann could not say he had been beaten. He had been "poked in the ribs and told to write," he said, and he had been kept without sleep "for a long time."

He did, however, make the specific charge that the police had dictated to him the misspelling of simple words in the "request" writings, and proudly showed how he could spell *n-o-t*, *b-o-a-t*, and *s-i-g-n-a-t-u-r-e* correctly.

The defendant was turned over to David T. Wilentz for cross-examination. From that moment Hauptmann's entire attitude changed. His eyes, which had been soft and pleading under the attention of Reilly, became hard. His frame became tense. He leaned forward and gripped the arms of his chair as though to prepare for an impact from a fist.

Wilentz pounded him with his criminal record in Germany, making him admit—or say he could not remember—every occasion on which he had been convicted and every crime he committed. The ordeal was not pleasant for Hauptmann. He appeared to shrink, to become small, to retire to the back of his chair. His replies were given sullenly. . . .

The Attorney General forced him to admit he had "lied about some things after he was arrested in the Bronx," and that many of the first stories he told about the ransom money were untrue. Then he thrust in front of him a little red book, an account book, taken from the Hauptmann home after his arrest.

"Is that your handwriting?" Wilentz asked.

"Yes, it is," Hauptmann said. There was fear in his eyes, fear of the unknown. He leaned far forward, and his face was a foot away from the prosecutor's.

Wilentz pointed to a written word.

"Now tell me, how do you spell 'boat'?"

"B-O-A-T."

The Attorney General appeared to spring at him. His voice rose to a shout. "Then why did you spell it, in this book, 'B-O-A-D'?" he demanded.

Hauptmann stumbled and halted. His face grew red. He asked whether it wasn't an old book, and suggested that "you make improvements in your writing." He said he wasn't sure he wrote the word in the book. For the first time since the beginning of the trial he was floundering, at a loss for a ready explanation.

Wilentz dropped the book and turned to the block of wood in which Hauptmann had concealed, in five small holes and one large one, ransom currency amounting to $840 and a small German pistol. He forced the witness to admit he had bored the hole for the pistol so that the block of wood, fitting into the wall, would come flush to the rest of the wall.

On that day, Hauptmann underwent only half an hour of cross-examination. It was the most gruelling half hour of his life.

Over the week-end the prosecution forces were jubilant. Over in Trenton, where the Attorney General's staff made its headquarters, New York columnists patted Wilentz on the back and predicted he would "break Bruno" in another court session. They advised him—and flattered him—into the belief that he was at last penetrating the prisoner's armor of sullen stolidity. They were mistaken, and if Wilentz himself entertained the belief, he was also mistaken. No person and no set of circumstances, at that time, could have wrested from Hauptmann an admission that he committed the kidnaping or was responsible for the death of the Lindbergh child.

When court resumed on Monday, January 28th, Hauptmann had enjoyed a long rest over the week-end. He came into court prepared to beat back all Wilentz's assaults on his story.

For five hours, that day, the defendant was badgered, wheedled, coaxed and hammered alternately in an obvious attempt to extract a confession from him—or at least to force from him admissions so damaging that he would throw up his hands and become mute. The attack failed, although Hauptmann did admit he had lied. And Hauptmann was angry.

"You think you're a big shot, don't you?" Wilentz asked with a sneer. "You think you're bigger than anybody and everybody. You're the man who has will power. You wouldn't tell if they murdered you. Will power is everything with you."

To the rapid volley of questions, asked in a crescendo, the prisoner shouted, "No, no, no!" with rising temper.

Wilentz asked whether Hauptmann had not sworn to untruths in the Bronx.

"Stop that!" Hauptmann shouted, shaking a long finger under the Attorney General's nose.

"You lied, didn't you? Lies, lies, LIES!"

"Well you lied to me, too, right in this court room here!"

Hauptmann was shaking. His face changed color, from white to red and red to white again.

Actually, the day's proceedings were devoid of much meat for the prosecution. Hauptmann repeated, over and over, his story of finding the ransom money in the broom closet. He reversed the testimony he had given in the Bronx, to say that if he wrote down the telephone number and address of Dr. Condon in his closet, it was only because he made a habit of recording historical dates!

Wilentz's most damaging evidence against the defendant, during the session, came with the introduction of a letter from Hauptmann to the family of the late Isidor Fisch, in which the defendant had told them he had taken $5,500 "from my private bank account" to lend his fur-cutter friend. He was forced to admit that the private bank account was a myth, but explained it by saying he had told his friend's relatives that story "because it would have been difficult to explain the deal otherwise."

In the letter, Hauptmann had asked whether he could not be appointed administrator of Fisch's estate. But he didn't tell Fisch's brother that he had a shoe box full of money, left him by Isidor. He intended to keep that as a surprise—and to give him all the money except what Fisch owed him, a matter of $7,500, when they should come to America to collect the estate.

On Tuesday, January 29th, the following day, Wilentz established the fact that during 1932, Hauptmann made many deposits of silver coin in his various bank accounts. The inference was that Hauptmann was making small purchases with the ransom bills, receiving change in silver, and depositing this in his bank. Hauptmann insisted that where deposit slips showed entries opposite the word "silver," this was merely an error.

He left the stand after seventeen hours of questioning, eleven of them under the pitiless cross-examination of Wilentz. He had been what lawyers call "a good witness." He was, in fact, one of the few "good witnesses" Bruno Richard Hauptmann was to have in his own behalf. When he left the stand, he turned and with deliberation, smiled at the jury.

Of his testimony, one significant phrase remained with the jury, however. When Wilentz asked him about his visit to California, he had said "the trip was planned for a year already." There were those who remembered the phrasing of a ransom note—"the case was prepared for a year already."

Mrs. Anna Hauptmann, who for four weeks had watched, with reddened eyes, the State's efforts to send her husband to the electric chair, was called to elaborate on his alibi for the three important dates in the history of the Lindbergh crime—March 1, 1932, when the kidnaping was committed, April 2, 1932, when the ransom was paid, and November 26, 1933, when he was accused of passing a ransom bill in Greenwich Village.

Her face was a mask. It had been a mask throughout the trial except for the brief, vivid flash of anger when her one-time friend, Mrs. Ella Achenbach had turned against her. Now, her face was composed. Only the rapid blinking of her eyelids as she groped for replies to the questions betrayed her nervousness. . . . She was dressed in dull navy blue, with a small hat from beneath which her rust-blonde hair straggled uncertainly.

Mrs. Hauptmann was on the stand for two hours and ten minutes. She remembered the night of March 1, 1932, she said, because it was on the following day she learned about the kidnaping. She distinctly remembered "Richard's" calling for her—because March 1st was a Tuesday, and he "always" called for her on Tuesdays at the bakery.

She remembered the "music evening" of April 2nd, and swore her husband was at home with her in the Bronx on that night, with a small group of friends.

She particularly recalled November 26, 1933, because that

was her husband's birthday, and there was a little party—
not exactly a party, but at any rate a friendly gathering, at
her home on that night. Richard had been present throughout the evening, she said firmly.

Wilentz, in cross-examination, paid little attention to the
three alibis. Instead, he plunged into the episode of the
mysterious shoe box on the upper shelf of the kitchen closet.
Mrs. Hauptmann was forced to admit she never saw the
box, although she kept her cleaning rags, soap, coupons,
cloths, and other articles on the shelf, and had constant recourse to the closet. And the Attorney General made her
say—a blow to her housewifely pride—that although she
cleaned two other shelves in the broom closet, she never
cleaned the shelf on which, according to her husband, the
shoe box full of money reposed.

It seemed to observers that this admission hurt Anna
Hauptmann more than anything else she said.

Then the Attorney General carried her back over the
testimony she had given in the Bronx, where she had said
she didn't know where her husband was on March 1, 1932—
that she couldn't say positively that he had been with her.

Altogether, the drab and loyal wife did her best, but her
best afforded little support for her husband's involved story.
It was evident that Hauptmann told his wife nothing, absolutely nothing, about his mysterious affairs.

At this point the trial degenerated into a tragic type of
burlesque. Mrs. Hauptmann left the stand and was succeeded by the strangest array of alibi witnesses ever gathered
together in one court room. Reilly called "Elvert Carlstrom."

Carlstrom was a pink-cheeked young Swede who, at the

time of the kidnaping, was caretaker for a vacant house in Dunellen, N. J., for which labor he received $5 a week and was permitted to sleep on a cot in the empty building.

Carlstrom's story was that March 1st was his birthday. In celebration of it, he deserted the Dunellen house, went to the Bronx to call on a young lady, and wandered by chance into Christian Frederiksen's bakery. There, of course, he "saw Hauptmann," having a cup of coffee. He knew Anna Hauptmann (as a matter of fact his lady love was one of Anna's best friends) but he had never seen Anna's husband before. He remembered the incident because Hauptmann had laughed at him because of his poor command of the English language.

Carlstrom became confused under cross-examination, and resisted efforts of the prosecution to draw from him an admission regarding his later activities. He was finally forced to admit that he spent the remainder of the night "in the company of women" in Brooklyn. Later, his best friend knocked down the entire story by testifying that Carlstrom spent the entire night of March 1st in Dunellen, asleep on his cot bed.

Yet Carlstom was the best of the alibi witnesses. There came to the stand one August von Henke, who said he met Hauptmann, out for a walk with a police dog, on the night of March 1st. Under cross-examination, August admitted he had changed his name twice, that he ran a speakeasy that had been raided countless times, and that he operated a questionable resort in Harlem.

After von Henke, or Marhenke, or whatever his name was, there came Louis Kiss, a Hungarian who also "happened to be in Frederiksen's bakery on the night of March 1st, 1932." He, too, saw Hauptmann there, drinking coffee.

The spectators marveled at the popularity of Frederiksen's bakery. It seemed, as a New York lawyer remarked, busier than the Grand Central Station. All night long people were rushing in, having a cup of coffee, looking at Hauptmann, and rushing out about their business.

The business of Louis Kiss, it developed on cross-examination, was bootlegging. On March 1st, he said, he made two pints of rum "in ten minutes," and apparently aged it on the subway while he was taking it to a friend in the Bronx, to whom he sold it for $1.25 a pint. Becoming confused while riding around town, he found himself near the bakery and dropped in to rest himself.

The testimony of Kiss was nullified in rebuttal when Leo Singer, the "friend," to whom he was delivering his homemade rum, testified that the delivery was not made until March 10th.

Then there was Lou Harding, an out-at-the-elbows laborer who told a rambling story of having seen two men with a ladder in an automobile near Hopewell about the time of the kidnaping. Harding admitted under pressure that he had been in jail twice, once for assault and once for an offense against a woman.

Peter Sommer, who told a vague story of seeing persons resembling Isidor Fisch and Violet Sharpe "on the Weehawken ferry, with a baby, about midnight on March 1st," was later discovered to be a "professional witness" who had changed his testimony in previous cases "because he hadn't been paid his fee." On cross-examination he contradicted himself, forgot his story, altered his testimony, and floundered in a sea of uncertainty. Finally, he had recourse to a phrase that was to become famous. To every question asked by the prosecutor he replied:

"Well, I wouldn't say yes, and I wouldn't say no." Before he stepped down it had become almost a chant—"I wouldn't say yes, and I wouldn't say no."

In keeping with the character of these witnesses, one Benjamin Heier, in a resplendent new suit, testified that he was parked at St. Raymond's cemetery on the night of April 2, 1932, in dalliance with a young woman whom he tried not to name, and that he saw Isidor Fisch leap over the cemetery fence and come directly within the range of his headlights. The State proved that at the time he said he saw this vision, he was eight miles away, in an automobile accident. The record of this accident was in the New York police files.

Then there was Philip Moses, another taxicab driver who had boasted for a week, around Flemington, that he was going to "crack this case wide open." He announced himself as a "song-writer, plumber's helper, farmer, amateur actor, news-stand operator and amateur dancer," and said he had seen "a gang" in or near St. Raymond's cemetery on the night the ransom was paid. His "gang" turned out to be two men, in trouble with a balky automobile, and a third who was helping them to get it started.

The testimony of Sam Streppone, who said Fisch once left a shoe box in his keeping, was beaten down by Wilentz who forced the witness to admit he had been adjudged insane, and that he had been confined to institutions "five or eight times."

"Vere are dey getting dese vitnesses?" Hauptmann asked Lloyd Fisher in alarm. "Dey're hurting me."

Mrs. Anna Bonesteel, a Yonkers restaurant proprietor, told of having seen a young woman resembling Violet Sharpe, nervously sitting in her establishment on the night of March 1, 1932, with a blanket in her arms. She was taken aback by Wilentz's question:

"Madame, what would you say if we should show you that Violet Sharpe was in Englewood when you say she was in your restaurant?"

Mrs. Bonesteel made no reply.

Bertha Hoff, like Sam Streppone, recalled that Isidor Fisch once went to her house with a mysterious package which he wanted to leave with her. He was accompanied, she said, by "a farmer named Budreau." The State promptly found the "farmer named Budreau," who swore the event never occurred.

The amazing rapidity with which the State ran down the records of the defense witnesses brought admiring comment from observers. The prosecution appeared to have at its finger tips the histories of all the strange assortment of men and women who projected themselves into the case, despite the defense's attempt to conceal them from view until they took the stand. The method of operation was this:

As soon as a defense witness had given his name and address, Colonel Schwarzkopf left the room and sent a brief dispatch to State Police headquarters. Within five minutes the entire detective departments of New York and New

Jersey, by teletype, telephone, and sometimes cable to Europe, were checking the witness's career.

Meanwhile, in court, Attorney General Wilentz dragged out his cross-examination until a flood of incoming police reports reached the prosecution table. Then he would begin his series of embarrassing questions.

The police ran through the records of every hospital for the insane, every penal institution. They interviewed neighbors of the witnesses, pried into his habits, talked with his employers. In the case of Elvert Carlstrom, four hundred police worked from mid-afternoon until dawn the next day assembling data on his career. When court opened the next morning, the Attorney General had a dossier containing information about the young man that not even Carlstrom suspected another person in the world of knowing.

Ben Lupica who, months before, had promised to make an excellent witness for the prosecution, was not called by the State. He had become uncertain in his story of seeing Hauptmann, with the ladder in his car, on the day of the kidnaping.

The defense, however, called him to the stand, and extracted from him a statement that the man he saw "was not Hauptmann."

Thereupon Wilentz took him over for cross-examination and obtained a completely contradictory reply.

"The man resembled Hauptmann," Lupica declared.

"I don't know," he said after leaving the stand, "which side I helped more. I guess it was an even break."

The defense did produce three witnesses, however, of better quality than these. John M. Trendley, a handwriting expert of repute, testified to his belief that it would have been "absolutely impossible for Hauptmann to have written the ransom letters." But he admitted he had examined the writings only two hours and a half.

Dr. E. M. Hudson, fingerprint expert was likewise an upright witness. But he said he saw only one nail hole in the kidnap ladder when he examined it in March of 1932. The State produced photographs taken on March 8th of that year, with the four nail holes prominently displayed.

Hans Kloppenburg, a handsome young German, told a straightforward story of the various "moosic evenings" at the Hauptmann home, and confirmed the story that the defendant was at home on the night of April 2, 1932, at the time Dr. Condon was paying $50,000 to the St. Raymond's cemetery extortioner. He also told of seeing Fisch bring a package to the Hauptmann apartment, shortly before he sailed for Germany. He was one of the best defense witnesses.

The trial rolled speedily to its conclusion. Relatives of the Sourland mountaineer, Millard Whited, who had identified Hauptmann as the man he saw twice near the Lindbergh home, testified that his reputation for veracity "ain't no good." Charles DeBisschop, a "practical lumberman" who brought whole pine trees into court to support his testimony, displayed two boards which, he said, matched perfectly— like the ladder rail and the attic board—and yet which came from wholly different trees.

Finally, Brevoort Bolmer, a filling station proprietor, told of seeing a man, a woman, and a car with a ladder in it, on the morning of the kidnaping.

The defense rested.

In rebuttal, a piece of business that ran from the grim to the hilarious in character, the State knocked to earth the carefully constructed alibis, and tore to pieces the contention that Violet Sharpe was concerned in the kidnaping.

Three companions with whom Miss Sharpe spent the evening on which the kidnaping took place testified they were with her at the Peanut Grill until nearly 11 o'clock. And finally, an aristocrat of aristocrats, Mrs. Dwight W. Morrow, grandmother of the kidnaped child, closed the government's rebuttal by confirming the true story of her serving maid's activities on the fateful night.

The testimony was concluded. Hauptmann was led back to his cell. He knew at that moment that there was very little hope for an acquittal, and he was resentful of the manner in which his case had been handled. He paced the floor of his cell over the long week-end.

CHAPTER TWENTY-ONE

BEFORE THE END OF THE TRIAL, BRUNO RICHARD HAUPTMANN
had become a puppet, jerked across the stage on the strings
of publicity, personal aggrandizement and political ambition. Guilty or innocent, it was impossible not to feel some
pity for the man who was fighting such a single-handed
battle against death while the world around him was making a Roman holiday.

True, his attorneys were waging a desperate legal battle
to save him but of these attorneys only one seemed to have a
personal interest in him as a human being, and that was
C. Lloyd Fisher.

Furthermore, even his attorneys had come almost to the
parting of the ways, and more than one of them would
have withdrawn from the case if there had been an ethical
way out.

On the one side were the so-called "country lawyers,"
Fisher, Egbert Rosecrans, and Frederick A. Pope. On the
other was Edward J. Reilly, who had been brought into the
case by the same interests in New York which dominated
Mrs. Anna Schoeffler Hauptmann.

The country lawyers resented Reilly's appearance in the
case. They resented his clothes and his manner. They dis-
liked his bombast and disagreed with his methods. They
regarded him as an alien who could not talk the language

of Hunterdon County folk, and who would do more to alienate than to cultivate the sympathies of the jury.

"We have been taught," one of them said to me, when Reilly had completed half of his defense, "the principle of establishing one theory of defense and clinging to it. Mr. Reilly has opened up a dozen different theories."

It had been known that one of the strongest defenses, as developed by the country lawyers, was that "the body found in the Sourlands mountains was not that of the Lindbergh child." The State would have had to go to extreme lengths to prove the *corpus delicti,* if the issue had been pressed. C. Lloyd Fisher's examination of those who testified to the discovery of the body had been based on this defense theory. Every question he asked had been directed to the determination of whether the prosecution had absolute, unbeatable proof that the body was that of the Lindbergh child.

In the midst of this development, Reilly said to the court that "the defense, of course, does not question at all that this was Colonel Lindbergh's child."

C. Lloyd Fisher left the room, and Bruno Hauptmann, who saw part of his case crumbling beneath his feet, became almost frantic. Unquestionably in a panic when he saw a lawyer he trusted passing through the door, he was provoked into making his strange outburst against Thomas Sisk, at whom he shouted "liar."

If the country lawyers were outraged by the presence of Reilly on the defense, Reilly in turn was impatient with some of his colleagues. He could see little reason for the long and technical cross-examinations of handwriting and wood experts as conducted by Frederick A. Pope, for example.

Yet behind those tedious examinations lay the country lawyer's strategy. The purpose behind them was to render the jury impatient of such technical evidence, and thus incline them to disregard *all* technical evidence, whether for prosecution or defense.

The attempt to turn the Hauptmann trial into a circus, however, had begun long before the lawyers were engaged, and every sensational New York newspaper wanted to be the ring-master. Anna Schoeffler Hauptmann was as well guarded by the *New York Journal* as her husband was by the State of New Jersey. She was guarded, day and night, as that newspaper's prized possession, and not an alien newspaper correspondent was permitted to talk to her, confer with her, or interview her.

Her living quarters were chosen by agents of the newspaper. Her "guards" escorted her to court, sat behind her, warded off all strangers, and escorted her home again when court was out. When she went back to the Bronx, on weekends, to visit "Bubi" and rest, one of her guards went with her. Waking, sleeping, eating or drowsing in court, she was always under watchful eyes.

It was realized, of course, in the more sensational New York newspaper circles that the biggest possible story that could have come out of the trial would have been a confession from Bruno Richard Hauptmann. The prize would have been "How I Killed the Lindbergh Baby." The profits from it would have been enormous, and there were rumors of offers as high as $150,000.

Besides, there were efforts to obtain from the sheriff's office and staff many special privileges, such as: exclusive seating arrangements and tacit permission to bring into court machinery for expediting the news reports or for flashing the verdict—which had been expressly forbidden by Justice Thomas W. Trenchard; second, favored rooms in the court house; third, extra tickets for special correspondents, additional artists, columnists, sob sisters, and visiting circulation managers; fourth, the privilege of photographing Hauptmann in his cell—a privilege which was at first frowned upon by Hauptmann.

The newspaper correspondents, all of them, were a hardworking lot. They were on the story of the century and they were constantly spurred to more prodigious feats of journalism by their New York offices which were constantly crying for "beats."

In the early weeks, therefore, no story was too weird or impossible to find its way over the wires into the metropolitan dailies—some of the dailies, that is. And ten minutes after the edition containing the new sensation had reached the streets, all the other correspondents would be queried by their editors and a new wild-goose chase would begin.

"I can stand twenty-four hours a day of straight reporting," one of the newspaper men remarked, "but this chase after stories that I know are false before I start out is driving me into a nervous breakdown."

The center of activity, outside of court hours, was the Union Hotel, across the street, to the top floor of which, like a herd of ponderous elephants, the jury was escorted each night and there locked up under an impressive guard of five constables—three male and two female.

And the center of activity in the hotel was Nellie's Tap

Room, an additional bar set up to cater to the overwhelming hosts that descended upon the hostelry at dusk each day.

An estimable young New York reporter, Travis Fulton, had rescued a stray dog from the streets one day—a frowzy, down-and-out black and white dog of uncertain ancestry, with a face that bore in it the depths of canine misery and despondency. Under his care, she had become sleek and shiny, contented with life, and worshipful of her master. Travis named her Nellie, and she became the adopted mascot of the press.

In her honor, the hotel proprietors named their new bar "Nellie's Tap Room," and within a week, Nellie was to become the most famous dog in America.

The tap room, therefore, became the news exchange of Flemington. There the evidence was discussed. There the following day's stories were mapped out and there, lightening the tragedy and the tedium, voices were often raised in song.

The newspaper work was exacting and nerve-wracking. A million words a day, or thereabouts, were leaving Flemington, much of it in long-hand, for typewriters, even of the noiseless variety, were banned in the court room. The very natural result was that as soon as the day's work was over, the tension was relaxed and thereafter the correspondents were inclined to ease their nerves by playing as hard as they had worked.

Out of one evening of such communion, for instance, grew the "schnitzel-bank" song—a parody on the ancient singing-school jingles that used to hang in every German *bierhaus*. The first verses of the parody ran:

Ist das nicht ein dowel pin?
Ja, das ist ein dowel pin.
Fitted das not nicely in?
Ja, it fitted nicely in.

Ist das nicht ein ransom note?
Ja, das ist ein ransom note.
Ist das nicht ein Nelly b-o-a-d?
Ja, das ist ein Nelly b-o-a-d.

So it went, with new verses every day when additional testimony was offered. And a New York correspondent with artistic ability drew charts to go with the song, which was sung with relish and abandon on every occasion when there was a let-down from the grimmer business in hand.

As a community, the newspaper correspondents, as a rule, kept their own exclusive company, and they resented the intrusion of outsiders—of the Broadway celebrities and hoofers and opera singers and tragediennes and blonde-haired beauties from sundry choruses. They equally resented the hordes of morbid sensation seekers who swarmed into town, tried to usurp the court house, did usurp the hotel, and generally ran riot through Flemington. There was an excuse for the celebrities, who came to be seen and to add to their publicity files. The only excuse for the others was unhealthy curiosity and a desire for strange souvenirs, such as autographs of the semi-great, miniature ladders—at ten cents apiece—picture post-cards of the court house and jury, and discarded admission tickets.

In the corridor fronting on Nellie's Tap Room, there was a long row of benches with typewriters for the correspondents and telegraph instruments for their operators. Nightly a dozen men and women would be pounding out their morning stories at this battery.

The crowds discovered that this was one of the centers of newspaper activity. So they came, to stand three deep behind the writers, to watch them operate, to peer at their signatures, and to stick their heads over the correspondents' shoulders and comment on their ability and workmanship. Writing under such conditions became difficult.

One correspondent, writing three paragraphs which he found not to his liking, and discarding it, found a spectator picking it up and thrusting it under his nose.

"Are you going to use this?" the spectator asked.

"No," said the correspondent in the shortest possible tone.

"Well, if you'll autograph it, I'll pay you five dollars for it," the spectator said.

Eventually, driven from Nellie's Tap Room by the horde, a majority of the correspondents shunned the place and resorted to the quieter precincts of the dining room for their conferences.

Justice Trenchard had endeavored, throughout the trial, to maintain an air of dignity and to prevent the case from degenerating into a burlesque. From the standpoint of his own court and the conduct within it, he had succeeded admirably, against overwhelming odds. Each day saw increasing crowds jammed into the suffocating room. Clouds of human steam rose, to congeal and run down the windows— as in the poor debtors' court in Pickwick papers—and the place was stifling and unhealthy.

The crowds stood in the aisles and packed themselves solidly into the window recesses. They sat on radiators and stood on tables. The entrances were so crowded that the court officers had difficulty in forcing their way through.

Finally, Justice Trenchard issued an order that no person might enter the court room after the seats were filled. Thereafter those who were fortunate enough to be admitted breathed much easier.

The height of publicity—and the height of commercial folly—was reached, however, in the taking of sound-films of the trial. From the first day of the action a great camera had stood in one corner of the gallery, housed in a casing. The justice had forbidden the taking of photographs, motion or still, when he was on the bench.

After the trial was under way, engineers ran a cable down to a point just behind the jury, where a microphone was concealed by an electric fan. The action of the camera was silent. None except the engineers and the camera men knew what was going on. Experts from a film manufacturing company had been consulted, and a test of the court room light had been made. As a result the company made a special film, designed to catch every ray of light in the room. The film was so delicate that it had to be kept on ice. Otherwise it would have been worthless in four hours.

Several witnesses—including Hauptmann—were recorded in that manner and the films were sent to New York, for joint distribution to those companies that had coöperated in the scheme.

Here the producers or their executives made their mistake. They released the sections of films already in hand and permitted them to be shown in movie houses. Henceforth they were stopped by an angry justice and an indignant attorney general. Their machine was dismantled and their microphone was thrown out.

Had the temptation to release the film not been so strong, and had they been able to wait until the end of the trial, they would have had a masterpiece.

In contrast to the amazing hippodrome produced by all manner of publicity agents, was the patient, humane, dignified manner and method of Justice Trenchard both on and off the bench.

The justice realized that the thing most greatly to be feared was a mistrial. He was forced to lean backward, at times, to prevent it. There were occasions when persons in the court room leaped to their feet—like the Rev. Vincent Burns—to throw the proceedings into an uproar and break into the continuity of the testimony. There were other times when the bickering between defense and prosecution lawyers reached such intense heights that words were spoken which might likewise have caused the withdrawal of a juror and a consequent mistrial. All of these dangers Justice Trenchard avoided with caution and good common sense.

But the most striking and attractive attribute of the presiding judge was his humanity—the homely tenderness with which he guarded over the health and well-being of his jury.

"One of your constables," he told them on a Friday, "owns a large sight-seeing 'bus. He has been good enough to suggest that since you are not to be in court tomorrow, you might like to go for a ride. I am agreed, and counsel are agreed, that if you will follow a certain route that will not take you near any of the places mentioned in this case, you may take the ride, and I hope it will do you good.

"I want you to go, however, only if the weather is good. If the weather is inclement, I want you to stay indoors. And whether the weather is good or bad, I must insist that you dress warmly and wear your rubbers. If any juror lacks rubbers, I will be glad to supply them."

Verna Snyder, Juror Number Three, lacked rubbers. A bailiff bought her a pair, put them on for her, and charged the purchase to the Justice.

Justice Trenchard was tolerant of the working press because he realized they had their work to do. He was insistent there should be no special privileges and that there should be an even break between all services and all correspondents. More than once, when reports of discrimination reached his ears, he intervened to protect the rights of those who had been "frozen out."

He was less tolerant of the sight-seers who came to make holiday in his court, and he was extremely impatient at the constant interruptions, the giggling and hysterical laughter, that came from the crowd when it was tickled or amused by some bit of evidence.

"Upon the next outburst of the sort," he would say, "I shall order the officers to clear the court of all but the press. I am amazed that you should come here to laugh."

On the Monday when the last chapter of the trial was begun, the circus crowds reached their greatest proportions. Throughout the morning they had poured into town by automobile and on foot. They had no places to sleep for every bed in town was occupied or engaged. They confiscated cots and slept in corridors. They slept in their own automobiles, under piles of rugs. Or they went room-hunting in neighboring towns—in Clinton and Stockton and Califon. Many of them made Trenton their base and "commuted" over icy roads, to Flemington.

By Wednesday, when the judge's charge was delivered and the case was given to the jury, they were doomed to disappointment, for justice, thoroughly outraged, announced a new deal. The spectators were driven from their vantage points. Their tickets, however obtained, were not honored. State Police held them outside in the cold. And the cold forced them back, into the hotel, or still farther away, to Trenton or wherever they made their headquarters. On that day one could move fairly easily within the court house.

Differences between the defense lawyers had increased in the previous days. Bruno Hauptmann, unsure about what Reilly would do for him in the summation, specifically wanted his friend, Lloyd Fisher, to make the closing address to the jury. He felt intuitively that Fisher had a greater knowledge of the temper of the Hunterdon County farmer than had Reilly and that he could talk to them in a language they would understand.

Others of the "country lawyers" agreed with Hauptmann. But Reilly himself, as chief counsel, elected to make the summation himself.

The prisoner's uneasiness had increased as the calibre of the various witnesses brought forward in his defense was exposed. He liked not at all the character and testimony of some of his "friends."

"That witness iss no good," he hissed after one of them had left the stand. "He's doing me harm."

Talk of an impending confession grew, and with it rumors began to grow throughout the country, first that Hauptmann had committed suicide, and, second, that he had left behind him a confession. The rumors were easily disposed of by rapid telephone calls to the jail, but they persisted.

One man shook his head whenever one of these reports reached his ears. He was Deputy Sheriff Hovey Low who, more than any other man had gone below the surface of Bruno Hauptmann and discovered something of his mental makeup.

"He will never commit suicide," said Low, "and he will never make a confession. No one on earth would be able to make him confess. He will say, even if he goes to the chair, 'I didn't do it—I have nothing to confess.'"

On a certain morning the florid-faced chief counsel swung into the jail and marched to Bruno Hauptmann's cell. He was breezy and brusque.

"Good morning, Richard," he said, "how do you feel today?"

"Not so good," said the prisoner.

"Well, now, I just wanted to tell you, Richard, that if we're going to save you, we've got to have the whole story, you'll have to tell us all about it. If you do tell us, we can do something for you. Otherwise——."

"But there's nothing to confess," said Hauptmann. "I am innocent. I didn't do it."

A little later Mrs. Hauptmann saw her husband and talked with him a few moments in German.

"What did he tell you? Did he say anything to you?" a member of the defense counsel asked.

Mrs. Hauptmann's eyes flashed.

"He says he is innocent—that there is nothing to tell— nothing to confess—and he's telling the truth," she declared.

Outside the crowds swelled, bought their post-cards, hung their little ladders by ribbons around their necks, jostled the State Police, jammed the bars, broke bottles, tore up newspapers, gulped sandwiches, and—waited.

CHAPTER TWENTY-TWO

THROUGHOUT THE TRIAL, ANTHONY M. HAUCK, JR., PROSECUTOR of record for Hunterdon County, had been kept in the background, while George K. Large, "brains" of the prosecution, prepared the case and David T. Wilentz, the attorney general, basked in the glory of presenting it.

On Monday, February 11th, however, Hauck was given his first opportunity to show the neighbors that he was something more than a silent partner in the prosecution. His superiors let him make a little speech to the jury, the first of the summations.

Hauck did very well, although he didn't tell the jury anything they didn't know already. He discoursed for a moment upon the law, advised the jury that the State had proved its case, asked them to find Hauptmann guilty, and sat down without demanding an electric-chair verdict. Edward J. Reilly followed him, for the defense.

Out of deference to the homely ways of the jury, Mr. Reilly had refrained from wearing the usual carnation in the lapel of his coat. That was his only concession, however. He refused to divest himself of his striped pants which, after all, might be deemed the badge of office of a successful Brooklyn lawyer.

Mr. Reilly, urban and urbane, talked down to the country-folk of the jury. He reminded them, over and over again, that they were simple people with honest hearts and common sense—"David Harum horse sense," he put it—and whenever he found himself in danger of indulging in rhetorical flights, he checked himself abruptly. His manner was that of one who said, "come, now, we are all yokels together."

The chief defense counsel talked well and ably until midafternoon. After that he appeared to tire, and he was forced to resort to time-worn legal cliches. Interest lagged, and Hauptmann's gaze wandered away from the jury and became fixed on the top of his brown shoes.

Mr. Reilly advanced several theories for the consideration of the jury. He declared the State had failed to prove the kidnaping was committed by means of the ladder that had been traced to Hauptmann. He denied there was the slightest evidence that Hauptmann had ever built, seen or handled the ladder. He suggested that the crime was engineered by some of the Lindbergh servants, perhaps under the guidance of Butler Oliver Whately.

"And as for Betty Gow," he cried, "do you believe her story for one moment? I don't."

He reviewed the testimony of Peter Sommers, of "I wouldn't say yes and I wouldn't say no" fame, as demonstrating beyond a doubt that Violet Sharpe, deceased like Whately, had a hand in the plot. He took a long-distance shot at Henry (Red) Johnson, demanding to know why the State had not brought him back from Europe to testify.

Reilly made a particularly bitter attack on Dr. John F. Condon, "that eccentric old man of the Bronx," described his testimony as fantastic beyond belief, and asked why the police had not investigated him more thoroughly. Again, as in the case of Betty Gow, the defense counsel declared he didn't believe a word of the doctor's testimony.

Brutal in his denunciation of the minor figures who had given evidence against his client, Reilly was a little softer in his characterization of such witnesses as Colonel Lindbergh and Mrs. Dwight W. Morrow.

"They were merely mistaken—honestly mistaken," he conceded. All the others were "perjurers, liars, publicity seekers, and movie contract hunters."

After denouncing the New Jersey State Police for the "bungling of this case that has cost so much pain and so much money to the taxpayers," he embarked on the most amazing phase of his summation.

"This case was a frameup from beginning to end," was his theme. He inferred that the police constructed the kidnap ladder, created the marks that traced it to Hauptmann's hands, themselves removed the board from Hauptmann's attic in order to fit it to the ladder rail, and "bought the eight noted handwriting experts" who testified Hauptmann penned the ransom notes. And as a matter of fact, he added, the jury's own conclusions regarding the authorship of those notes would be as good as those of any handwriting expert who ever lived.

Returning to the actual kidnaping, he shouted:

"Who knew the baby had a cold and had to remain in Hopewell on that Tuesday? Not Hauptmann. Nobody in God's world but Colonel Lindbergh, his lovely wife, his butler's wife, Betty Gow, the servants in the Morrow home and 'Red' Johnson knew the Colonel was going to be in

New York that night. . . . Now the Colonel can have all the confidence in the world in Betty Gow. I have none. . . . I say the circumstances point absolutely along a straight line of guilt toward that butler and the servants who were disloyal to Colonel Lindbergh."

He insinuated that Inspector Henry Bruckman of the Bronx police wrote the tell-tale telephone number and address of Dr. John F. Condon on the panel in Hauptmann's closet, and that his client was thereafter so brutally treated by the police that he didn't know what he was saying when he gave uncertain or contradictory statements in reply to their questions.

Of his own alibi witnesses he said little, beyond the fact that they had established that Hauptmann was not in or near Hopewell at the time of the kidnaping. He regarded Amandus Hochmuth, who had seen Hauptmann in the Lindbergh lane as "a man who had hallucinations" and inferred that other identification witnesses testified for the sake of publicity or because they were in fear of the police.

The jury's common sense, he declared, should tell them that one man alone could not have kidnaped the child. He prayed they would not send "an innocent man" to the chair, and concluded by painting a picture of the infant "in Heaven."

Attorney General Wilentz, on the following day, delivered himself of a summation which made up in vituperation what it may have lacked in logical argument. Instead of devoting himself to a review of the undeniably strong evidence piled up by the State, he gave almost his entire address over to replying to his "delightful adversary" as he

termed Mr. Reilly, and to shouting epithets at Hauptmann
—"Public Enemy of the World Number One—a man in
whose veins runs icewater."

The Attorney General did show, at least, a fine sense of
dramatics. He bade his witnesses stand up, one after another—Colonel H. Norman Schwarzkopf, Inspector Henry
Bruckman, William E. Frank—and as they stood, erect in
front of the jury, he asked whether they looked like "crooks,
men who would frame another man and take away his life
on perjured evidence—Schwarzkopf, a graduate of West
Point. . . . Bruckman, one of the highest and finest officers in the New York police. . . . Frank, a man of honor
and an official of the United States government."

He scoffed at the defense witnesses as "ex-convicts, luna-
tics, idiots," and then excoriated the "perjurers, who came
to the defense of this man, prompted by the defense radio
broadcasts."

"What type of man," he asked, "would kill the child of
Colonel Lindbergh and Anne Morrow? He wouldn't be an
American. No American gangster and no American racka-
teer ever sank to the level of killing babies. . . . It had to be
a fellow who was an egomaniac, who thought he was om-
nipotent. It had to be a secretive fellow. It had to be a fellow
who wouldn't tell his wife about his money, who would
conceal the truth from her. It had to be a man you could
kill and still he wouldn't tell if he didn't want to. . . . It
had to be the type of man who would hold up women at
the point of a gun—women wheeling baby carriages. We
have found Public Enemy of the World Number One. He
is here for your judgment."

Through the long day, Wilentz continued his summation. He stopped a while for the luncheon recess, and Juror Verna Snyder was so affected by his discourse that she left her luncheon untouched.

His most startling observation appeared to be a reversal of the State's theory that the child was killed when the ladder broke while the kidnaper was descending his ladder from the nursery.

"Let me tell you why the child didn't cry," he said. "This fellow took no chance on the child awakening. He crushed that child right in that room into insensibility. He smothered and choked that child right in the room. He wasn't interested in the life of the child. Life meant nothing to him. That's the type of the man I told you about, Public Enemy of the World Number One."

Wilentz picked up one of the ransom notes and called attention to the crude symbol at the bottom, the blue and red circles and the three holes.

"Blue—B for Bruno," he shouted. "Red—R for Richard. . . . Holes—H for Hauptmann."

The Attorney General pointed out the similarities in Hauptmann's handwriting and that in the ransom notes. He recalled the evidence as to the accused man's financial transactions, and traced the chain of circumstantial and direct evidence from the ransom payment to the sleeping suit, from the sleeping suit to the nursery, from the nursery to the kidnap ladder, from the ladder to Hauptmann—"a complete chain."

He asked for the death penalty.

Hauptmann, cautioned by counsel to remain quiet, sat

with a flushed countenance through the oration. Occasionally he muttered "dat's a lie," but he was careful to keep his voice low. None heard his words except his counsel and those correspondents nearest him.

As Wilentz turned from the jury a commotion arose. A man in clerical garb, from among the spectators, leaped to his feet shouting, "a man has confessed in my church———."

Bailiff's leaped upon him. State Police sprang at him, muffling his voice, covering his mouth with their hands, rushing him out of doors, kicking and struggling.

Counsel for both sides were on their feet. The Attorney General was trembling. After six weeks of frantic effort to send Hauptmann to the chair, a mistrial might have been declared and the whole cause would have to be fought over again.

Justice Trenchard called the opposing counsel to the bench and inquired if they had heard the words. By common consent it was agreed that since the interrupter's voice had been so promptly choked off, it was probable the jury hadn't heard much more than a meaningless phrase. The Justice elected to ignore the matter.

The spectator, a Rev. Vincent Burns, was had up for a hearing, and released to go home under police guard, to return later for action on possible charges of contempt of court.

Wednesday, February 13th, 1935. Verdict Day.

Justice Trenchard ordered the exclusion of every person who had not been accorded a seat. Then he ordered the court room 'doors locked, and declared that no person should enter or leave the room while he was delivering his charge to the jury.

There was nothing indefinite in Justice Trenchard's charge. True, he charged on the evidence, and the strength of his instructions to the jury was predicated upon the strength of the State's case. But he told the jury, among other things, that they must ask themselves:

"Is there any doubt in your minds as to the reliability of Dr. Condon's testimony? It is argued that his testimony is inherently improbable and should be, in part, rejected by you, but you will observe that his testimony is corroborated in large part by several witnesses whose credibility has not been impeached in any manner whatsoever."

Concerning the defense claim that a "gang" committed the kidnaping:

"Is there any evidence in this case whatsoever to support this conclusion?"

Concerning the ladder:

"If it was not there for the purpose of reaching the window, for what purpose was it there?"

Of the wood from which the ladder was constructed:

"Does not the evidence satisfy you that at least a part of the wood came out of the flooring of the attic of the defendant?"

Of the ransom money:

"Does it not appear that many thousands of dollars of ransom bills were found in his garage, hidden in the walls or under the floor, that others were found on his person, and others passed by him from time to time? . . . The defendant says that these were left with him by one Fisch, now dead. Do you believe that?"

Of the shoe box, said to have contained the ransom money:

"His wife said she never saw the box, and I do not recall that any witness excepting the defendant testified they ever saw the shoe box there."

Of Amandus Hochmuth's testimony that he saw Hauptmann in Hopewell:

"May he not have well and easily remembered the circumstance in view of the fact that that very night the child was carried away? Do you think, on the whole, that there is any reason to doubt the old man's testimony?"

Justice Trenchard charged the jury that they should return one of three verdicts, guilty of murder in the first degree, guilty of murder in the first degree with a recommendation for life imprisonment (a sentence being mandatory), or acquittal.

The jury retired at 11:23 o'clock in the morning, to consider the evidence and more than 300 exhibits prepared for them.

Spectators were driven from the court room. Justice Trenchard retired to his chambers for sandwiches. Members of the press were permitted to remain in the building, and all others were herded outside. At noon, the Justice ordered Sheriff Curtiss to send food to the jurors, who were considering the case in a room directly beneath the cell where Hauptmann was walking nervously back and forth—four paces to the window, four paces to the barred door.

The privileged one hundred and fifty correspondents,

under-sheriffs, bailiffs, tipstaves, clerks and messengers idled in the court or wandered through the corridors and up and down the long flights of stairs. Wire chiefs checked their equipment and installed duplicate transmission sets to guard against failure of their lines when the verdict should be returned. The hours went by.

At mid-afternoon there was a flurry of excitement. The jury had sent for a magnifying glass. Obviously they were studying the handwriting and wood exhibits. But no other message came from behind the locked door.

A blue haze of smoke filled the court room, for a majority of the correspondents, scribbling descriptions of the scene, were smoking furiously. Accredited messengers, the only persons permitted to pass in or out of the court house doors, brought in bags of sandwiches and containers of coffee. The floor was littered, inches deep, with discarded newspapers, copy paper, torn paper sacks.

In one corner of the room several correspondents started checker games. In another they tossed pennies at a crack in the floor. A dice game was in progress in the library, and at one time the stakes rose to $880—on a single throw. Justice Trenchard, seeking a law book, strolled from his chambers to the library. The players had a moment's warning, and when he entered the room, they were engrossed in reading law books themselves. Whether the Justice realized he had broken up the game may never be known, but he emerged from the library smiling, like a proctor who had caught his students in embarrassing pursuits.

Dusk came and the lights were turned on. The smoke grew thicker. Correspondents who had vantage points in the front benches practiced signaling "flashes" to the gallery, where their runners were stationed for a rapid dash to the wire rooms.

Several of the news men smuggled brief cases past the guards at the doors. In them were small portable wireless sets, capable of transmitting signals perhaps half a mile. It was their intention to "flash" the verdict from these sets to their own stations, whence the word would go out on the regular wires.

Justice Trenchard ordered more food sent in to the jury. Under the law he was privileged to keep the jury without sustenance until a verdict had been reached, but he is a humane man. It was, however, against the New Jersey law for the jury, or any member of it, to leave the room where the deliberations were taking place, until a decision had been made. Waking or sleeping, the four women and eight men had to remain in that room.

"Of course, that is nothing but a species of coercion," C. Lloyd Fisher remarked.

The smoke became more dense and the floor became more littered. Isolated groups indulged in a little harmony. Edward J. Reilly sat blandly in the witness chair and chatted with the correspondents.

At 9:30 o'clock in the evening, Sheriff Curtiss said: "I believe they will reach a verdict tonight." Meanwhile the more sensational newspapers had published reports—wholly fictitious—that the jury stood "ten to two for conviction." There was no possible way by which any human being, outside of the twelve men and women concerned in the deliberations, could have known the trend of the discussion in the jury room.

Half an hour later the court room was thrown into tumult, when Sheriff Curtiss was called from his office and summoned to the ante-room for a conference with the constables who were guarding the jury. He returned and disappeared into Justice Trenchard's chambers. Word spread through the court house that the jury had arrived at a verdict—or, alternately, that Justice Trenchard had decided to leave the court for the night, in which case a verdict could not have been returned until 10 o'clock the following morning.

The correspondents took their accustomed seats. Suddenly every light in the court room was extinguished. It might have been a signal. The reporters held lighted matches in their left hands and scribbled with their right. Singing and laughter arose in the darkness.

The lights flashed on again, and in the blue haze Attorney General Wilentz was shouting orders to the State Police.

"Close and lock those doors. I want every man in this room seated. I want this noise stopped." He was pacing angrily up and down in front of the judge's bench. Deputy sheriffs howled "quiet, quiet, quiet!" State troopers passed along the rows of correspondents, demanding to see their red tickets. Those who had forgotten or lost them were escorted out.

At this point, the elaborate signal service of the Associated Press went wrong. An operator, it was said, unwittingly flashed a number over his portable radio, from within the court room to the wire room. Over the association's network went an erroneous "flash."

"Hauptmann Convicted—Gets Life."

The flash was transmitted to all Associated Press clients. Presses rolled and thousands of newspapers poured out into the streets of major American cities with the false news. The radio picked it up and the error was duplicated in theaters, restaurants and public gathering places.

When it was realized that an error had been made, and that the jury had not even entered the court room, frantic attempts were made to straighten out the error. But between the correspondents inside and those in the wire room there was no communication. The doors were locked, and the man who had unconsciously sent the wrong flash was blissfully ignorant of the turmoil outside.

At 10:28 o'clock from the belfry of the court house came the solemn tolling of a bell. To those in the court it sounded far away, as in a distant village. A hush fell over the crowd, because they knew it marked the end of the jury's deliberations.

Outside the court house, the street was a glare from the powerful flood lights and flares of the motion picture companies. So dense was the crowd that it was impossible to move. But with the tolling of the bell there were cheers, shouts, noise. Someone in the crowd threw a stone, shattering the fan-shaped glass above the portico.

Deputy sheriffs moved quickly to the court room windows and drew down the shades. Thus they blocked intentions of some enterprising newspapers to flash the verdict by signal to reporters waiting atop neighboring buildings.

At 10:29 o'clock there was a stir at the library door. Hauptmann appeared, hustled along by Lieutenant Smith and Deputy Sheriff Low. But this time the glint of steel handcuffs showed below his coat sleeves. He was manacled to his guards.

One minute later the jury entered. Mrs. Verna Snyder was weeping. Mrs. Ethel Stockton was pale.

Mrs. Anna Hauptmann, her face a death mask, was escorted into court and seated at the defense table. She looked at her husband and her lips moved reassuringly.

C. Lloyd Fisher, from whose face every particle of color had been drained, stepped quickly to Bruno Hauptmann and put his hand on the prisoner's shoulder.

"Now whatever happens, remember, whatever happens, don't you make any outcry, any sound at all. Leave everything to me. Not a sound!"

He repeated the admonition to Anna Hauptmann, who nodded.

There was a wait, a seemingly interminable wait. It was 10:44 o'clock, fourteen minutes after the white-faced jury had reached the jury box, before Justice Trenchard, in his black robes, mounted the bench. The audience rose and then were seated as he rapped on the bench with his gavel. The jury remained standing.

Justice Trenchard ordered the defendant to rise. Hauptmann did so, clumsily, awkwardly. The fingers of his left hand, below the shackles, groped and clung on to Hovey Low's hand. He stood like a soldier of the Kaiser's army, straight as a ramrod, stiff, his heels close together and his pointed chin raised in the air. A surge of emotion had flushed his face to a deep red. Mrs. Hauptmann studied the jury.

And in this last scene of the drama one familiar face was absent. Colonel Lindbergh refused to be present.

"Ladies and Gentlemen of the Jury, have you arrived at a verdict?"

"We have."

"Who shall speak for you?"

"Our foreman."

"How say you, Mr. Foreman?"

Charles Walton, his face an ashen gray, took a paper from his pocket. His hands were trembling. Then he raised his head and his voice.

"We, the jury," he said, "find the defendant, Bruno Richard Hauptmann, guilty of murder in the first degree."

Hauptmann's clutch on the hand of Hovey Low slowly relaxed. His face remained immobile. Not a muscle twitched and he made no sound. His wife, not daring to look at him, gazed steadily at the floor, and her lips trembled.

"May we have a poll?" Edward J. Reilly asked in a low voice.

One by one the jurors answered to their names. One by one they repeated the formula, some clearly, some in tones so low that only the front benches could hear—"guilty of murder in the first degree."

For a moment the scene resembled a slow-motion picture. Ages passed before there was a sound. The Attorney General seemed stunned. Defense counsel made no motion. Hauptmann, still erect, still without indication of shock, stood watching the judge.

Justice Trenchard reminded Wilentz of his duty.

"Do you wish to make a motion for sentence?" he asked.

Wilentz mumbled the motion. Justice Trenchard cut the words of his sentence mercifully short. He said:

"Bruno Richard Hauptmann, you have been convicted of murder in the first degree. The sentence is that you, Bruno Richard Hauptmann, suffer death at a time and place and in a manner provided by law."

He set the date for execution as "the week beginning March 18th." And signed the death warrant.

"The prisoner is remanded to the custody of the sheriff."

Hauptmann's guards rose quickly with him and rushed, rather than walked, with him. The condemned man stumbled as he passed the defense table. Not once did he look at his wife.

.   .   .   .   .

Through the night the correspondents wrote the last chapter of the Flemington story. The crowds, cheering, melted away. Nellie's Tap Room was empty. The desertion of the village was under way.

At dawn all that remained in front of the Court House were a few tired State Troopers, their collars wilted, their gaudy uniforms rumpled. The litter of thousands was scattered in the street. Papers and broken bottles. Flash light bulbs, discarded torches. Mud, crushed and dirty ice, rubbish, the cast-off impedimenta of a departing host.

In his cell, Bruno Richard Hauptmann's face was wet with tears. His strange voice was broken and racked with sobs. He held in his hand a cablegram from Kamenz, Germany. It said:

BRUNO RICHARD HAUPTMANN
ICH GLAUBE ALLES GUT WIRD
DEINE TREUE MUTTER